# RELIGION AND CONFLICT IN SOUTH AND SOUTHEAST ASIA

Although conflict both between and within religious traditions has long been a feature of the political and social environment across Asia, it has assumed greater political significance with recent waves of communal violence and the rise of radical Islam.

This multidisciplinary volume analyses the causes and dynamics of religiously inflected violence. Relying primarily upon illustrative case studies from a range of countries in South and Southeast Asia, the chapters are grouped around three main themes: the causes of religiously justified collective violence; the international and transnational settings for religious violence; and strategies for disrupting religious violence.

While the book makes clear that religiously inflected violence is a general term that encompasses analytically distinct types which have to be countered or prevented in different ways, the studies also demonstrate the fluidity of the boundary between them. For example, communal violence lends itself to discursive reframing as religious warfare, thereby translating what is essentially a local conflict into global discourses of religious violence. The book also underscores the crucial role of the state in provoking religious violence or failing to intervene and highlights the contentions for political, legal and cultural authority between the secular state and religiously motivated actors.

Bringing together scholars from religious studies, political science, sociology, anthropology and international relations, this volume brings much needed attention to the role of religion in fostering violence in South and Southeast Asia and addresses strategies for its containment or resolution.

This book will be of great interest to advanced undergraduate and postgraduate students of Asian politics, security studies and conflict studies.

**Linell E. Cady** is Franca Oreffice Dean's Distinguished Professor of Religious Studies and director of the Center for the Study of Religion and Conflict at Arizona State University. Her publications include *Religion, Theology, and American Public Life* and the co-edited volume *Religious Studies, Theology and the University: Conflicting Maps, Changing Terrain.*

**Sheldon W. Simon** is Professor of Political Science and faculty associate of the Center for Asian Studies and Program in Southeast Asian Studies at Arizona State University. He is the author or editor of nine books, including *The Many Faces of Asian Security* and *East Asian Security in the Post-Cold War Era.*

ASIAN SECURITY STUDIES
Series editors:
Sumit Ganguly, Indiana University, Bloomington,
and Andrew Scobell, US Army War College

Few regions of the world are fraught with as many security questions as Asia.
Within this region it is possible to study great power rivalries, irredentist conflicts,
nuclear and ballistic missile proliferation, secessionist movements, ethnoreligious
conflicts and inter-state wars. This new book series will publish the best possible
scholarships on the security issues affecting the region, and will include detailed
empirical studies, theoretically oriented case studies and policy-relevant analyses
as well as more general works.

# RELIGION AND CONFLICT IN SOUTH AND SOUTHEAST ASIA

## Disrupting violence

### Edited by Linell E. Cady and Sheldon W. Simon

NBR   THE NATIONAL BUREAU *of* ASIAN RESEARCH

Routledge
Taylor & Francis Group

LONDON AND NEW YORK

First published 2007
by Routledge
2 Park Square, Milton Park, Abingdon, Oxon OX14 4RN

Simultaneously published in the USA and Canada
by Routledge
270 Madison Ave, New York, NY 10016

*Routledge is an imprint of the Taylor & Francis Group,
an informa business*

© 2007 Center for the Study of Religion and Conflict
and The National Bureau of Asian Research

Typeset in Times New Roman by
HWA Text and Data Management, Tunbridge Wells
Printed and bound in Great Britain by
Biddles Ltd, King's Lynn

*British Library Cataloguing in Publication Data*
A catalogue record for this book is available from the British Library

*Library of Congress Cataloging-in-Publication Data*
Religion and conflict in South and Southeast Asia : disrupting violence /
edited by Linell E. Cady and Sheldon W. Simon.
p. cm. -- (Asian security studies)
Revised papers originally presented at a conference held at Arizona State
University in October, 2004.
Includes bibliographical references and index.
1. Violence – South Asia – Congresses. 2. Violence – Southeast Asia
– Congresses. 3. Religion and politics – South Asia – Congresses.
4. Religion and politics – Southeast Asia – Congresses. 5. South Asia
– Social conditions – Congresses. 6. Southeast Asia – Social conditions
– Congresses. I. Cady, Linell Elizabeth, 1952– II. Simon, Sheldon W.,
1937– III. Title. IV. Series.
HN670.3.Z9 .R45 2006
306.60954                                                              2006019046

ISBN10: 0–415–39734–0 (hbk)
ISBN10: 0–203–96748–8 (ebk)

ISBN13: 978–0–415–39734–6 (hbk)
ISBN13: 978–0–203–96748–5 (ebk)

# CONTENTS

CONTENTS

# CONTRIBUTORS

**Alyssa Ayres** is Deputy Director of the Center for the Advanced Study of India at the University of Pennsylvania, and associate editor (acting managing editor) of the journal *India Review*.

**Linell E. Cady** is the Franca G. Oreffice Dean's Distinguished Professor of Religious Studies, and the Director of the Center for the Study of Religion and Conflict, at Arizona State University. She is the author of *Religion, Theology and American Public Life*, and the co-editor of *Religious Studies, Theology, and the University: Conflicting Maps, Changing Terrain*.

**Maya Chadda** is Professor of Political Science at William Paterson University of New Jersey and a research fellow at the Southern Asian Institute, Columbia University. She is the author of *Indo-Soviet Relations*; *Paradox of Power: The United States Policy in Southwest Asia*; *Ethnicity Security and Separatism in South Asia* and *Building Democracy in South Asia: India, Pakistan and Nepal*.

**Sumit Ganguly** holds the Rabindranath Tagore Chair in Indian Cultures and Civilizations and is the Director of the India Studies Program at Indiana University in Bloomington. He is the author, editor or co-editor of some ten books on South and Southeast Asia. His most recent book is *Conflict Unending: India–Pakistan Tensions Since 1947*.

**Robert W. Hefner** is Professor of Anthropology and Associate Director of the Institute for Culture, Religion, and International Affairs at Boston University. He is the author of *Remaking Muslim Politics: Pluralism, Contestation, Democratization* and *Schooling Islam: The Culture and Politics of Modern Muslim Education*.

**Mark Juergensmeyer** is Director of Global and International Studies and professor of sociology and religious studies at the University of California, Santa Barbara. His widely read *Terror in the Mind of God: The Global Rise of Religious Violence*, is based on interviews with violent religious activists around the world.

**Joseph Chinyong Liow** is Assistant Professor at the Institute of Defence and Strategic Studies, Singapore. His book, *The Politics of Indonesia–Malaysia Relations: One Kin, Two Nations*, will be released shortly.

**Kumar Ramakrishna** is Assistant Professor and Head of Studies at the Institute of Defence and Strategic Studies (IDSS), Nanyang Technological University, Singapore. Recently published books he has authored or edited include *Emergency Propaganda: The Winning of Malayan Hearts and Minds 1948–1958*; *The New Terrorism: Anatomy, Trends and Counter-Strategies* and *After Bali: The Threat of Terrorism in Southeast Asia*.

**Juliane Schober** is Associate Professor of Religious Studies at Arizona State University, specializing in Theravada Buddhism, modernity and politics in Southeast Asia. She is the editor of *Sacred Biography in the Buddhist Traditions of South and Southeast Asia*.

**Sheldon W. Simon** is Professor of Political Science and Faculty Affiliate of the Center for Asian Studies and Program in Southeast Asian Studies at Arizona State University. He is author or editor of nine books, most recently *The Many Faces of Asian Security*.

**See Seng Tan** is an Assistant Professor at the Institute of Defence and Strategic Studies, Nanyang Technological University, Singapore. He is the co-editor of "Asia-Pacific Security Cooperation: National Interests and Regional Order" and "After Bali: The Threat of Terrorism in Southeast Asia."

**Mark Woodward** is Associate Professor of Religious Studies at Arizona State University. His research specializations include religion and modernity, and religion and politics. He is the author or co-author of *Defenders of Reason in Islam: Mutazilism from Medieval School to Modern Symbol*; *Islam in Java: Normative Piety and Mysticism in the Sultanate of Yogyakarta* and the editor of *Towards a New Paradigm: Intellectual Developments in Indonesian Islam*.

# PREFACE

This volume is a collection of essays exploring the intersections of religion and violence in South and Southeast Asia, primarily through a series of illustrative case studies. It draws together leading Asia specialists from the United States and Asia who represent a variety of disciplinary orientations, including political science, religious studies, anthropology, and security studies. It has become increasingly apparent that understanding the roots and dynamics of religiously inflected violence calls for collaboration that crosses disciplinary boundaries. The relative lack of attention to religion in international relations and security studies, combined with a tendency to privilege moderate expressions of religion and discrete traditions in religious studies, has conspired to keep religious violence on the margins of academic inquiry. This volume explicitly seeks to redress this situation.

This collection is also attentive to questions of policy. The title, "disrupting violence," is deliberately ambiguous: it calls attention to the personal and societal damage that violence inflicts, as well as the efforts needed to contain, mitigate, or defuse it. Developing more imaginative and effective policies, however, cannot be separated from an accurate diagnosis of the nature and causes of episodes of religious violence. Taken together, the essays in this volume do both, though each contribution makes one or the other emphasis its priority.

The volume grew out of a conference titled "Religion and Conflict in Asia: Disrupting Violence" that was held at Arizona State University (ASU) in October 2004, and the chapters are revised versions of presentations originally given at that event. The conference was co-sponsored by The Center for the Study of Religion and Conflict (CSRC) at ASU, the Institute of Southeast Asian Studies (ISEAS) in Singapore, and The National Bureau of Asian Research (NBR) of Seattle and Washington DC. The Center for the Study of Religion and Conflict is a recently launched ASU initiative promoting transdisciplinary research and education on issues of religious conflict and violence. ISEAS is a research centre dedicated to the study of socio-political, security and economic trends and developments in Southeast Asia. NBR is a nonpartisan research institution dedicated to informing and strengthening policy in the Asia-Pacific. Together, the complementary strengths of these three institutions allowed us to thoroughly examine the nature of religious violence in Asia, and to begin to identify possible strategies and policies to counter it.

As the conference conveners, we would like to thank our colleagues Mark Woodward and Juliane Schober at ASU for their advice in the formative stages of the conference planning. We are grateful to Ambassador K. Kesavapany, director of ISEAS, and Professor K. S. Nathan, senior fellow at ISEAS, for their commitment to the initiative and participation in the conference. We also want to thank Richard Ellings, president of NBR, for his support and participation in the conference. In planning and organizing the conference, and in editing this volume, we have worked very closely with Michael Wills, Director of Southeast Asia Studies at NBR. We gratefully acknowledge his substantial contribution to this project. We also want to thank Gustav Brown, Kaleb Brownlow and Jessica Keough, NBR staff in the Southeast Asia Studies Program, for their help. In the Center for the Study of Religion and Conflict, we want to thank Matt Correa, research assistant, and Carolyn Forbes, assistant director, who provided critical support along the way.

Linell Cady<br>
Sheldon Simon<br>
Arizona State University

## About The National Bureau of Asian Research

NBR is a nonprofit, nonpartisan research institution that focuses on major policy issues in the Asia-Pacific and their impact on the United States. Major themes in NBR's research agenda include strategic and diplomatic relations, regional economic integration and development, trade, globalization, terrorism, energy, and health. Drawing upon an extensive network of the world's leading specialists and leveraging the latest technology, NBR conducts advanced, policy-oriented analysis on these issues, and disseminates the results through briefings, studies, conferences, television, and email fora.

## About The Center for the Study of Religion and Conflict

The Center for the Study of Religion and Conflict at Arizona State University promotes research and education on the intersections of religion and conflict, from the civil to the violent. Serving as a hub that fosters exchange and collaboration across the university as well as with its broader publics – local, national, and global – the Center stimulates scholarly work that is problem focused and broadly disseminated.

# Part I

# RELIGION AND VIOLENCE
## An overview

# 1

# INTRODUCTION

## Reflections on the nexus of religion and violence

*Linell E. Cady and Sheldon W. Simon*

The attacks of September 11, 2001 have done more to focus attention on the conjunction of religion and violence than any other event in recent memory. They have served as a wake up call to the rise and increasing political significance of religiously inflected violence around the world. Questions abound: Is there an intrinsic connection between religion and violence, making religion part of the problem not the solution? Or, perhaps, is religious violence a misnomer, a clear indication that authentic religion has been hijacked by criminals, evildoers, and thugs? Do we get sidetracked by focusing on religious violence, failing to recognize the real causes of the turn to violence and terrorist acts? What difference, if any, does it make when violence is aligned with religious discourses and identities? What accounts for the rise of religiously inflected violence in recent decades?

Although the questions are daunting, they have not prevented the formation of broad interpretive frameworks seeking to explain the global rise of religious violence. The most prevalent is a version of the "clash of civilizations" theory first advanced by Samuel Huntington a decade ago. Seeking to illuminate global politics in a post-Cold War world, Huntington argued that in the world into which we are moving "the most important distinctions among peoples are not ideological, political, or economic. They are cultural."[1] Civilizations are the broadest cultural formations, and religion is a "central defining characteristic."[2] Although Huntington identified seven major civilizations in the contemporary world, after September 11 his paradigm quickly morphed into versions of "the West against the Rest" or, even more commonly, "Islam against the West." Whatever the limitations of his paradigm – perhaps most especially its essentializing of complex civilizations – it proved prescient in linking religion and violent conflict, and underscoring their increasing saliency in global politics.

During the Cold War the role of religion was virtually ignored by government policymakers and by international relations analysts. The dominant global ideological competitors from the 1950s through the 1980s were liberal-capitalism, socialism, and communism. These ideas found a battleground in the new states that were created by post-World War II decolonization. These states were, in many cases, culturally fragmented and unstable, with rapidly growing populations; ordinary people were caught up in their governments' efforts to modernize along Western lines, often at the expense of their traditional religious beliefs and communal structures.[3] In the 1970s and 1980s, in many developing states, government legitimacy declined in the wake of corruption, economic failure, and political repression – all associated with modern secular ideologies. People turned to the older culturally familiar institutions of ethnicity and religion as alternatives.

Today, different and largely polarized conceptions of political and legal legitimacy exist in the world.[4] In the West, this legitimacy is primarily secular, rational, and pragmatic. In much of the developing world, secular forms contest with cultural definitions of the sacred and spiritual for political and legal dominance. This contest reflects disillusion with Western-style modernization. Those in the West often characterize religiously-based violence as terrorism because it challenges Western concepts of reason and legal order. However, many in the non-Western world reject the legitimacy of secular politics and a secular state, with jihadists even identifying them as a form of terrorism.[5]

Across Asia, conflict and violence within and among religious groups have long been features of the political and social environment. Long-running religious conflicts have assumed greater political significance following recent waves of communal violence and the rise of radical Islamism in South and Southeast Asia. The Israeli–Palestinian conflict, invasion of Iraq, and the broader US-led war on terrorism (which many Muslims perceive as explicitly anti-Islam) to some extent serve as rallying points for those Muslim groups advocating religious violence. Alongside the increased prominence of Islamist terrorism, is the growth of violence from other religious groups. Moreover, with a religious resurgence under way in many parts of this broad region in the past three decades, other conflicts are emerging between religious and secular models of government that are compounding the immediate challenges of how best to understand and respond to religious violence and terrorism. Scholars, policymakers, and conflict resolution practitioners need to understand the forces that are driving the religious resurgence and the politicization of religion, and the factors that lead to, or escalate, religious violence.

## Focusing the problem

"Religious violence" is a broad category that includes several analytically distinct types: communal religious violence, religious war, and its subset, religious terrorism. The quintessential form of communal religious violence is the sporadic riot that tends to be local, provoked, and driven primarily by concerns for equality and political representation. In these episodes of violent conflict, religion is primarily a marker of identity, leading to common designations as communal or ethnic violence. Religious war and religious terrorism, on the other hand, evidence greater organization and scope, and a more explicit religious ideology framing the conflict and legitimating the violence. As this collection makes clear, it is important to distinguish them because their causes and dynamics differ as, consequently, do effective strategies for their prevention or disruption. On the other hand, this volume also makes clear that analyzing these forms of religious violence in isolation from each other can obscure significant continuities. Communal religious violence, for example, lends itself to discursive reframing as religious warfare. To the extent that such reframing takes hold, the form can morph in some discursive contexts, though not all. Hence, outbreaks of communal religious violence may also be situated within a broader pattern of religious warfare, suggesting that forms of religious violence are analytically distinct though perhaps not always mutually exclusive. Indeed a number of the essays point to an increasing tendency for localized communal religious violence to become discursively relocated within regional and global dynamics, a development linked to globalizing trends.

Although not the central focus of this volume, the phenomenon of contemporary religious terrorism looms large in a number of the studies. "Sacred" terrorism of the kind perpetrated by Al Qaeda and similar groups is part of a religiously inspired "fourth wave." This wave follows three earlier historical phases in which terrorism was tied to the breakup of empires, decolonization, and Marxist-oriented anti-Westernism.[6] While the newest international terrorist threat emanates largely from Muslim communities and/or countries, it is part of a larger phenomenon of resistance to globalization, in which groups and individuals reject the underlying values of a market-based, free trade-driven global economy in favor of a society based on religious rules and mores.

Internationally, the main targets of the "sacred" terrorists are the United States, the US-led global system, and those within developing countries who benefit from these arrangements – primarily the ruling elites – as well as the majority of Muslims. The jihad era is animated by widespread alienation combined with elements of extremist religious identity and doctrine. The hyper-religious motivation of small groups of terrorists targeting large numbers of people in the service of their beliefs takes place most readily within environments of weak governance, dysfunctional social services, poverty, and/or political repression (whether perceived or real) of religious organization and expression. Parts of South and Southeast Asia exhibit significant deficits in measures of human development. Different manifestations of religious-inspired terrorism and inter-communal violence are found in countries as diverse as Indonesia, the Philippines, Thailand, Burma, India, Sri Lanka, Bangladesh, and Pakistan.

Much international attention has focused, since the September 11 attacks, on the role Islam, or more specifically Islamism, plays in such violence, appearing to lend credence to those arguing that we are witnessing a clash of civilizations.[7] Yet, despite the many serious security challenges that are arising from the Muslim world, there are many elements within mainstream Islam that reject the radical Islamist vision. Islam's tradition of equality and its notion that the state serves the community make representative government compatible with its beliefs. The importance of charity and an earlier tradition of religious tolerance going back to the time of the Ottoman Empire can be invoked by moderates in Muslim countries. In Southeast Asia, for example, despite the emergence of transnational terrorist groups such as Jemaah Islamiyah (JI), major forces for moderate Islam can be found – in the two largest Muslim social organizations in Indonesia – Nahdlatul Ulama and Muhammadiyah – and in the ruling Barisan Nasional party in Malaysia.

Even though Islam provides the most currently obvious examples, Southeast Asia also offers an interesting example, in the case of Burma, not just of another religion but of the state appropriating religion for the legitimation of violence. In modern Burma, Buddhist monks have been both perpetrators and victims of violent clashes; the ruling military junta has repeatedly invoked Buddhist symbols of authority to instigate violence against its political opponents and Muslim and tribal minorities. Much of the opposition to the current regime has also invoked Buddhist sentiments and practices, but in this instance to espouse non-violent resistance to the state.

South Asia similarly presents illustrations of religion used as justification for political violence. In Pakistan, growing disillusionment with the weakness of political institutions and opposition to the current military regime has led to a surge of support for religiously-motivated political movements, many of them with radical Islamist tendencies. The rise of Sunni-based Islamism in Pakistan has aggravated existing tensions between the majority Sunni and minority Shia communities. In India, the increased influence of radical Hindu nationalism, instances of anti-Muslim violence such as the Gujarat massacre in 2002, as well as the spate of recent violent incidents against Christian missionaries, adds a new dimension to the underlying, politically motivated, transnational religious tension in the region. In marked contrast to the usual Indian inclination to blame Pakistan-based militants for terrorist attacks, Indian security forces attributed the August 2003 bombings in Bombay to a new wave of indigenous militant Islamists arising from the traditionally quiescent Indian Muslim community. In Bangladesh, meanwhile, the 2001 legislative elections brought to power an alliance that includes two Islamist political parties and resulted in a significant upsurge in violence against the country's Hindu minority, causing widespread internal displacement and an exodus of tens of thousands of Hindus seeking refuge in India.

## Shifting optics: the need for new analytic frameworks

Although the problem of violent religious conflict has burst into public consciousness since September 11, it is hardly a new phenomenon. Communal violence, pogroms, crusades, and jihads litter the historical landscape. That makes it all the more striking that exploration of the intersection of religion and violence remains such an underdeveloped field of study within the contemporary university. To a great extent this is a result of the interpretive frames that have dominated scholarship in the latter half of the twentieth century. These include the disciplinary lenses that have shaped academic inquiry in recent decades, and the distorting influences of a largely unexamined secularization paradigm within which they have operated. It is also the case that rapidly accelerating globalizing developments are exposing the limitations of conventional analytic frameworks that tend to disassemble the parts of a whole for closer study. The growing mutual dependencies within our world call for new optics that can bring together – in the same frame – attention to the local and the global.

Disciplinary specialization has conspired to keep violent religious conflict largely off the radar screen. Scholars from the social sciences and policy arenas have, for the most part, ignored religious dimensions in their analyses. The secularization of society, and most especially the university which has been a primary secularizing agent, helps to account for this fact. By defining religion separately from politics, economics, and science, and locating it within a private domain, scholars have proceeded to focus on a secularized model of the public realm and the actors within it. Deeply influenced by the theory of secularization that dominated the social sciences until recently, scholars have largely assumed that religion is a private option of the individual, a matter of personal faith, that has little public expression or salience. If addressed, religion tends to be a marker of demographic identification, but not a reservoir of beliefs, symbols, and rituals that deeply shape personal and collective life. In a recent scathing critique titled "How Academia Failed the Nation," Francis Fukuyama cites the erosion of area studies coupled with the ascendancy of economic models within the social sciences for Americans' deeply impoverished understanding of the rest of the world. As he points out, the trajectories are linked as the quest for generalizable laws of human behavior sidelined interest in that which was more specifically tied to place and time. "Rational choice" approaches have attained a privileged position in political science in the past two decades. This method seeks "to create broad, universally applicable laws of political behavior by generalizing across large numbers of countries rather than focusing intensively on the history and context of individual countries or regions."[8] It is not a method that can illuminate the continuing power of diverse religious traditions in shaping the assumptions, attitudes, and sensibilities of individuals and collectivities around the world.

Foreign policy, which depends upon an understanding of the "subtleties and nuances of how foreign societies work" has been exceedingly ill served.[9] Western policymakers, like academics, have shared in the secular liberal discursive framework that sharply distinguishes between the religious and the secular. Located within this horizon, they have focused on secular forces and institutions, ignoring the religious assumptions and values that shape individual and collective life throughout most of the world.

The study of religion has primarily been left to scholars of religion. But this division of labor has not been without its costs. They, too, have operated out of the secular liberal paradigm that has presumed and sustained a separate religious domain. Hence they have tended to focus on religious communities and traditions in isolation from broader political, economic, and sociological forces. The humanistic roots of religious studies have also favored, especially in recent decades, a historical lens that focuses on single traditions or regions. This has particularly been the case since the eclipse of the older paradigm of "comparative religion" epitomized in the work of Mircea Eliade. As a result, there has been relatively little attention to identifying broader patterns through comparative study, and even less devoted to addressing questions of public policy. And, finally, the field of religious studies, with its deep commitment to liberal principles of tolerance and respect for all religions, has tended to smuggle in implicit assumptions about authentic religion. From this perspective, religious violence is in the province of the deviant, not "authentic" religion: perhaps driven by a political agenda to be studied by political scientists or even sociopathic, to be studied by psychologists. Because religious violence is deemed aberrant, it has been located at the margins of academic inquiry.

Recent scholarship has begun to emphasize the need to build bridges between fields that seldom interact if religious conflict is to be adequately understood and contained. Douglas Johnston, for example, underscores the critical importance of bringing scholars of religion and political science and policymakers into conversation to craft international policy and develop more effective forms of conflict resolution.[10] Located primarily within the conflict resolution field, Mark Gopin similarly argues for the need to pay much greater attention to the role of religion around the world not just in fostering violence but in shaping effective peacemaking strategies.[11] For too long the field has remained wedded to models of intervention that rely on notions of individuals acting out of enlightened self-interest that do not comport with the experiences or communal identities of most religious believers. The spread of suicide bombers who value their cause more than their life surely exposes the fatal limitations of the dominant model.

Rapidly accelerating globalizing trends also point to the limitations of analytic frameworks that separate the local or national from a regional or global horizon. Human migration patterns and the communications revolution have made such distinctions increasingly problematic. This does not mean that local and national factors, including the geography, particular histories, and established institutions of countries, have been displaced as the primary contextual determinants. Indeed a number of contributors underscore the importance of attending to local and national contexts in the analysis of the causes of religious violence. This is especially important to counter the desire for general theories of religious violence or "one-size-fits-all explanations" as Robert Hefner calls them. Even so, the increasing size and power of diaspora communities, the role of TV and the internet in facilitating communication, and the transnational identities that religions often promote, make it impossible to ignore the regional and global dynamics in the incitement and legitimation of religious violence.

## Themes and patterns

This volume contributes to the recent scholarship calling for comparative, multi-disciplinary, and collaborative work to address the conjunction of religion and violence. By bringing together scholars of religion, political scientists, and anthropologists, the collection seeks to advance scholarly understanding of violent religious conflict in South and Southeast Asia. The essays do not presume any single model of the alignment of religion and violence, a presumption that would prematurely foreclose reflection on some of the most important questions. Is, for example, religious terrorism rooted in religion, or is it cloaked by religion? What difference, if any, does this make for policy interventions? The authors identify possible patterns of religious violence and suggest countermeasures by various actors, including the state and co-religionists. Through discussion of illustrative case studies drawn from a range of countries, religions, and two Asian subregions, the authors discern patterns in the development of religious movements and religious violence. The essays are grouped around several themes:

- What are the causes of religiously justified collective violence? Which groups have initiated violence, and why have they done so (e.g., ideological or socio-economic reasons)? How have these dynamics changed over time?
- What are the international and transnational settings for religious violence? How have these settings reconfigured the dynamics and effects of religious violence?
- What are some strategies for disrupting religious violence? Is religiously legitimated violence less susceptible to a negotiated solution?

Several authors in this volume examine Hinduism and Buddhism in South and Southeast Asia and explain their varying religious and organizational characteristics as well as the manner in which they engage the state and other religious traditions in their territories. Unsurprisingly, though, much of this volume assesses Islam, which dominates Indonesia, Malaysia, Brunei, southern Thailand, the southern Philippines, Pakistan, Bangladesh, and is also the religion of a significant portion of India's population.[12] In Southeast Asia, most of the region's Muslims, unlike those in the Arab world, live in successful modernizing countries with multicultural societies. Nevertheless, fundamentalist versions of Islam are making headway. A US-funded Freedom Institute poll on Indonesia published in November 2004 revealed that 16 percent of those polled refused to condemn the terrorist organization, JI, as long as it fought those oppressing Muslims, while more than 50 percent surveyed opposed the existence of churches in Muslim majority areas.[13]

More fundamentally, some Muslim scholars point to the difficulty modern democracy encounters in Muslim societies – the widely held notion by the elite that the masses who are not qualified to interpret *sharia* are therefore not qualified to govern themselves. As Muhammad Khalid Masud, of Allama Iqbal University in Pakistan, put it at an Indonesian seminar sponsored by the International Center for Islam and Pluralism: "In Islam, sovereignty belongs to God alone, and this is expressed through *sharia* because it is revealed by God. Since only experts in Islamic tradition can properly interpret *sharia*, they alone can represent the sovereignty of God."[14] This thinking gives rise to the denial of popular participation in politics in many predominantly Muslim countries.

Religious extremists in South and Southeast Asia drink from a volatile brew of economic crises, diminished state capacities, and ethno-religious tensions. The governments of the Philippines, Indonesia, Pakistan, and India, unable effectively to suppress armed extremists, also seem reticent about backing religious moderates. Moreover, Muslim moderates generally are not adept at creating cohesive groups to respond to jihadist violence.[15] Although most jihadist groups have strictly local agendas – such as the Indonesian *laskars* (militia units) and Abu Sayyaf in the Philippines – JI has region-wide aspirations and has been funded from Al Qaeda and other Arab sources. Fortunately, neither constitutes a major force within the Philippine or Indonesian Muslim communities. However, the legacy of authoritarian rule, corrupt political elites, and sectarian "trawling" by extremists willing to worsen ethno-religious tensions will likely continue to breed religious violence.

Looking at various cases across South and Southeast Asia, it is possible to discern certain patterns. There appear to be some common negative trends: the tendency of both the state and non-state actors to invoke religion as the justification for violence against other faith communities, and the likelihood, in the case of Islam, that limiting the political "space" available to Islamist political parties drives them underground and radicalizes them. But there are also positive signs, most notably the continued moderation of large majorities in most communities even where religious violence has occurred or is occurring. One of the key questions facing scholars, policymakers, and conflict resolution practitioners is whether and how these moderates can be empowered. Empowering moderates would help to reduce religious tensions in countries that have suffered sectarian violence or "sacred" terrorism, and thus reduce the risk of conflict.

## Orientation to the volume

Drawing upon his extensive personal experiences studying religious terrorists from across the world, Mark Juergensmeyer's opening essay addresses the global rise of religious violence. His is not an illustrative case study of one country or region, as are the other essays, but a synthetic overview of the nature of religious violence to which, he argues, all religious traditions have a propensity. Although violent religious conflict has multiple causes, with the feeling of humiliation an especially common thread, Juergensmeyer emphasizes that the addition of a religious ingredient qualitatively transforms it. By invoking images of a cosmic war, evident in all cases of religious militancy he has encountered, the conflict takes on a transcendent reference with absolute oppositions between good and evil. He notes that strategic considerations become less salient, and violence takes on a personally redemptive or purgative function. Particularly important, Juergensmeyer argues, is the role that religion plays in justifying the violence, a role that "challenges the state's monopoly on morally-sanctioned killing." He points out that dissatisfaction with secular nationalisms and the secular nation-state is a recurring theme within religious militancy across the globe in recent decades. The transnational dimensions of violent religious movements stem from acceleration of human migration, as well as explicit ideologies of global conflict. Despite the rise of heightened passions associated with religious militancy, Juergensmeyer notes that it can also quickly dissipate. He concludes that it is especially important that authorities avoid engaging in a parallel rhetoric of cosmic war in their response to terrorism as that only maintains the master narrative of holy war and the cycle of violence.

10

Robert Hefner's chapter, "The Sword Against the Crescent," examines historical experiences of Islam in the southern Philippines, southern Thailand, Indonesia, and Malaysia that account for differing susceptibilities to religiously-legitimated violence. He assesses the frequently testy relationships between Christian colonial governments and Muslim populations, concluding that central government efforts at assimilation by both colonial regimes and their nationalist successors in southern Thailand, the southern Philippines, and Aceh province in Indonesia had the counterproductive effect of spurring local populations to move from ethno-nationalism to secession. Although Islamist violence exists in almost all Southeast Asian Muslim states, jihadists are a small, often fractionalized minority. Abu Sayyaf and Jemaah Islamiyah have been severely weakened by military and police actions in the Philippines and Indonesia. Nevertheless, Professor Hefner warns that weakened jihadist organizations have spawned spin-offs consisting of new, freelance paramilitarists who are difficult to track and suppress. Islamic moderates are re-centering Muslim politics away from violence in Indonesia and Malaysia. However, radicals still dominate in the southern Philippines and southern Thailand. Generally, though, militant Islam's agenda in Southeast Asia is regional not global. Nor does there seem to be significant spillover between Southeast Asian jihadists and Al Qaeda's anti-American and anti-Arab government agendas.

Juliane Schober's contribution explores the intersections of Buddhism and violence, focusing primarily on modern Burmese politics. Buddhism is deeply rooted in Burmese history, and closely aligned with its national identity. Despite a reputation for and doctrinal commitment to nonviolence, the Buddhist tradition has been appropriated to incite and legitimate violence by both state and non-state actors. Schober concentrates attention on two major episodes of collective violence: the 1988 popular uprising against the state that elicited a powerful military clamp down, and the 1997 riots against Muslims. She analyzes the role of the sangha, the decentralized Buddhist communities of monks and nuns, in organizing and facilitating violence in the popular uprising, and its participation in communal violence against Muslims in the 1997 riots. She also addresses the manner in which the Burmese state has appropriated the symbols, rituals, and institutions of Buddhism to legitimate its own power, as well as incited anti-Muslim sentiments among Buddhists for essentially diversionary purposes. Schober notes that Buddhism has been similarly linked with national identity in Sri Lanka, with the Sinhalese sangha assuming a more direct political role in Sri Lankan public life. The monks have essentially developed Buddhist justifications for the armed struggle in the civil war against the Tamil Tigers, imagining the war as their religious obligation to create a Sinhalese Buddhist nation. Schober argues, as do other contributors, that collective religious violence must be interpreted within its broader economic, political, and social context. Its roots are as varied as other sources of conflict. However, like Juergensmeyer, Schober argues that religion is a transforming ingredient, a recurring theme through a number of the case studies. Drawing upon mythic, transcendentalizing narratives and symbols and rituals with deep emotional roots, religion serves to intensify and absolutize the conflict, rendering it far less susceptible to negotiated settlement.

In examining India, Pakistan, and Bangladesh, Sumit Ganguly argues that polyethnic states constitute a breeding ground for ethno-religious conflict when governments lack a commitment to ethno-religious pluralism, the protection of minority rights, and democratic procedures. In his chapter, "The Roots of Religious Violence in India, Pakistan, and Bangladesh," however, he cautions that dominant majorities installed through democratic procedures may still foment violence if they ignore the need for ethnic and religious pluralism. Emphasizing the politics of inter-religious violence in South Asia, Professor Ganguly notes that even at India's outset, the dominant secular Indian nationalist Congress Party failed to provide explicit guarantees to protect the country's large Muslim population, thus encouraging the separatist sentiments that led to Pakistan's creation. The latter's dominant party, the Muslim League, had neither the Indian Congress commitment to secularism nor its intra-party democracy. Religious riots occurred in Pakistan as early as 1953. By the 1970s, the country formally divided its citizens into Muslims and non-Muslims. As a predominantly Sunni country, religious violence in Pakistan has been directed at the Shia community. Weak political institutions have been unable to contain this violence. Professor Ganguly concludes pessimistically that all three South Asian states, characterized by strong societies and weak governments, have led political leaders to make sectarian appeals to bolster their shaky political standing. These actions subvert the law and promote ethno-religious discord. Of the three states, he sees hope for dampening sectarian violence only in India because its democratic procedures are well embedded, its judiciary is independent, and freedom of the press and respect for personal rights and civil liberties are the norm. Unfortunately, these safeguards prevail neither in Pakistan nor in Bangladesh.

Mark Woodward's essay explores the nature and dynamics of collective religious violence in Indonesia, paying particular attention to its interface with rapidly globalizing trends of recent decades. Woodward notes that religion has been a major source of conflict in Indonesia since its independence from the Dutch in 1945, and religious violence marked both the beginning and the end of the Suharto regime (1967–98). Rejecting the orthodox Muslims' vision of an Islamic state in favor of a form of civil religion, the military-dominated Suharto regime effectively managed religious conflict as it focused on rapid economic development. The economic collapse in 1997, combined with probable military provocation and organization, sparked serious rioting and violence against the economically successful ethnic Chinese, leading to Suharto's resignation. Woodward explores the ethnic, economic, and religious fault lines that structured the outbreaks of violence. He underscores the manner in which globalizing developments facilitated the transformation of this local political crisis into a strand of a larger global struggle, with the communications revolution facilitating its dissemination. A similar trajectory marks the rise of Laskar Jihad, an Islamist militia with ties to elements within the Indonesian military, and its response to the Muslim–Christian violence in Ambon. Although neutral security forces preventing violence are essential, Woodward urges that the underlying causes of conflict and violence be addressed, with perpetrators of violence being held accountable by the state as well as their own religious-ethnic communities.

Alyssa Ayres, in "Religious Violence Beyond Borders: Reframing South Asian Cases," examines the transnational components of religious violence through the cross-border flow of ideas, people, and, as she aptly puts it: "the basic capital of violence (arms and money)." Professor Ayres emphasizes the symbiotic historical memory of the 1947 Partition that informs Hindu and Muslim visions of the other as enemy. Analyzing the Kashmir conflict as emblematic of externally driven religious violence, Professor Ayres discusses the evolution of what began as an autonomy movement among Kashmiri Muslims but evolved into a Pakistan-backed religious battle accompanied by the forced expulsion of Kashmir's Hindu minority. By the last half of the 1990s, non-Kashmiris dominated the anti-Indian insurgency. Led by Islamist extremists, the fight for Kashmir now replicates the Hindu–Muslim conflict between India and Pakistan. The Afghan war against the Soviet Union in the 1970s also permitted Pakistan's president, General Zia, to leverage his Islamization policies with aid from the United States and Saudi Arabia, resulting in the strengthening of Pakistan's most conservative Sunni elements. Strengthened Sunni Islamists have also moved against Pakistan's minority Shia community. In Bangladesh, too, Islamic radicalization in the 1990s led to attacks on that country's Hindu minority for alleged alliances with the forces of secularism in India. Thus, neither Pakistan nor Bangladesh protects religious minorities. Militias in the former openly recruit young men to perpetrate jihad in Kashmir; and Bangladesh's founding commitment to provide a home for Bengalis, irrespective of religion, is only a bitter memory. Professor Ayres, like Professor Ganguly, concludes pessimistically that the governments of the subcontinent show little political inclination to protect minorities or control extremist organizations bent on destroying what they see as communal enemies in neighboring states as well as local "fifth columns."

In contrast to other chapters in this book that focus on states and religious movements as organizations, Kumar Ramakrishna presents a different level of analysis in "The (Psychic) Roots of Religious Violence in South and Southeast Asia." Arguing that since states and religions are socially constructed, understanding how they behave requires an examination of individual psychologies for, after all, individuals bonding together comprise social groups. Professor Ramakrishna concentrates on how jihadist and other extreme religious organizations are able to induce their members to violent actions. Drawing on social psychological literature dealing with ingroups and outgroups and how hatred is generated by the former toward the latter, Professor Ramakrishna argues that religious extremists are often "yoked" to political objectives via a religious ideology that becomes a political ideology. He also notes that ingroup frustration fuels violence because of the belief that dominant outgroups work to block ingroup aspirations. A heightened sense of group awareness serves to subordinate the individual to the group's identity. Shared grievances, then, against the stereotyped outgroup motivate violent action that is also justified through ingroup ideology. Professor Ramakrishna revisits Mark Woodward's discussion of the 1998 anti-Chinese pogroms in Indonesia

13

in terms of mimetic group frustration, adding an individual/group dimension to Woodward's analysis. He then concludes that religious violence is less about religion per se than underlying social psychological frustrations. Religion becomes the legitimation for violence that warring parties commit because of frustration. These arrangements are difficult to disrupt because they have become absolutized through sacralized ideology. Moreover, because Westernization/globalization promotes desacralization as well as religious and moral relativism, those groups committed to a sacred social space believe they are mortally threatened and respond accordingly. Ramakrishna is not optimistic that jihadist groups can be defanged.

In "Debating Strategies for Disrupting Violence: Lessons from South Asia" Maya Chadda turns her attention to questions of policy and prevention. She underscores that effective strategies for disrupting violence depend upon an accurate diagnosis of the problem. Recognizing the multiple variants of religious violence, including civil wars, holy wars, and communal violence and riots, Chadda focuses on the religious violence between Muslims and Hindus in India. Most pronounced at the time of partition in 1947, Hindu–Muslim violence has been a recurrent feature in India, although neither constant nor ubiquitous. This violence, Chadda contends, stems primarily from "economic inequalities, social discrimination, and victimization." Chadda identifies two major strategies for preventing communal religious violence in India. The first strategy, typically the recommendation of commissions, focuses on what can be done primarily by the state "before, during, and after the riots to prevent reoccurrence." The second strategy, more attentive to resources of civil society, focuses on longer term societal solutions for enhancing communal harmony. Reviewing a number of proposals that exemplify these two main strategies, Chadda rejects single cause approaches, advocating a "coalition strategy" that incorporates insights from both. She observes that religious or communal violence in India has taken on more dangerous valences with the rise of Hindu nationalism and the insurgency in Kashmir, with its Pakistani and jihadist influences. Although Indian Muslims have sought to maintain a domestic framework for interpreting Hindu–Muslim conflicts, other actors in India, Pakistan, and Bangladesh, have pushed regional and transnational religious alliances that are potentially explosive. Although some strategies for developing a coalition to disrupt communal religious violence are evident, Chadda cautions that our understanding of the relationship between such violence and larger forces of globalization and modernization remains very limited.

Joseph Liow's "Violence and the Long Road to Reconciliation in Southern Thailand" is a cautionary tale of how a myopic Thai government following a culturally insensitive assimilationist policy can actually exacerbate the conflict it hopes to resolve. Thailand's predominantly Malay-Muslim southern provinces have resisted the dominant Buddhist central government's efforts to dilute Malay-Muslim culture for a century. While waxing and waning, what had been primarily an ethno-nationalist resistance – and not a particularly Islamic revolt – has acquired an increasingly religious character in the last few years. Though not yet

14

absolutized, growing Islamic fervor in opposition to the central government has rendered the conflict increasingly violent and potentially intractable so long as Bangkok maintains its present course of privileging the use of force to contain the resistance. Professor Liow's analysis examines an issue that several of this book's authors raise: Is Islamic religious violence a product of indigenous Muslim complaints or has it been induced or exacerbated by external jihadists either from Southeast Asia or the Arab world? In southern Thailand's case, Liow insists the dynamics are strictly local and not driven by abstract ideological rejection of modernity but rather by Bangkok's clumsy attempts at assimilation. Resolution, then, must be based on the Thai government's acceptance that the southern Thai community possesses an ethno-cultural identity distinct from the dominant Thai nation. Nonetheless, local militants have been energized by the US invasion and occupation of Afghanistan and Iraq and Bangkok's collaboration with the US war on terrorism. Thus far, the central government's inept response under Prime Minister Thaksin has been characterized by institutional conflicts between the army and police combined with efforts to invasively monitor Muslim schools (*pondoks*), all of which only serve to inflame anti-government sentiment. A continuation of current policies could well encourage external jihadists to join the fray and further destabilize an already sensitive border region between southern Thailand and northern Malaysia.

In "Lévinas and the Question of Civilizational Amity After September 11" See Seng Tan provides a concluding meditation on the causes and prevention of religious violence in our deeply fractured world. Any long-term and sustainable strategies for disrupting violence across civilizational boundaries, he argues, must address fundamental ontological, ethical, and epistemological assumptions that are built into the very way in which the conflicts are framed – by both militants and their opponents. Tan notes that this claim has very little purchase among international relations scholars, security analysts and practitioners. Taking Liow's and Chadda's contributions as illustrative of reflections on effective policy concerning religious violence, Tan notes that strategies commonly address two levels: first, a focus on the state's maintaining or restoring law and order and second, attention to longer term political, social, and economic policies to redress underlying causes of the turn to violence. Although Tan judges these policy recommendations to be both comprehensive and necessary, he also concludes that they are insufficient for addressing deeper dynamics of civilizational conflict. Drawing upon the philosophy of Emmanuel Lévinas, Tan targets the modern ontology of the subject as independent, autonomous, and sovereign – rather than fundamentally relational – as a major contributing factor in civilizational conflict. Most importantly, he argues that this contributes to the pattern of demonizing the "other" that is evident not only in the discourse and practices of religious militants, but also in their secular opponents. As a result, both sides conclude that violent extermination of the other is both necessary and moral, a conclusion that deepens civilizational enmity and perpetuates the cycle of violence. Only a thoroughly relational, mutually dependent, vision of human life on this planet will, Tan argues, facilitate the global amity that is so essential to our future.

## Conclusion

This collection of case studies makes clear that religious violence is a general term that encompasses various forms that must be analytically separated. Communal religious violence and religious militancy receive the greatest attention in these studies. Their respective nature, causes, and dynamics differ, as do the most effective strategies for their disruption or prevention. Religious violence can be a misleading term if it fosters the impression that religion is the primary or root cause. Virtually all the contributors caution against making this mistake, insisting that the causes of conflicts that lead to violence in general are equally salient in the case of religious violence. Hence it is critical to consider the economic, social, and political grievances, for example, that may be factors in, and most likely originating causes of, cases of religious violence. A recurring theme in the volume addresses the difference that the religious ingredient makes in episodes of violence. The emotional resonance of religious narratives, symbols, and rituals, their power to shape individual and collective identity, and their transcendental frames qualitatively transform violent religious conflict. When religion enters the mix, as many authors emphasize, the violent conflict becomes less susceptible to negotiation.

This appears to be especially the case in religious militancy, and less so in communal religious conflicts where religion tends to function more as a marker of identity. A largely localized phenomenon, communal religious violence is primarily driven by grievances over equality and political representation. A minor triggering event and the work of provocateurs in promoting rumors tap into the underlying discontent and intercommunal tensions. Woodward argues that the 1997 riots targeting Indonesia's Chinese community epitomize this model, as do the 2002 Muslim–Hindu riots in Gujarat, India. Although religion functions primarily as a marker of collective identity in episodes of communal religious violence, the religious ingredient is far from inert. Its sacralizing presence arouses deep passions, evident, for example, in the role that sacred space plays in the incitement to and escalation of violence. The destruction or desecration of mosques, temples, or shrines, for example, is a deliberately provocative and deeply symbolic act that incites retaliation.

The religious dimension of localized communal violence, moreover, allows it to be discursively relocated within regional and global dynamics. Globalizing developments, including the increase in diaspora communities and the communications revolution, have facilitated this trend. A largely local and territorial conflict between Christians and Muslims in Indonesia, for example, morphs into a global struggle through the broadly disseminated internet postings of religious compatriots. Mutual demonization and misinformation about atrocities committed combine to harden religious identities, foster hatred, and sustain the cycle of violence. A number of case studies suggest that perception trumps fact in the dynamics of violence, evident in the extraordinarily powerful role of rumors and propaganda in its incitement.

One of the interpretive challenges in the analysis of religious violence concerns the respective weight placed on local grievances and dynamics versus broader regional and transnational factors. Robert Hefner's and Mark Woodward's respective explorations of religious militancy in Indonesia exemplify this point. Hefner emphasizes the local dynamics in the Islamic jihadist movement, and views its presence in Southeast Asia as primarily a regional and not a global struggle. Woodward, on the other hand, highlights the ways in which parochial violent conflicts, with local roots, become embedded within global discourses of religious conflict. Joseph Liow's interpretation of the Muslim insurgency in southern Thailand also underscores this dilemma. Portraying it as primarily a local movement against an assimilationist national project, Liow also discerns increasing signs that it is taking on more religious valences, including religious martyrdom and the mutual destruction of sacred sites. This worrisome trend indicates its potential as a magnet for jihadists seeking to reconfigure the conflict within the pattern of global religious war.

The relationship between religious violence and the state is a recurring theme in this volume. As a number of contributors note, communal religious violence is aligned with states that lack the power or the will to protect and respect religious minorities. This is particularly the case for South Asia, especially Pakistan and Bangladesh who, Ganguly argues, abandoned their identity and commitment to secular democracy. India remains committed to this ideal, yet the rise of Hindu nationalism in the past decade has deeply compromised this commitment. Southeast Asia evinces a stronger commitment to the ideals of secular democracy, most especially Indonesia, Thailand, and Malaysia. Countries with close alliances between national identity and religion, as in Burma and Sri Lanka, have experienced communal religious violence, as state and non-state actors use religion to further their respective political agendas. In addition to other precipitating grievances that foster communal religious violence, provocation by the state or its failure to intervene to defuse a triggering incident from escalating into a major riot must be accounted among the causes of such violence.

The relationship between religious violence and the secular state is also critical for understanding the rise of global religious militancy. Rejecting the legitimacy of the secular state, and its privatization of religion, religious movements from various traditions and regions have appropriated religious narratives and symbols to mobilize opposition and justify the use of violence. Multiple factors have contributed to the disillusionment with the secular state, including rising education levels combined with stagnant economies, corruption, and obstacles to political dissent. Religions provide a culturally powerful alternative tradition from which to challenge the secular state. Through creative bricolage, religious narratives, symbols and rituals, and the organizational networks that sustain them, can be appropriated to advance dissenting agendas and sanction violence on their behalf.

The foregoing case studies document the transnational activities of many South and Southeast Asian religiously motivated terrorist groups. Jihadists from both regions trained together with Al Qaeda in Pakistan and Afghanistan during the anti-Soviet and Taliban eras, forming personal bonds that persist to this day even after they relocated to their home countries.

17

Illustrative of mutual support was the sectarian violence in Indonesia between 1999 and 2003 in which 5,000 people died and another 350,000 were displaced. Members of foreign or transnational extremist groups, such as Kumpulan Militan Malaysia and Jemaah Islamiyah, fought against Christians alongside – though independently of – Laskar Jihad in Muslim–Christian battles in Maluku and Sulawesi.[16]

Although many of the first generation of Asian jihadists have been captured, killed, or abandoned the battlefield, a new generation has replaced them. Training camps for jihadists supported by JI and with funding from the Arabian Peninsula operate in Moro Islamic Liberation Front (MILF)-controlled areas of Mindanao in the southern Philippines where militias from throughout Southeast Asia still gather. The Philippine government has yet to secure that region. With an ineffective maritime interdiction capability and corrupt local officials, jihadists regularly train and disperse back primarily to Indonesia and possibly to southern Thailand and northern Malaysia; or possibly remain in the Philippines as part of the MILF or Abu Sayyaf.

Of particular concern is the large number of Malaysians, Indonesians, and Filipino Muslim students attending Muslim religious schools in Arab countries and Pakistan where they can come under the influence of hard-line Islamic teachers. Although some of this overseas Islamic education has been discouraged by Southeast Asian governments, local Muslim schools in southern Thailand and Indonesia are still subsidized by foreign donations – frequently from Saudi Arabia; and the teachers in these schools have often been educated there.[17] In sum, Islamist education in Southeast Asia constitutes the end of a chain, the links of which include financial support from Arab states, fundamentalist teachers from these states as well as Pakistan, and recruiters from JI, the Indonesian *laskars*, the MILF in the Philippines, and other like-minded jihadist groups. In South Asia, the incendiary Kashmir conflict has been a focal point for deadly violence between Hindu nationalists and Pakistan-based jihadists. For the latter particularly, Kashmir's future has become absolutized and brooks no compromise. Therefore, efforts by President Musharaf to rein in the militants will probably not succeed.

Strategies to disrupt religiously motivated violence depend on at least two underlying conditions: 1) Is the violence instrumental for the groups involved, that is, is it a marker for groups' goals such as regional autonomy (southern Philippines, southern Thailand) or a greater voice in the country's affairs (Muslims in India). Alternatively, 2) Is the violence absolutized such that it serves a fundamental group identity that cannot be compromised or even permit peaceful coexistence with members of other communities. The latter constitutes a zero-sum relationship with others and is, therefore, particularly difficult to disrupt or erode.

The political and social contexts in which religious violence thrives are difficult to change in the short to medium term. They include weak governance and an inability to protect targeted minorities, reduce poverty, and improve dysfunctional social services. Nevertheless, conditions in Southeast Asia seem more propitious for moderating religious extremism than in South Asia. In the former, most of the region's Muslims live in successful, modernizing countries with plural societies that either aspire to democracy or already practice it. In these environments, religious moderates should thrive and promote their constituents' religious needs peacefully. To overcome smaller, vocal extremist organizations, the moderates must themselves organize and publicize their agendas, discrediting those who engage in violence. Yet, until recently, moderate Muslim organizations in Southeast Asia have seemed reticent. A recent promising development occurred in December 2004 when Indonesian President Yudhoyono sponsored an International Dialogue on Interfaith Cooperation that included Muslims, Christians, Jews, Buddhists, Hindus, and Confucians from 13 Asia-Pacific countries. Its declared goal was to empower religious moderates.[18]

For those groups practicing instrumental violence, policy changes by governments may point the way to a solution. In southern Thailand and the southern Philippines, Bangkok and Manila have pursued unsuccessful policies of assimilation and dilution respectively. In the former, the Thai government has tried to acculturate southern Muslims to the majority Thai Buddhist life style, ignoring the Malay-Muslim culture of its southern citizens. Better acceptance of the legitimacy of this subculture as well as investment in traditional occupations such as agriculture and fisheries would provide a beginning for conflict reduction. Similarly, in the southern Philippines, greater autonomy for this Moro region and a larger share of national investment might spur development and dampen violent resistance.

Prospects for amelioration in South Asia seem less propitious because Pakistan-based jihadist resistance, to a secular Kashmir as well as Sunni attacks against the Shia community within Pakistan, has become absolutized. Hindus in Kashmir are unacceptable too, as a matter of sacred doctrine. Unfortunately, even in India, where the government is committed to protecting all its citizens, Hindu nationalism is on the rise, defining itself through anti-Muslim depredations. When religious attitudes toward other faiths and lifestyles become sacralized, prospects for conflict amelioration seem remote.

## Notes

1  Samuel P. Huntington, *The Clash of Civilizations and the Remaking of World Order* (New York: Touchstone Books, 1996), 21. This book is an elaboration of an article titled "The Clash of Civilizations?" that first appeared in the summer 1993 issue of *Foreign Affairs*.
2  Ibid., 47.
3  This discussion is drawn from James F. Rinehart, "Religion in World Politics: Why the Resurgence?" *International Studies Review* 6, no. 2 (June 2004): 271–4.
4  Although illuminating critical dynamics in international affairs, this polarized model risks obscuring more subtle similarities. See Bruce Lincoln, *Holy Terrors: Thinking About Religion After September 11* (Chicago: University of Chicago Press, 2003), especially Chapter 2, for a comparative analysis of speeches of Osama bin Laden and George Bush addressing the jihadist global conflict, which underscores this point. On one level, bin Laden, exemplifying charismatic religious leadership, makes frequent use of religious discourse to legitimate the attacks on America, whereas Bush, representing official secular state authority, avoids explicitly religious discourse in an effort to frame the conflict as a moral one. On another level, however, Bush's explicit

biblical allusions and closing benediction that accentuates God's blessings on America point to a "vast subtextual iceberg" that "helped Bush assert the religious nature of the conflict in the same moment he sought to deny it." (30) That Bush's religious references were primarily coded rather than explicit points to the applicability of the model that contrasts Western and non-Western forms of political legitimacy, but their very presence at all points to its limitations.

5  Scott Thomas, "Taking Religious and Cultural Pluralism Seriously," in *Religion in International Relations: The Return From Exile*, ed. Fabio Peliot and Pavlow Hatzopoulos (New York: Palgrave Macmillan, 2003).

6  David C. Rapoport, "The Fourth Wave: September 11 in the History of Terrorism," *Current History* 100, no. 650 (December 2001): 438–42.

7  Islamism has become a term to designate a fundamentalist version of Islam that advocates strict adherence to *shariah*; a subset of this group advocates violence.

8  Francis Fukuyama, "How Academia Failed the Nation: The Decline of Regional Studies," *Chronicle of Higher Education*, January 3, 2005.

9  Ibid.

10  Douglas Johnston, *Faith-Based Diplomacy: Trumping Realpolitik* (New York: Oxford University Press, 2003); and Johnston Sampson and Cynthia Sampson, eds., *Religion: The Missing Dimension of Statecraft* (New York: Oxford University Press, 2000).

11  Marc Gopin, *Between Eden and Armageddon: The Future of World Religions, Violence, and Peacemaking* (New York: Oxford University Press, 2000).

12  It is worth noting that 52 percent of Muslims live in parts of Asia other than the Middle East, and that nearly half of all Muslims live in South and Southeast Asia (44 percent), as opposed to just 28 percent in the Middle East.

13  Stephen Ulph, "…While Indonesia Makes Progress Against JI," *Terrorism Focus* (published by Jamestown Foundation) 1, no. 9 (November 30, 2004), http://www.jamestown.org/terrorism/news/ article.php?articleid=2368926.

14  M. Taufiqurrahman, "Islam Compatible with Democracy, Scholars Say," *Jakarta Post* (Jakarta), December 7, 2004, in United States Technical Information Service, Foreign Broadcast Information Service (hereafter cited as *FBIS*), December 8, 1999, via internet.

15  Robert W. Hefner, "Political Islam in Southeast Asia: Assessing the Trends" (paper in the *Political Islam in Southeast Asia: Conference Report*, Johns Hopkins School of Advanced International Studies, Washington DC, March 25, 2003), 5–9.

16  Dana R. Dillon, "Southeast Asia and the Brotherhood of Terrorism," Heritage Lectures, no. 860, Heritage Foundation, Washington DC, November 19, 2004, 2.

17  Sheldon W. Simon, "Southeast Asia: Back to the Future?" in *Strategic Asia 2004–05: Confronting Terrorism in the Pursuit of Power*, ed. Ashley J. Tellis and Michael Wills (Seattle, WA: National Bureau of Asian Research, 2004), 265, 272.

18  Sheldon W. Simon, "US-Southeast Asian Relations: Elections, Unrest, and ASEAN Controversies," *Comparative Connections – An E-Journal of East Asian Bilateral Relations* 6, no. 4 (January 2005): 65.

# 2

# FROM BHINDRANWALE
# TO BIN LADEN

## A search for understanding religious violence

*Mark Juergensmeyer*

My involvement in the study of religious terrorism began with the Sikhs. I had lived in Punjab for several years during the early part of my academic career when my focus was on the relationship between religion and politics in India in general and Punjab in particular. During the 1980s, therefore, I watched with mounting horror as a spiral of violence developed between Sikh militants and the government. How could such affable, intelligent people be swept up in an encounter that was so vicious, so unforgiving?

I embarked on a project to try to understand why – to try to enter into the mindset of people whom I knew well and whom I had come to respect. I wanted to understand how some of the best and brightest of their generation of youth could be engaged in a confrontation that was so suicidal, so horrendous, so beyond rationality, a situation where the demands and the interests of the movement seemed to be beyond ordinary calculation. It is relatively easy to understand a movement that is motivated towards a strategic purpose – that is, one created to gain ground, perhaps even literally ground in the sense of land and property to be taken. But when the war in which a movement is engaged seems so religiously ideological – as the Khalistani movement seemed to be – it is beyond simple comprehension. It appears to be so irrational, so mythological, that it is difficult to imagine how intelligent people could enter into it with such passion and with such risk to themselves. I wanted to know why.

I also wanted to know whether this situation was idiosyncratic to the Sikhs, or, for that matter, to India. In the 1980s violent movements of religious activism were relatively infrequent phenomena. This was prior to the rise of Hamas in the intifada of the Palestinian movement, and only the Islamic revolution in Iran bore witness to a new kind of virulent anti-modern religious politics that in time would cast its shadow over much of the globe. At that time, in the 1980s, I wanted to know whether the characteristics of the Punjab situation were unique to India, or whether there were patterns that were replicated in other forms of religious politics emerging around the world.

So I took a year off in 1986 to study the speeches of the symbolic leader of the Khalistan movement, Sant Jarnail Singh Bhindranwale, and spend some time again in that area of India that I knew well and in which I was reasonably trusted. What I discovered at that time continues to resonate through my work even today, some twenty years later.[1]

Let me give an example. On one occasion I was able to talk with a group of Sikh militants who were members of a martyr brigade. They were Sikh versions of what would later be thought of as Islamic martyrs, the suicide bombers associated with Hamas and Al Qaeda. Late at night in the back room of a Gurdwara, a Sikh house of worship, in Delhi, six young men entered the room. They were disguised when they came in – they had scarves over their faces so that initially I could not see them. They came in armed with guns and there was tension as they entered the room. Then they sat down and took off their scarves and I felt a wave of astonishment. They were just teenagers, perhaps seventeen or eighteen years old. They reminded me of the undergraduates I had taught at Punjab University. I did not know them personally, but I felt I could have known any of them. There was nothing savage about their demeanor or their intensity. They exuded compassion towards their people and towards their religious tradition. They were in some ways the best of the younger generation of Jat Sikhs, the privileged community within Punjab. These were bright and promising young men who would ordinarily have been playing soccer and receiving prizes for their competition. But there they were, engaged in what was for them an extraordinary struggle.

I could ask anything I wanted, I was told. Their English was not bad, and I knew enough Hindi and Punjabi to supplement it. I wanted to know why, just – why? They knew what I meant, but it was a question that was as perplexing to them as it was to me. To them it was so obvious. There was a great and historical conflict, a war in which they felt totally enmeshed. To them this war was so palpable.

"We're at a time of crisis," they said. "We're in a great moment of history and it's a time of conflict between good and evil, and truth and untruth, and religion and untruth. And we have a chance to make the difference."

For them to be soldiers in a great struggle was not only intensely ennobling, it was a religious experience that was almost redemptive in its quality. That is, they felt that they could take part in this movement, in this struggle, and not only change their society but be transformed in some way. I had a sense that whatever rewards they might have obtained in a material sense were unimportant. In the case of these Sikh martyrs, since they were not Muslims, there were no heavenly rewards and no virgins waiting. The reward for these young men was the religious experience in the struggle itself: the sense that they were participating in something greater than themselves. Like any kind of religious transformation, it would not only bring great honor to their families but also redeem them personally.

What the young Sikh warriors taught me was that the religious activism of their movement was not simply a struggle over land or politics. It was an ideological struggle. Their social involvement had an intensely personal commitment, and it was motivated by the heady sense of spiritual fulfillment and the passion of holy war. Their enemy was not, however, another religion: it was the a-religion, or irreligion as they imagined it, of modernity.

This observation led me to other parts of South Asia – Sri Lanka, Kashmir, and elsewhere in India – and to other parts of the world, especially the Middle East, to see if the emerging religious activism in these regions in the 1990s was similar in character to the anti-modern religious activism of the Sikhs. Though in many places, from Kashmir to Palestine, practical issues of sovereignty and political control were touted as their goals, the passion and rhetoric of their activism was religious. In this sense it was not just that religion was politicized, the opposite was also true: politics were religionized. Social differences were cast into religious terms, and political struggle became personal and spiritual.[2]

The Khalistani paradigm of religious struggle persists in movements of religious activism around the world. The Khalistani paradigm is one where religion provides both the critique and the antidote to the secular life-style associated with modernity. The condemnation of the corruption of modern secular life – and in particular modern secular politics – is couched in religious terms. And the act of struggling against the secular state in a sacred war is itself redemptive. Fighting becomes an almost ritual act.

Years later I thought of the Sikh militants I met in a side room of a Delhi Gurdwara when I interviewed another activist, one from a different religious tradition. The young Sikhs' language of religious conviction and transformative warfare was echoed by this activist, Mahmud Abouhalima, one of the men convicted in the 1993 bombing of the World Trade Center. I interviewed Abouhalima on two occasions in the Federal Penitentiary at Lompoc in California. Mahmud is an affable, friendly, pleasant guy, a tall Egyptian with freckles and red hair – they called him Mahmud the Red. He was an easy conversationalist. He liked Western women. I was going to Denmark for a conference soon after the interview and he warned me about those Scandinavian women – "they are beautiful and treacherous," he said. He himself had had two European wives, one after the other. Mahmud swore on occasion – he was not a pious person – he would say "damn this," "shit this," in casual conversation.[3]

But when the subject came around to the role of religion in public life his eyes would begin to glaze and you would see an almost transformative change in his face. He would look at me with a sense of deep frustration and say, "Mr Mark, you just don't get it."

"You people are like sheep," Abouhalima said. "You don't see what's going on, what's really going on. Your media just won't let you see it. There's a war going on, there's a war between truth and evil, and good and bad, of religion and unreligion, and your government is the enemy."

I tried to understand why bombing buildings would make a difference in this struggle. Abouhalima didn't want to talk about the World Trade Center bombing because he was still hoping to appeal his conviction for conspiracy in the attack. But he would talk about the Oklahoma City federal building. After all nobody had accused him of that crime, and the trial of Timothy McVeigh was being conducted at the time.

"Mr Mark, if you want to understand why these people bomb buildings, I'll tell you," Abouhalima said. "Don't think it's for no reason. They have a reason."

And what reason is that? I asked him.

"They said they want to send a message," he said.

A message to whom?

"To you, Mr Mark," Abouhalima answered, explaining, "they want to send a message that the government is the enemy."

And then he sat back and looked at me and smiled. With a look of satisfaction he said, "And now you know."

And after September 11, we all knew.

In a curious kind of way what Abouhalima was telling me was how he defined terrorism. What he said was that one should not think of these recent acts of religious terrorism as simply matters of tactics or strategy in a war that can be won through other means, but as performances of very important symbolic acts. After all, what was the point of bombing the World Trade Center? What was the next thing to come? Were there going to be waves of submarines of Islamic fighters washing up on the shores of California and beginning to attack the Golden Gate? No. There hasn't been any attack by Al Qaeda on American soil in the several years since September 11. For that matter, they hadn't attacked in the nine years before – that is, the nine years after the 1993 attack. There was a great gap between the 1993 and 2001 attacks on the very same building.

Yet what a building to choose for a symbolic attack, the World Trade Center. If you were going to look for a symbol of America's economic power throughout the world in an era of globalization, the World Trade Center would be it. Its height, its domination of New York's skyline, its very name says it all. If one were also looking for a similar symbolic target to exemplify America's military power throughout the world, one might also want to choose the Pentagon. So in one day to get both was quite a feat. The event captured the enormous symbolic significance of those two sets of buildings. The choice of the buildings told us a lot about their message, a message that didn't need to be conveyed in any other way. There was no need for some sort of terrorist public relations man from Al Qaeda to come running out and say, "Well now, we bombed these two buildings for this reason or that ..." There was no need for that. The medium was the message. In this particular case the symbolic power of the buildings was enormous – not only throughout American society but I suspect even more importantly throughout the Islamic world. They were trying to impress their own people, their own potential supporters, by showing not only that the United States was the enemy but also that it was vulnerable. It could be wounded, and it could be angered into fighting back.

So it seems to me that in the post-modern era we have a post-verbal, image-driven kind of radical political message. It is conveyed by a kind of terrorism that is wholly different from traditional terrorism. These terrorist acts are less tactical than symbolic. They are less engaged in a real struggle, one that has immediate goals and gains, than one that is transcendent. I began to think of it in the terms that were presented to me by the people I was interviewing, as forms of war. I called it "cosmic war," by which I mean a war beyond human imagination, a war touched with religious weight. These are the great wars of good and bad, of truth and evil that are part of every religious tradition.[4]

Christianity also contains such images of cosmic war. When I was a boy growing up in the American Midwest in a pious Protestant family, I used to go out and see revival preachers who would come around during the summer. They would set up tents almost like a traveling carnival or a road show, and put on a great performance. The music was electrifying and the preaching terrific, and often at the end there would be an altar call. We were supposed to make a decision for Christ.

I remember one preacher who used to dress up in camouflage battle costume. He would look out as us, midwestern innocents, and growl, "There's a war going on." He went on to explain that what he had in mind was not just a metaphor. "It's a real war," he said. "It's a war between truth and evil, and good and bad. Within your own soul you've got to make a decision now – are you going to be one of the victims or are you going to be one of the victors? Are you going to make a decision for Jesus?"

He told us we had to decide on the spot and come to the Lord, and some of us did. The moment was so great, and the pressure so intense, how could anybody not want to be on the side of good? How could anybody not want to be on the side of the Lord?

Years later, when I talked with people like Abouhalima and the young Sikh men in the Delhi Gurdwara, I found myself thinking that it is only a bit of a stretch to connect my revival preachers in southern Illinois to the ideologies of Osama bin Laden or Sant Jarnail Singh Bhindranwale. Bhindranwale looked out over his sea of young Sikh men and he saw those who had shaved their beards and those who were wearing slick pants and shiny shoes and he said, "You've strayed, you've strayed, you've gone against the guru and the teachings of the book and you've strayed. It's time now to make a decision. Are you going to get right with the Lord?"

Bhindranwale, like my revival preacher, challenged his followers to straighten up, to make something out of their messy lives. And, of course, each of us has a messy life, which is why the message of religion speaks so quickly and sharply to the heart of one's private experience. Are we going to make something out of our messy lives, he wanted to know, and decide to be on the side of the right, to be soldiers for God?

The only difference between the revival preachers and bin Laden and Bhindranwale is that the followers of Al Qaeda and Khalistan were real soldiers. They had real targets, so the evil was not just the shadowy sin that is within the heart of every person but it was also externalized. In the case of bin Laden it was America; in the case of Bhindranwale it was that evil woman who was "born in the house of Brahmans," as he put it, which was his way of talking about Indira Gandhi, India's Prime Minister.[5] In some ways their struggle was a more satisfying kind of religious war than the revival preacher's. Since the enemy was not only within but also outside, the enemy could be more easily attacked. If you were a soldier in their cosmic war, you could actually do something. You really could put on your armament, you really could get weapons, and you really could do something about destroying evil.

In some ways, bin Laden and Bhindranwale preached a gloriously simplified version of the message of religion that has been a part of every tradition, the battle – that almost Manichaean battle – between oppositions, and the way in which one's own life can be purified by taking on the stand of the good. In every case of religious militancy that I have studied I have found echoes of this cosmic war. I discovered what one Christian militia member who is a supporter of Timothy McVeigh, called "an aha experience."

This "aha experience" that the Christian militia member described – this realization that there was a great war going on and the US government was the enemy – was remarkably similar to what Mahmud Abouhalima told me about his own awareness of a great war in which the US was the enemy. The two could have been the same person, though one was a Christian militia supporter of Timothy McVeigh and the other was an Al Qaeda supporter of Osama bin Laden. Both said that it changed their lives, this "aha experience." It suddenly gave clarity when they were confused, angry, frustrated, and humiliated.

The sense of humiliation was a remarkably common emotion, one described by almost everyone with whom I talked who was a supporter of, or involved in, religious violence. I have no way of knowing whether they felt a greater sense of humiliation than those who did not turn to violence, and yet it seemed to me that the frequency with which they characterized their struggle in this way indicated that this may have been the case. They said that they felt an enormous sense of frustration and humiliation over not being able to know what was going on or knowing what to do about it when the world appeared to be going out of control.

Then in the midst of their frustration many of them said that they experienced a clarifying insight, an "aha experience." The ideology of great warfare that they accepted suddenly made everything click into focus. It was in the midst of a blurry image of the world around them that the moral contours of life suddenly sharpened into view. "Aha," they seemed to say, "now I know why I've been made to feel so humiliated and frustrated, it's because there's this evil enemy and it's out to control the world." For members of the Christian militia at the time of the Oklahoma City bombing, the evil enemies were Bill Clinton and Janet Reno. The enemy list also included the forces of globalization and the new world order. They saw these forces taking away their firearms and centralizing the government and doing other things to deprive them of individual rights. But now they could do something about it, they could fight back. But more importantly than even fighting back in any kind of strategic and tactical way was to fight for the sake of fighting – in order to overcome the frustration, the utter frustration, that they felt about the world.

It was this frustration that Mahmud Abouhalima expressed to me when he said, "Mr Mark, you people are like sheep."

I usually try not to argue with the people whom I interview. It is not so much that I want to be nice, but I want to keep myself out of the picture in order to understand their point of view. In the case of Abouhalima, however, I couldn't take it any more.

"I'm not a sheep," I told him. I said that I was a Christian and I feel strongly about issues of morality in public life.

He said, "Oh no, Mr Mark, you're a sheep. You're a sheep, I know." And then he said, "I know you. I've lived your life, but you haven't lived mine. I know how you people think. You are fooled. You read what you read, you see what you see on television, and you are fooled. You don't know what is really going on."

Abouhalima had this enormous frustration about us. He thought that we really didn't get it. Not just we Americans, but most people in the Muslim world. I want to stress this because I think especially for jihadi militants associated with Al Qaeda, the Muslim audience is very important. They have the sense that the rest of the Muslim world doesn't get it. So the point of attacks such as the one on the World Trade Center is to show the Muslim world as well as us that there is a war going on. And now, as Abouhalima says, now they get it. We, Americans and Middle Easterners, now know that there are people who feel that the world is at war, that there is a great battle going on, and that the United States can be taunted into seeing the world the same way. So these acts of terror are meant to be a kind of performance, a kind of demonstration. These are acts of theater meant for television – and not just for CNN, but for Al Jazeera, television within the wider Muslim world.

So the conclusion to my search for understanding these acts of religious violence perpetrated by activists around the world, from Bhindranwale to bin Laden, is that these are religious responses to a political problem. They are responses to the perception that the world has gone awry. Let me indicate some of the implications about this way of thinking about these acts.

## Religious violence is very religious

Though every situation of religious activism has a social context in which economic and political issues have been important, these issues have never been the whole story – an ideologically religious perspective was grafted onto them. In the case of Punjab, I knew that young rural Sikhs had perfectly good reasons for being unhappy. Economically, they saw their agricultural products receiving what they thought to be less than fair market; politically, they felt their own authority was being undercut by the ruling Congress party; and socially, they regarded their status and influence waning in comparison with the urban castes. None of these things, however, explained the vitriol and religious passion with which their opposition to the government was expressed.

In the Sikh case, as in cases of religious activism around the world, the religious ingredient changes the picture dramatically. For one thing it personalizes the conflict. It provides personal reward – religious merit, redemption, and the promise of heavenly luxuries – to those who struggle in conflicts that otherwise have only social benefits. It also provides vehicles of social mobilization that embrace vast numbers of supporters who otherwise would not be mobilized around social or political issues. In many cases, it provides an organizational network of local churches, mosques, temples, and religious associations into which patterns of leadership and support may be tapped. It gives the legitimacy of moral justification for political encounter. Even more important, it provides justification for violence that challenges the state's monopoly on morally-sanctioned killing. Using Max Weber's dictum that the state's authority is always rooted in the social approval of the state to enforce its power through the use of bloodshed – in police authority, punishment, and armed defense – religion is the only other entity that can give moral sanction for violence and is therefore inherently at least potentially revolutionary.

## Religious activists critique the secular world and the secular nation-state

Movements such as the Sikh rebellion in Punjab are religious critiques of the deficiencies of the secular nation-state. In a paradoxical way, it seemed to me, the European Enlightenment's primary political creation, the modern nation-state, is both criticized and propped up by the Enlightenment's old enemy, religion. In some cases religion has become the ideological glue that holds together a sense of nationhood and supports a new kind of religious nation-state. This was the religious agenda of the revolution in Iran and also of the Hamas movement within the Palestinian liberation struggle. Nationhood became a defining part of the Sikh rebellion in Punjab – the "Khalistan" movement, as it came to be called – even though Bhindranwale said that he neither favored nor disfavored the idea. For many who lost faith in the idea of secular nationalism, religion has become the vehicle of collective identity, expressing what John Lie describes in a recent book as "peoplehood," the essential ingredient for the Enlightenment idea of the nation-state.[6]

## Religious activists sometimes have a global agenda

The remarkable mobility of the world's population in an era of mass transportation and easy communication means that most religious communities are now dispersed across the planet. Hence religious activism is often transnational in its networks of operation and its bases of support. The far-flung operations of Al Qaeda provide one case in point. The support for the Khalistani movement is another. The concept of Khalistan was coined among expatriate Punjabis in London, and the first currency for the cause was printed in Canada.

The ideology of these movements is, sometimes, transnational as well. In one of his videotaped statements after September 11, Osama bin Laden spoke about the oppression that the Islamic world has experienced in the last eighty years – evoking the image of the Ottoman Empire as the goal of his new form of transnational Islamic politics. In other instances bin Laden has been explicitly opposed to the Western style of globalization and its efforts to impose the values and power of one culture over the others. In this sense, bin Laden may be regarded as a kind of religiously-motivated guerilla anti-globalist. And yet as his Ottoman Empire reference and his transnational network indicate, he is something of a globalist himself, albeit one dedicated to an alternate Islamic vision of globalization.

## The religious passions of activists can vanish as quickly as they appear

Like summer storms, the passion of religious war can seize the consciousness of a people and allow for the most vicious acts of violence. Then just as rapidly the mood can change, the spiritual charge can dissipate, and the political differences return to a more worldly and civil form of interaction. The cultures of violence in which these activists are caught are ephemeral things. Although they dip into their cultural traditions for images and examples that will support their efforts, these battles can be fleeting fantasies. They are not wars between cultures; certainly not a "clash of civilizations."

Although war is a part of every religious tradition, no tradition teaches its followers to permanently hate other people. This idea is not traditionally Sikh or Hindu or Islamic. It is also not traditionally Christian or Jewish or anything else. It is an image of desperation that comes in response to deep frustration. In some cases, of course, there are real issues involved – such as the Palestinian movement for sovereignty to which Hamas is related. But Hamas does not express the whole of the Palestinian cause. The percentage of popular Palestinian support for Hamas has dropped dramatically in particular moments when it seemed that there would be peaceful solutions resulting from the negotiations between the Israelis and Palestinians. The terrorism of Hamas, like most terrorism, is not a permanent condition. It can change, and it can dissipate almost as rapidly as it appeared.

Why am I so confident in saying that? Because I have seen it happen in many cases. I remember the troubled days of Berkeley in the 1960s, and how the revolutionary spirit of that era that spawned the terrorism of the Weathermen movement became, in time, domesticated. The recent trial of a woman who in her youth was a member of that terrorist movement provided a poignant picture of a middle-aged woman baking brownies in a suburban home, harboring hidden and terrible memories of a violent past.

All of Northern Ireland is, in a sense, recovering from a violent past. In the case of Northern Ireland, where there were real issues of territoriality at stake, there was ability in the Good Friday agreement to move beyond the aura of ultimate confrontation. The way this happened was, I think, in part due to an astute political leadership that did not over-respond. In the Northern Ireland case, the spiral of violence began to wind down rather than to wind up.

A similar pattern happened in Punjab. I remember traveling through Punjab villages soon after the decade-long era of violence came to an end in the early 1990s. The villages had a war-ravaged look to them, an air of fatigue as if they had been swept by a hurricane, and now they were left to gather up the pieces. "The movement is over," one of the former militants told me. What he meant by that was not only that many of his colleagues were killed or in hiding, but also that

29

the mood of public support that had sustained the movement over the years had dissipated and was gone.[7] The powerful image of warfare now seemed distant, no longer related to the struggles in the world around it. The young militants who had been called "the boys" by most Punjabis, these overly-mature youngsters thrust into guerrilla war, had indeed become boys once again.

How quickly these moods of warfare can shatter and break. The lesson to be learned, I think, is that authorities have to find ways to respond to acts of terror without adopting the religious dissidents' own rhetoric of cosmic war. In an eerie kind of way the language of a "war on terrorism" buttresses the reality of those who espouse acts of terror. We need to move beyond images of ultimate confrontation. The more we can resist appearing like the evil enemy that the Bhindranwales and bin Ladens of this world say we are, the better off we are in diffusing the vicious spiral of violence and dissipating images of cosmic war.

# Notes

1 My first article on Sikh violence was published as "The Logic of Religious Violence," in *Contributions to Indian Sociology*, reprinted in David Rapoport, ed.., *Inside Terrorist Organizations* (London: Frank Cass, 1988), 172–93.

2 This comparative study of movements of religious nationalism was published as *The New Cold War? Religious Nationalism Confronts the Secular State* (Berkeley, CA: University of California Press, 1993).

3 Interview with Mahmud Abouhalima, convicted co-conspirator in the World Trade Center bombing case, federal penitentiary, Lompoc, California, September 30, 1997.

4 See Mark Juergensmeyer, *Terror in the Mind of God: The Global Rise of Religious Violence*, 3rd edn (Berkeley, CA: University of California Press, 2003).

5 Jarnail S. Bhindranwale, "Address to the Sikh Congregation" (sermon given in the Golden Temple, November 1983, trans. Ranbir S. Sandhu, April 1985, distributed by Sikh Religious and Educational Trust, Dublin, OH); and Jarnail S. Bhindranwale, "Two Lectures" (lecture given on July 19, 1983, trans. Ranbir S. Sandhu, September 20, 1983, distributed by Sikh Religious and Educational Trust, Dublin, OH).

6 John Lie, *Modern Peoplehood* (Cambridge, MA: Harvard University Press, 2004).

7 I appreciate the assistant of Prof. Harish Puri, Dept of Political Science, Guru Nanak Dev University, Amritsar, in facilitating this visit to Sultanwind village in Amritsar district.

# Part II

# THE DYNAMICS OF RELIGIOUS VIOLENCE

Case studies from South and Southeast Asia

# 3

# THE SWORD AGAINST THE CRESCENT

## Religion and violence in Muslim Southeast Asia

*Robert W. Hefner*

Surveying the vast expanse of Muslim Southeast Asia, one might be tempted to conclude that the programs of nation-building begun two generations ago are today in serious trouble. To many observers, the Muslim-majority territories of Southeast Asia – especially, Indonesia, the southern Philippines, and southern Thailand, with Malaysia a partial exception to the trend[1] – seem peculiarly afflicted with the twin blights of ineffective governance and religiously-legitimated violence. Since the overthrow of the authoritarian Suharto government in May 1998, Indonesia has seen the worst of this, with bitter battles between Christians and Muslims, terrorist attacks in Bali and Jakarta, and at least 15,000 dead in sectarian violence. The Bali bombing in October 2002, in which some 200 people were killed, was at the time the bloodiest terrorist assault since the events of September 11, 2001. The attack was not random, but the work of a shadowy, pan-Southeast Asian movement with ties to Osama bin Laden's Al Qaeda. Equally alarming, the Jemaah Islamiyah network, as it is known, was shown to have organizational links to Muslim rebels operating in the southern Philippines. In recent years, some rebels in this latter region have shifted from conventional armed struggle to terrorist attacks on civilians.

There is a bittersweet irony to the recent surge in radical Islamist violence. It is that Islam in Southeast Asia had long been regarded as more tolerant and inclusive than its Middle Eastern counterparts. When, in the early years of the twentieth century, movements for independence arose across island Southeast Asia, observant Muslims were at the forefront of those embracing the new nationalist and multireligious ideals. When, in the late 1970s and 1980s, a movement for Islamic revitalization swept the region, some of its leaders were celebrated proponents of democratic Islam. Notwithstanding this distinctive legacy, in the aftermath of the Asian economic crisis of 1998, Muslim communities across the region were shaken by the emergence of angry Islamist militias. Many observers saw their appearance as proof that, although some in the intellectual elite may be liberal-minded, Muslim politics at a mass level had become anything but democratic.

Which is it to be, then, for Muslim Southeast Asia: a civil Islam dedicated to pluralist and democratic politics, or a *jihadi* Islam determined to implement Islamic law at any price? In this chapter, I want to explore this question and the more general issue of religion and violence in Muslim-majority areas of Southeast Asia. I preface this discussion with three observations. First, radical Islamists have no monopoly on sectarian violence. In the Philippines during and after the Marcos period, Christian toughs also formed armed gangs, often with an eye toward bloodying Muslim rivals. After the overthrow of Indonesia's President Suharto in May 1998, Christian militias in Sulawesi and Kalimantan attacked hapless members of the local Muslim minority, most of whom were poor immigrants from nearby islands. Hundreds were slaughtered.[2] These and other examples remind us that *jihadi* Muslims are not the only ones to engage in sectarian violence.

My second point is that, notwithstanding the actions of non-Muslim vigilantes, the Islamist *jihadis* are a far more serious threat to Muslim Southeast Asia's long-term stability. This is so for the simple reason that Islamist paramilitaries are more numerous than their non-Muslim counterparts. Equally important, the radicals have not only targeted physical infrastructures, but have taken aim at the larger but less effectively organized community of moderate Muslims. Notwithstanding their small numbers, in other words, the radicals have damaged Southeast Asia's tradition of moderate Islam. The *jihadis* are also a threat because at least some of them have forged ties with internationalist groupings like the Al Qaeda. These linkages have allowed local militants to exercise a political influence disproportionate to their numbers in society.[3] In the most strife-torn regions, like the southern Philippines and eastern Indonesia, the *jihadis* have also succeeded in scaling up what were once local tensions and "riot systems"[4] into putative clashes of Muslim and Christian civilizations.

My third and final point is equally basic but important. It is that today's religious violence indicates that there is a struggle under way for the hearts and minds of Southeast Asian Muslims. The struggle is not the result of an unchanging "Islam" everywhere fated to extremism. Muslim politics is as varied as that in the West, and, although it gets less media attention than *jihadi* extremism, the movement for a pluralist and democratic Islam is important and growing. The struggle for the hearts and minds of Southeast Asian Muslims is the result, then, not of a uniform "Islam," but of highly varied interactions between a divided Muslim community, on the one hand, and state and society structures beset with their own problems of coordination, corruption, and sectarianism, on the other. Muslim politics in each country bears the imprint of nation-making programs and state–society interactions. As a result, the scale of each country's sectarian threat also varies.

The good news in all this is that events like the 2004 elections in Malaysia and Indonesia show that a solid majority of Muslims yearn for a political process that is moderate and pluralistic. The bad news is that containing the violent fringe will require not only the good will of the moderate majority, but heightened collaborations across the state–society divide to forge new institutions to contain the violent fringe and strengthen institutions for citizenship and social justice.

## From ethnic diversity to agonistic pluralism

Media discussions have tended to invoke either of two causes to explain recent outbursts of religious violence in Muslim Southeast Asia: the conspiratorial activities of internationalist *jihadis* like Al Qaeda or some immutably agonistic disposition in Islam itself. There *are* formidable *jihadi* groupings operating in Southeast Asia, and, as I shall discuss later, they have perpetrated awful acts of violence. The textual traditions of normative Islam dealing with jihad also contain tropes that, if moved to the center of Muslim politics, can be used to justify undemocratic and violent behaviors.[5] Neither of the above one-size-fits-all explanations, however, pays sufficient attention to either the political or the religious dynamics of Muslim Southeast Asia. An understanding of these factors is vital if we are to appreciate both the moderating strengths and the vulnerabilities of Southeast Asian Islam.

The Malay–Indonesian archipelago was a late entrant into the world of international Islam, and the way in which Islam diffused to the region has influenced the political temperament of the Muslim community to this day. Although small groups of Arab traders operated in the region from the late seventh century onwards, the first Islamic states were established only in the thirteenth and fourteenth centuries. Islam became the dominant religion in the maritime archipelago (with the notable exception of the Christian Philippines) only later, beginning around the seventeenth century. In Java, long the most populous region in island Southeast Asia, conversion to Islam was accompanied by battles between Muslim and non-Muslim kingdoms. In general, however, Islam spread not by war, but through the peaceful efforts of Muslim traders and teachers active in the region's spice trade, which linked maritime Southeast Asia to Muslim ports in India and southern Arabia. The primary impetus for conversion appears to have been the desire of local merchants and rulers to identify with what had become the dominant religion in the archipelagic macrocosm.[6]

In the aftermath of conversion, the political ecology of the archipelago continued to influence the organization and temperament of Southeast Asian Islam in three ways. First, with its thousands of islands and its ecology of alternating paddy fields, dense tropical forests, and remote uplands, the region's geographic diversity made effectively centralized government impossible, at least until the introduction of modern technologies of statecraft in the late nineteenth and twentieth centuries. Despite almost two millennia of state formation, and in striking contrast to the Middle East and East Asia, no local power ever dominated more than a portion of this region. Instead, the precolonial archipelago was fragmented into a pluricentric assortment of maritime principalities, inland agrarian states, upland and small-island chiefdoms, and stateless peoples roaming the region's vast interior forests.

A second feature of this region's political ecology was that its administrative fragmentation impeded efforts to impose religious or ethnic uniformity, creating a complex ethno-religious mosaic. The archipelago's larger ethnic populations, including the Javanese, Acehnese, Malays, and Buginese, all achieved a measure of ethnic uniformity in their respective spheres of influence. However, and again in striking contrast with events in China and the Arab Middle East, these populations never managed to homogenize ethnicity over a large territorial expanse. In religion, too, all of the Muslim ethnic groups were officially Sunni, but each was nonetheless internally divided by differences of doctrine and rite.

In their Philippine colony, the Spanish were more successful creators of a cultural empire, Christianizing the native population and creating a hybrid "Filipino" identity among the lowland peasantry in the northern and central Philippines. Even Spanish power proved no match, however, for the fractious Muslim statelets and chiefdoms in the south; these were never brought under Spanish control. The south's integration into the Philippine state would await the arrival of the Americans in the aftermath of the Spanish–American war, some three centuries after the Spanish conquest. Even then, the American pacification of the south required 15 years and took some 10,000 Muslim lives. Rather than converting the southerners to Christianity, however, the Americans provided them with the educational and organizational skills with which to begin the transition from fissiparous tribals to an imagined community of Muslims. The consolidation of that pan-Islamic identity is still far from complete; even today the south's Muslim groupings remain segmented by ethnicity, tribalism, and patronage. However, the combination of mass education, the Marcos regime's anti-Muslim policies (in the 1970s), and an influx of land-hungry Christians all worked to create a greater sense of Muslim community than ever before.[7]

Notwithstanding island Southeast Asia's ethno-religious fragmentation, then, the diffusion of Islam across most of the modern archipelago showed that local populations were not hermetically sealed from each other. The ease of maritime travel insured that, despite their ethnic differences, coastal Muslims came to share many cultural traits. For Muslim scholars (*ulama*), this included texts of Shafie jurisprudence, the only *madhab* or school of law to establish itself in the region. For what we now describe as "popular" Islam, the shared corpus included an assortment of healing rituals, midwifery techniques, saints' tales, and rites of life passage, many of which Islamic scholars regarded as of dubious orthodoxy. A small but steady stream of maritime Muslims also made the trek to southern Arabia and the Hijaz for study and pilgrimage. When, in the eighteenth and nineteenth centuries, these latter lands were swept by movements of Islamic reform, pilgrims from Southeast Asia were quick to bring the ideas back to the archipelago.[8]

More than their fellow-Muslims in maritime regions, interior peoples like the inland Javanese and the Sasak of Lombok preferred an Islam with a local or ethnic face. Even after the late twentieth century's Islamic resurgence, many among these Muslims practice a form of Islam that shows the distinctive imprint of local sensibilities.

It is, however, the tribal minorities living in the archipelago's hinterlands that have long been most resistant to the maritime ecumene's Islamic cultural flow. Many among these peoples remain non-Muslim to this day. Aware of the hinterland minorities' estrangement from their Muslim neighbors, the Dutch targeted the tribals for conversion when, late in their colonial rule, they finally allowed European missionaries access to the interior. In Malaya the British also

36

were never enthusiastic Christianizers, but they too allowed missionaries to operate among the non-Muslim peoples of Sabah and Sarawak (in what is today East Malaysia), creating ethno-religious divides that have persisted to this day.

The third and final legacy of Southeast Asia's cultural ecology brings us squarely to the issue of religion and violence in the postcolonial period. The features of political ecology that I have highlighted here – the unevenness of state penetration and the fissiparousness of ethno-religious identities – meant that those in power often found it easier to rule, not by creating a culturally cohesive citizenry, but by playing ethnic, religious, and patronage groupings against one another. The Dutch in the East Indies were ardent promoters of divide-and-rule tactics, using them to separate non-Muslims from Muslims, as well as secular Muslims from political Islamists. The British, the Spanish, and a host of native rulers never shied from the technique as well. This pattern of divide-and-conquer has had an enduring influence. In recent years it has been used not only by authoritarian leaders like Marcos of the Philippines or Suharto of Indonesia, but also by local big-men intent on exploiting ethno-religious tensions for personal gain.

## Nation-making and nation-pillaring

It would be only a slight simplification to summarize the above social history with the observation that governance in premodern and colonial Southeast Asia was based on scaling up pre-existing cleavages of sect, ethnicity, and clientage more than on creating inclusive institutions or, least of all, modern forms of citizenship.[9] For the most part, this legacy continued into the postcolonial period. However, the specific pattern varied from country to country, under the influence of state-sponsored programs of nation-building. These programs offer clues as to the reasons for the uneven incidence of religious violence across Muslim Southeast Asia today.

### Southern Philippines and Thailand: from ethno-nationalism to Muslim secessionism

In southern Thailand since the 1930s and the southern Philippines since the 1950s, the central government's efforts at nation-building were accompanied by heavy-handed efforts to assimilate the local population to non-Muslim ways. Even moderate Muslims saw the programs as deeply flawed. They cited three problems: first, the "nation" was defined in a manner that excluded or marginalized Muslims; second, the programs did little to address the Muslims' backwardness relative to the country as a whole; and third, especially after the 1960s, the cheery ideals of nationalist equality were belied by the flood of non-Muslim migrants pouring into once-Muslim lands. In Thailand's three southern provinces, Muslims retained a solid majority (about 80 percent of the local population) despite the immigration. By contrast, in the Philippines' Mindanao province, long the heartland of their settlement, Muslims had been reduced to just 40 percent of the local population by 1975.[10]

This marginalization of the Muslim population occurred at a time when the Muslim minority in both countries was increasing its contacts with the Middle East. From the 1970s on, private and state-sponsored organizations in Libya, Saudi Arabia, and the Gulf states provided scholarships for study in the Middle East. Middle Eastern patrons also subsidized local programs of mosque and *madrasah* construction, and dispatched religious proselytizers (*da'i*) to the region. In both countries, these new programs undercut traditional forms of Islamic piety, which had tended toward quietism on matters of state. Religious proselytization also accelerated the development of an overarching sense of Muslim identity, although this sentiment was weaker in the southern Philippines, where bossism and ethnic tensions remained rife.

Despite these problems, by the late 1970s the trend in both countries was for secular-nationalist organizations with only vaguely Islamic programs to give way to more explicitly Islamist groupings. Similarly, conflicts that had primarily originated in ethnic and territorial disputes slowly acquired a more religious cast, although even today this evolution is far from complete. In the Philippines, the transition is exemplified in the career of Salamat Hashim, the founder of the Moro Islamic Liberation Front (MILF). Hashim spent ten years studying at Al Azhar University in Egypt, returning to the Philippines in 1969. He soon went to work with the Moro National Liberation Front (MNLF), which, despite its nominal references to Islam, was primarily an ethno-nationalist organization. Hashim split with the MNLF leadership in 1977; in 1984, he founded the MILF. Although his disagreement with MNLF leaders was as much personal as ideological, for tactical reasons Hashim distinguished his organization from the MNLF by placing far more emphasis on the struggle to implement Islamic law.

Even as they turned to armed struggle, mainstream militants in both southern Thailand and the southern Philippines shied from incorporating terrorist violence into their tactical repertoire. From the start, however, both rebel movements were plagued by freelancers and criminals less interested in Islam than in advancing their own material interests. This, unfortunately, was a harbinger of things to come.

### *Indonesia: Muslim politics pillarized*

In Indonesia, the legacy of nation-making and ethno-religious segmentation gave rise to regionalist tensions in a few provinces, such as Aceh on the northern tip of Sumatra. However, rather than assuming a regional-secessionist form, the general pattern in this country was for sectarian and ideological rivalries to cut right into the heart of the Muslim community. In particular, the primary opposition pitted an eclectic assortment of secular, nominal, and heterodox Muslims against Islamists determined to establish an Islamic state.

One index of the intensity of this opposition was the fact that, notwithstanding the country's solid Muslim majority (about 88.7 percent of the total today), in the late 1950s Indonesia had the unusual distinction of having the largest Communist Party in the non-Communist world. The party's mass base lay primarily among ethnic Javanese, who comprise 50 percent of Indonesia's population and are predominantly Muslim. Although the communists used economic and class appeals, their popularity was also based on their opposition to Islamic government. Much the same secularist spirit prevailed among supporters of the Indonesian Nationalist Party (PNI). While predominantly Muslim, the PNI's rank and file were uncompromisingly secularist. Indeed, some of the most ardent supporters of new Javanese religions, and thus of apostasy from Islam, had their organizational base, not in the Communist Party, but in the PNI.[11]

In Indonesian studies, this pattern of ideologically-based political segmentation came to be known as the *aliran* ("stream") phenomenon, and was a regular topic of discussion in the writings of post-war authors like Clifford Geertz and Rex Mortimer.[12] Viewed in broader perspective, we can see that the *aliran* pattern was an Indonesian variant of the ethno-religious segmentation that was pervasive across much of Muslim Southeast Asia in the early independence period. What distinguished the Indonesian version from its counterparts elsewhere, however, was that the most explosive divide lay within the Muslim community rather than between Muslims and non-Muslims. Each vertically-integrated "stream" had its own political parties, religious bodies, social services, and, significantly, class hierarchy. The overall pattern resembled a phenomenon familiar to historians of Western politics: the "pillarization" of politics and religion in the Netherlands. The phrase refers to the fact that, in the nineteenth and early twentieth centuries, each of the country's major ethico-religious communities (Orthodox Calvinist, Reformed Calvinist, Catholic, and, in the late nineteenth century, secularist) developed its own political parties, schools, and social services.[13]

Notwithstanding these structural similarities, the difference between the Indonesian and Netherlands variants of pillarization is that the Dutch developed a political structure for containing communal passions within a more or less democratic framework. By contrast, *aliran* competition in Indonesia eventually overwhelmed the political system, as was tragically apparent in the violence of 1965–6. At that time, in the aftermath of a failed left-wing officers' coup, conservative army generals mobilized the army and, primarily, Muslim organizations for a systematic campaign of anti-communist killing. A half-million people died, most of them nominal or heterodox Muslims.[14]

Western scholars at first believed that the military-dominated, "New Order" government that emerged in the aftermath of the violence was determined to eliminate the *aliran* divisions once and for all. In two limited senses the New Order regime did have this ambition. First, by barring all but its own party from the countryside and reducing elections to state-managed theater, the regime circumscribed all forms of popular politics. Second, the regime policies so traumatized the communist and Marxist left that no genuinely mass-based movement for revolutionary socialism has ever re-emerged.

Despite these achievements, and despite the great socioeconomic changes of the Suharto period (1966–98), other features of the *aliran* phenomenon proved more enduring. The division between citizens of Muslim and secular-nationalist persuasion remained strong. In no small part this was the case because, notwithstanding its rhetorical appeals to national unity, the Suharto regime took every advantage of *aliran* tensions, keeping its opponents off guard by playing Muslims against non-Muslims, and secularists against observant Muslims. When, in its final years, the regime faced a growing opposition movement for democracy, it reached out to hardline Islamists, portraying the democracy movement as secularist and Christian. These efforts were not enough to save Suharto, but they provided a prototype for other old-regime supporters, who, in the post-Suharto period, recruited radical Islamists to fight proponents of democratic reform.

Despite the continuing salience of *aliran* oppositions, in one important respect things have changed, indeed decisively. The Islamic resurgence that swept Indonesia during the 1980s and 1990s left secular and nationalist Muslims more religiously observant than they and their parents had ever been. Curiously, however, the wave of pietization did not translate into greater support for radical Islam or even Muslim political parties. Indeed, the elections of 1999 and 2004 show that, if anything, support for formally Islamic parties has declined since the 1950s. Equally remarkable, in the 1980s, the leadership of the country's two largest Muslim associations, with a combined membership of about 70 million, renounced the goal of establishing an Islamic state in favor of pluralist democracy.[15] In other words, the trend in Indonesia was one of "pietization" of once-nominal Muslims, coupled with "civil-societization" of already pious Muslims. The pattern is not unique to Indonesia – recent religio-political developments in Turkey[16] bear a resemblance – but its scale is without precedent elsewhere in the Muslim world.

However remarkable these developments, they were not enough to prevent the emergence of a well-organized and radical Islamist fringe, the development of which I discuss in the next section. As background to recent developments, however, it is important to recognize that today's radicals have clear historic precedents. Unlike Malaysia (which is discussed below), Indonesia gained its independence after a long and bitter anti-colonial war. The republicans fielded a more-or-less conventional guerrilla army. In addition to these formal units, however, much of the fighting was carried out by poorly disciplined groups of young male fighters, some of whom mixed extortion and brigandery with their anticolonial heroics. Consistent with Indonesia's tradition of *aliran* mobilization, the militias tended to be organized along sectarian lines, with the primary division pitting Islamists against socialists, communists, and secular nationalists.

In the final phase of the independence struggle, two rebellions broke out that were a harbinger of paramilitarist violence to come. First, in West Java, the Darul Islam ("abode of Islam") movement took up arms demanding an Islamic state rather than republican government. And second, in east-central Java, communist rebels seized several towns and, in a club-footed attempt to spark a social revolution, slaughtered thousands of pious Muslims. Although the communist revolt was quickly extinguished, the Darul Islam (DI) rebellion dragged on for more than twelve years.[17] Even after the capture of the movement's leader in 1962, his supporters maintained a loose network of Islamic schools and study circles (*halaqa*). From these organizational perches, DI activists continued to spread their message that secular government is sinful, only God's law is legitimate, and the best way to achieve the latter is through the creation of small communities (*jemaah*) of believers dedicated to the implementation of Islamic law. It was from the ranks of these activists that, in the 1990s, a shadowy terrorist organization known as the Jemaah Islamiyah was to emerge.

## Malaysia: Islamism as ethno-politics

If in postcolonial Indonesia pillarization cut across the Muslim community, politics in independent Malaysia was based on a pillarized pluralism neatly segregated by ethnicity and religion. In other words, the basic social divide in Malaysian politics is not that separating Islamists from secular nationalists, but Malays, who are Muslim, from non-Muslim Chinese and Indians.

The pervasiveness of ethno-religious divisions reflects two historical facts. The first is that, under British rule, the Malay Peninsula experienced a flood of Chinese and (mostly) non-Muslim Indian immigration of such a scale that, on the eve of the Second World War, the Malays were on the verge of becoming a minority. Worse yet as far as the Malay leadership was concerned, Malays remained an overwhelmingly agrarian people, while non-Malays dominated the cities and the booming national economy.[18]

What made the situation of the Malays so different from their counterparts in southern Thailand and the southern Philippines, however, was that in the transition to independence the British handed control of the state to Malays. Although excluded from the commanding heights of the economy, then, the Malay leadership used the state and national media to instill a sense of ethnic solidarity in the Malay population. The Malay-dominated state also provided preferential contracts to Malay businesses, improved Malay education, lifted the economic fortunes of rural Malays, and, by the 1990s, brought a surprisingly confident Malay middle class into existence. Despite allegations of cronyism, Malaysia's forty-year experiment with affirmative action remains one of the modern world's most successful.[19]

For the last thirty years of these social programs, Malay society also underwent an Islamic resurgence every bit as intense as that in neighboring Indonesia. Two features, however, distinguished the Malaysian resurgence from its neighbor's. First, notwithstanding the efforts of a few liberal-minded scholars, the tone of the Malaysian resurgence was more intellectually conservative than its Indonesian counterpart. The conservatism was especially apparent in the statements of the leading Islamist party, the All-Malaysia Islamic Party, known by its acronym as PAS. Although in the 1950s it had originated as an alliance of religious scholars and populist progressives, since the 1970s PAS has taken a theologically conservative tack, aimed at implementing the letter of Islamic law, including its controversial provisions on adultery, theft, and apostasy.[20]

The second characteristic of the Malaysian resurgence is equally distinctive. Notwithstanding their theological conservatism, and notwithstanding their habit of casting caustic aspersions at the US (as when the PAS leadership called for holy war against the United States after the invasion of Afghanistan),

Malaysian Islamists have shown a willingness to work within the framework of constitutional government. Conversely, they have been reluctant to dabble in the paramilitarist adventurism so dear to the hearts of Islamist hardliners in Thailand, the Philippines, and Indonesia. Of course, over the past thirty years Malaysia has seen a few incidents of radical Islamist violence. In addition, during the 1980s, some two hundred Malaysian militants traveled to Afghanistan to train with the *mujahidin*. Several dozen of these *jihadis* eventually joined the Jemaah Islamiyah (see below). In contrast to Indonesia and the southern Philippines, however, in Malaysia the Jemaah Islamiyah has never succeeded in its goal of forging ties to a mass movement. However conservative their theology may be, Malaysian Islamists continue to focus their energies on elections, party-building, and constitutionally-regulated politics.

## Varieties of Islamist violence

In the aftermath of the US-led invasion of Afghanistan, the second territory on which US policy-makers trained their attention was the Philippines. This was the first country after Afghanistan to receive US ground forces. More generally, policy analysts and the media began to voice concerns that Southeast Asia was about to become a second front for Al Qaeda. To many observers, the sectarian clashes in eastern Indonesia, the Bali and Jakarta Marriott bombings, and terrorist attacks in the Philippines and southern Thailand seemed to indicate the front had indeed been opened.

The genealogy of Islamist violence in Muslim Southeast Asia is, however, more complex than these anxious analyses imply. To understand the origins and likely future of religiously legitimated violence, we need to examine its variation by country, its precise ideological rationale, and the relationship of local militants to transnational jihadism.

### *Regional variation in Islamist violence*

What is striking about recent outbreaks of Islamist violence in Southeast Asia is that their incidence and scale map neatly against the social history of nation-making and ethno-religious tension outlined above. For example, notwithstanding the force of the Asian economic crisis of 1998 and the furor surrounding the imprisonment of the popular Deputy Prime Minister, Anwar Ibrahim, in 1998, Malaysia has been largely free of religious violence. Even among Muslims of Islamist persuasion, there is little enthusiasm for paramilitary jihad. In part this reflects the pragmatism of the new Malay middle class, which Western social critics often simplistically deride as conservative. However, the achievement also reflects the fact that, whereas Indonesia, southern Thailand, and the Philippines have long traditions of paramilitarist rebellion, Malaysians have managed to keep the train of national politics on a largely constitutional track.

Since the late 1990s, southern Thailand and the Philippines have seen renewed outbreaks of secessionist violence. Events in the Philippines show their trademark mixture of bossist rivalry, tribal tension, and criminality. In southern Thailand, the primary catalyst for the violence remains dissatisfaction with what is seen as the repressive hand of the central government. Although in the late 1990s Thai authorities seemed to be making progress in their negotiations with Muslim leaders, violence erupted again in 2003–04. Although small-scale by comparison with the southern Philippines and eastern Indonesia, these incidents show that some among the younger generation hope to rekindle the secessionist fire, in response to what is seen as a hardening of the Thai government's attitude toward Muslims.

It is unclear whether some among the youthful militants have received assistance from Al Qaeda or the Jemaah Islamiyah, as Thai authorities have claimed. Although understandably upset with attacks on Thai civilians and officials in late 2003 and early 2004, the Thai authorities' methodical killing of more than 100 lightly-armed militants on April 28, 2004, and the suffocation death of another 78 protestors in police custody on October 26, 2004, are prime examples of the type of heavy-handed repression certain to deepen secessionist passions.

The situation in the southern Philippines remains the most serious in all of Muslim Southeast Asia, for two reasons.[21] First, the scale of the armed Islamic opposition is the region's largest. There are today some 10,000–15,000 fighters associated with the Moro Islamic Liberation Front (MILF), and another 1,000 or so associated with the more extremist Abu Sayyaf Group. More than 100,000 youth have also received some form of military training, and stand ready to assist the full-time fighters.[22] Second, recent developments in the southern Philippines also indicate that there is increasing cooperation between local rebels and transnational *jihadis*. With this, too, we have begun to see a worrying shift among some rebels from conventional armed resistance to terrorism. There is also evidence of heightened collaboration between the MILF and the Jemaah Islamiyah, a development discussed below.

### *The special case of Indonesia*

It is in Indonesia, however, that the complex genealogy of recent violence is most apparent. In 1999 and 2004, the country conducted its first free elections since the 1950s. Both elections saw the great majority of citizens cast their vote for parties of either a secular nationalist or moderate Islamic orientation. True to earlier patterns of paramilitarist violence, however, a radical Islamist fringe defied public opinion and organized armed militias; attacked discothèques, bars, and other alleged centers of vice; and coordinated a violent counterattack against Christian militias in the eastern provinces of Maluku, North Maluku, and Central Sulawesi. As noted earlier, during the first phase of the conflict in the latter provinces, Christian gangs – some with secessionist aspirations of their own – carried out mass killings of Muslims. Islamist militias then responded in kind. In these three eastern provinces, more than 15,000 people have died; a million people have been displaced; and, despite the signing of a peace deal in 2002, the violence continues to this day.

The recruitment methods and organization of Indonesia's largest Islamist paramilitaries vary in a way that demonstrates that there is no single ideology, organization, or international mastermind behind the militia phenomenon as a whole. The largest group in the early post-Suharto period was the Islamic Defenders Front (Front Pembela Islam or FPI). The FPI grew out of an Islamist paramilitary organized by Arab–Indonesian Islamists with the support of the commander of the Jakarta police force and the commander of the armed forces, General Wiranto (a candidate for the presidency in Indonesia's 2004 elections). The FPI was first mobilized to defend a special session of the People's Consultative Assembly held in November 1998, six months after Suharto's resignation. The Assembly was to prepare the way for national elections and, it was widely assumed, the election of Suharto's designated successor, B.J. Habibie, to the presidency. Muslim sources in the capital whom I interviewed in these years reported that former President Suharto provided some of the funds for this militia effort. The fact that General Wiranto – a man previously regarded as having strong nationalist, not Islamist sympathies – became involved with the FPI, shows that the motive for the cooperation had less to do with religion than it did with elite jockeying for political influence.

However cordial their ties with some commanders, the leadership of the FPI was never merely a pawn of its military backers. In the capital city of Jakarta, where the organization had its base, FPI militants clashed repeatedly with police during 2000 and 2001. After one especially violent exchange, FPI leaders threatened to kill police officials who got in their way. The police responded with threats of their own. These incidents indicated that, although the FPI had powerful backers, some in the security elite were unhappy with the arrangement. In the aftermath of the Bali bombings in October 2002, domestic opinion swung solidly against the FPI, and, just a week after the violence, the FPI suspended operations.

The second largest Islamist paramilitary, the Laskar Jihad, also enjoyed a special relationship with a faction in the military command. Whereas the FPI specialized in combating vice and battling democracy activists, the Laskar Jihad was formed in early 2000 with the aim of combating "secessionist" activity in Christian regions of eastern Indonesia. The Laskar Jihad soon became the largest and best coordinated of Islamist paramilitaries operating in Maluku and Central Sulawesi. At one point, the leader of the Laskar Jihad, Jafar Umar Thalib, announced plans to dispatch militants to the province of Aceh, to fight secessionist rebels. The announcement provoked an angry reaction among Acehnese – who denounced Thalib as an army stooge. Shortly thereafter, Thalib scuttled his plan.

The Laskar Jihad appears to have enjoyed the backing of old-regime supporters because, of all the Islamist paramilitaries, it was the most willing to take on the government of Abdurrahman Wahid. Wahid was the near-blind democracy activist and leader of the Nahdlatul Ulama who was elected president in October 1999. In interviews with me in November 1999, Laskar Jihad officials stated bluntly that they regarded Wahid as a "communist and apostate," and were willing to work with anyone who opposed his presidency. In early 2000, the Laskar Jihad opened a military camp in West Java, where, as the International Crisis Group reported in

44

February 2002,[23] out-of-uniform members of the Indonesian military helped train the organization's jihad fighters. The Laskar Jihad also sponsored fiery rallies in cities, including one in front of the presidential palace where, as army officials stood by, machete-wielding activists threatened the president. Shortly thereafter, the Laskar Jihad moved hundreds of fighters from its camp in West Java across Java to Surabaya. From there they sailed on government-owned ferries to Maluku. They made the passage despite repeated appeals from the president, the minister of defense, and the governor of Maluku province that they not be allowed to travel.

A former mid-level field commander of the Laskar Jihad, whom I interviewed in August 2001 in Yogyakarta, explained how Jafar Umar Thalib came to enjoy this tactical support. Military retirees, explained the activist, had approached Thalib, in January 2000, with the message that they were willing to support his campaign in Maluku. The intermediaries made clear that they also shared Thalib's desire to undermine the reform government of Abdurrahman Wahid. Once the deal was agreed, a leading Arab-Indonesian businessman and two other allies of former President Suharto coordinated a flow of funds and arms to the jihad forces.

In the aftermath of the Bali bombings in October 2002, the Laskar Jihad was quickly disbanded, as was the Islamic Defenders Front. Although media reports and some Western scholars claimed that financial difficulties caused the organization's collapse, my contacts in the former organization confirmed that military backers had ordered Thalib to cease operations because of "international concerns." As I learned in Yogyakarta in August 2003, some sub-commanders in the organization opposed Thalib's decision and went on to form new militias of their own. None of these has sent troops into battle. In fact, one of the disgruntled militants told me that quite a few Muslims no longer had the appetite for jihad.

### The Jemaah Islamiyah and Jihadi internationalism

The third and final paramilitary organization I shall discuss here, the Jemaah Islamiyah (JI), is the most distinctive of the three, not least of all because it is the only one that is truly internationalist in organization.[24] Founded by Indonesians in exile in Malaysia in January 1993, the Jemaah Islamiyah is also the oldest of Indonesia's three main paramilitaries. Its leadership has an even deeper history, having earlier had ties to the Darul Islam movement, a group that had rebelled against the republican government in 1948 and continued armed resistance until 1962. Many of the second-tier leadership of the JI have an additional item in their internationalist portfolio, having undergone military training in Afghanistan in the late 1980s and early 1990s. It was in the Afghan camps that some of the future leaders of the JI made contact with Salamat Hashim, the founder of the MILF.

These international contacts were the basis for cooperation between the Jemaah Islamiyah and the MILF from the mid-1990s on. There is, one should add, no evidence to indicate that these early contacts had anything to do with Al Qaeda, although the latter organization had emissaries in the southern Philippines at this time. Al Qaeda's earliest contacts in Southeast Asia were most likely with the Abu Sayyaf Group, not the JI.

45

Formal cooperation between the JI and the MILF began in 1994, with an agreement allowing the JI to establish a camp-within-a-camp at the MILF's Abu Bakar complex in Mindanao. The Philippine army captured Abu Bakar in July 2000, after an offensive that displaced almost a million people. Sidney Jones and the International Crisis Group report, however, that to this day the JI continues to operate a training camp at a more remote mountain location.[25] The ICG remarked, "JI's training program in Mindanao was crucial in producing a new generation of operatives capable of filling the shoes of the Afghan veterans, increasingly depleted by post-Bali arrests in Indonesia, Malaysia, Singapore and Thailand."[26]

In recent years, the Jemaah Islamiyah and the MILF – or, at the very least, factions within each of these groups – have also collaborated in terror attacks. These include the attempted assassination of the Philippine ambassador to Indonesia on August 1, 2000, and the Davao bombings of March and April 2003, in which 38 people died. Inasmuch as the MILF is the region's largest Muslim secessionist movement and the Jemaah Islamiyah is its most ambitious terrorist network, this collaboration is a serious development indeed.

The long-term prospects for this collaboration, however, remain unclear. With significant arrests in Singapore, Malaysia, Indonesia, and the Philippines, Southeast Asian governments have dealt the JI leadership a serious blow. The Philippine army's attacks on MILF camps have also damaged the MILF infrastructure. Complicating matters further, in July 2003, the MILF's leader, Salamat Hashim, died of natural causes. True to the long-standing pattern of Philippine Muslim politics, aspirants to the MILF leadership quickly split along ethnic, tribal, and bossist lines. The result has been a decentralization of the day-to-day command, with some lower-ranking units now operating independently. Although this fissioning has weakened the organization, it also makes negotiation with MILF leaders more difficult. Recent developments have also made it difficult to determine to what degree MILF collaboration with the Jemaah Islamiyah, the Abu Sayyaf Group, and the Al Qaeda is a matter of formal policy, or an arrangement made by individual MILF commanders.

The Jemaah Islamiyah remains the most elusive of Muslim Southeast Asia's terrorist groups. Although media reports often present the organization as a branch of the Al Qaeda, the JI came into existence in 1993, probably before its leadership had made formal contact with Al Qaeda operatives. Moreover, the JI leadership appears divided on questions of long-term strategy. My interviews with JI sympathizers in central Java confirm the excellent reports of Sidney Jones and her ICG research team that there is a *jihadi* faction, linked primarily to associates of Hambali (the now-imprisoned commander for JI military operations), committed to carrying out terrorist actions. However, another faction, perhaps linked to the JI emir, Abu Bakar Ba'asyir (although his precise disposition is still not clear), believes that, before sustained jihad operations can be undertaken, the Muslim population must be prepared through religious education. One expression of the latter conviction was Abu Bakar Ba'asyir's decision to work with the "Council of Indonesian Mujahidin" (Majelis Mujahidin Indonesia, or MMI), founded in Yogyakarta in August 2000. The ICG has reported, and my own interviews have confirmed, that some Jemaah Islamiyah militants viewed Ba'asyir's involvement in this organization as a waste of time.

Inspired by Osama bin Laden's appeals in 1996 and 1998 calling for attacks on Americans, the Hambali faction of the JI carried out bombings in Bali in October 2002 and Jakarta in August 2003. In interviews in May 2003 with my Indonesian research assistant, Ba'asyir made clear that he did not regard the Bali bombings as sinful – merely a tactical blunder. "All those Westerners were going to hell anyway," he observed, on tape, and aware that the Indonesian interviewer was conducting the interview for an American.[27] He then added, however, that he worried that such attacks might undermine support for implementation of the *shariah*.

## Conclusion

This split in the JI leadership – between *jihadis* infatuated with purgative violence,[28] and militants determined to build a more enduring, if still jihadist organization – has its counterpart in radical Islamist circles across the Muslim world. In Southeast Asia, the tension between the two camps has increased in recent years. During this same period, army regulars in the southern Philippines seized the main MILF rebel camp. This weakened the rebel leadership's control over its units, leaving many free to launch attacks on their own. In Indonesia over the past two years, security officials have also dealt severe blows to the Jemaah Islamiyah. In the meantime, however, new paramilitarists have come on the scene, many less disciplined than the JI. As my interviews with returned Maluku fighters in Yogyakarta have revealed, some among these freelance *jihadis* are ex-criminals who dabbled in extortion and gangsterism before discovering Islam. The presence of freelancers like these in the *mujahidin* movement is a worrying development. It suggests that, even if security officials contain the Jemaah Islamiyah, less disciplined groups may emerge in its wake.

The decentralization of terrorist organizations has been counteracted, however, by three important developments: the continuing crackdown on *jihadis*; a relative, if not total, decline in Indonesian armed-forces support for Islamist paramilitaries; and, at least in Indonesia and Malaysia, the Muslim public's growing irritation with *jihadism*. The 2004 elections in Malaysia and Indonesia showed that the Muslim public has little appetite for radical paramilitarism. Mainstream groupings like the Nahdlatul Ulama and the Muhammadiyah have also launched major campaigns to discredit proponents of *jihadi* violence. What makes these trends all the more noteworthy is that they have taken place against the backdrop of what are, by any measure, extraordinary levels of public anger with US policies in the Middle East. If there's a silver lining in this cloud, then, it is that the Muslim public in these two countries seems to have developed a rational ability to distinguish opposition to US policies from support for paramilitarist Islam. The achievement has been facilitated by the hard-fought efforts of moderates attempting to recenter Muslim politics away from violence toward democratic government. The process is incomplete, but it is promising. The effort seeks to scale up resources for civility and pluralism long endemic to the region, albeit in a latent or uninstitutionalized form.[29]

The same generalization does not yet apply to southern Thailand or the southern Philippines. In the latter territory, in particular, the organization for the production of violence is well entrenched, and both conventional resistance and unconventional terrorism may continue for some time. Equally worrying, some militants in these regions may again try to export *jihadi* fighters to other parts of Southeast Asia.

Developments in Malaysia and Indonesia nonetheless provide grounds for cautious hope. They show that, even if the battle for the soul of Islam is far from over, there are extensive local resources for Muslim pluralism and civility. The most important of these include the many moderate Muslims determined to win the clash *within* Muslim civilization once and for all. The lesson for Western policy analysts is that the campaign against terrorism must not be seen in purely military terms, because its ultimate success depends on the efforts of Islamic moderates to win Muslim hearts and minds.

## Notes

1  The small Sultanate of Brunei is also a Muslim-majority country, and there are significant Muslim minorities in Cambodia and Burma as well.

2  On the Kalimantan violence, see, "Communal Violence in Indonesia: Lessons from Kalimantan," ICG Asia Report, no. 19, International Crisis Group, June 27, 2001; on Central Sulawesi, see Lorraine V. Aragon, "Communal Violence in Poso, Central Sulawesi: Where People Eat Fish and Fish Eat People," *Indonesia* 72, (2001): 45–79.

3  See Robert W. Hefner, "Muslim Democrats and Islamist Violence in Post-Suharto Indonesia," in *Remaking Muslim Politics: Pluralism, Contestation, Democratization*, ed. Robert W. Hefner (Princeton, NJ: Princeton University Press, 2005), 273–301.

4  The phrase is from Paul R. Brass, *The Production of Hindu–Muslim Violence in Contemporary India* (Seattle: University of Washington Press, 2003), 12–16.

5  For a discussion of the normative precedents for authoritarianism and antidemocratic violence in Islamic tradition, see Khaled A. El Fadl, *Rebellion and Violence in Islamic Law* (Cambridge: Cambridge University Press, 2001).

6  On the culture and political economy of early Islamic conversion, see Alijah Gordon, ed., *The Propagation of Islam in the Indonesian–Malay Archipelago* (Kuala Lumpur: Malaysian Sociological Research Institute, 2001); and Anthony Reid, *Southeast Asia in the Age of Commerce, 1450–1680, Volume 2: Expansion and Crisis* (New Haven, CT: Yale University Press, 1993), 132–201.

7  On the process of ethno-religious change in the twentieth-century south, see Thomas M. McKenna, *Muslim Rulers and Rebels: Everyday Politics and Armed Separatism in the Southern Philippines* (Berkeley, CA: University of California Press, 1998).

8  On popular and normative Islam, see Denys Lombard, *Le Carrefour Javanais: Essai d'Histoire Globale, Volume II: Les Réseaux Asiatique* (Paris: Éditions de l'École des Hautes Études en Sciences Sociales, 1990); Roy F. Ellen, "Social Theory, Ethnography and the Understanding of Practical Islam in South-East Asia," in *Islam in South-East Asia*, ed. M.B. Hooker (Leiden: E.J. Brill, 1983), 50–91; and John R. Bowen, *Muslims Through Discourse: Religion and Ritual in Gayo Society* (Princeton, NJ: Princeton University Press, 1993).

9  A theme explored in Robert W. Hefner, "Introduction: Multiculturalism and Citizenship in Malaysia, Singapore, and Indonesia," in *The Politics of Multiculturalism: Pluralism*

*and Citizenship in Malaysia, Singapore, and Indonesia*, ed. Robert W. Hefner (Honolulu: University of Hawaii Press, 2001), 1–58.

10  On southern Thailand, see Peter Chalk, "Militant Islamic Separatism in Southern Thailand," in *Islam in Asia: Changing Political Realities*, ed. Jason F. Isaacson and Colin Rubenstein (New Brunswick: Transaction Publishers, 2002), 165–86; on the southern Philippines, see McKenna, *Muslim Rulers*; and, for an earlier view, Cesar A. Majul, *The Contemporary Muslim Movement in the Philippines* (Berkeley, CA: Mizan Press, 1985).

11  On the Nationalist Party's support for new religious movements and, therefore, apostasy from Islam, see Robert W. Hefner, "Islamizing Java? Religion and Politics in Rural East Java," *Journal of Asian Studies* 46, no. 3 (August 1987): 533–54.

12  Clifford Geertz, *Religion of Java* (Glencoe, IL: Free Press, 1960); and Rex Mortimer, *Indonesian Communism Under Sukarno: Ideology and Politics 1959–1965* (Ithaca, NY: Cornell University Press, 1974).

13  On pillarization in the Netherlands, see Arend Lijphart, *Democracy in Plural Societies: A Comparative Exploration* (New Haven, CT: Yale University Press, 1977); and Anton C. Zijderveld, "Civil Society, Pillarization, and the Welfare State," in *Democratic Civility: The History and Cross-Cultural Possibility of a Modern Political Ideal*, ed. Robert W. Hefner (New Brunswick: Transaction Publishers, 1998), 153–71.

14  Robert Cribb, ed., *The Indonesian Killings: Studies from Java and Bali* (Clayton, Victoria: Centre of Southeast Asian Studies, Monash University, 1990). Hindu–Balinese communities also saw great violence; see Geoffrey Robinson, *The Dark Side of Paradise: Political Violence in Bali* (Ithaca, NY: Cornell University Press, 1995).

15  Robert W. Hefner, *Civil Islam: Muslims and Democratization in Indonesia* (Princeton, NJ: Princeton University Press, 2000).

16  See Jenny B. White, *Islamist Mobilization in Turkey: A Study in Vernacular Politics* (Seattle: University of Washington Press, 2002).

17  C. van Dijk, *Rebellion under the Banner of Islam: the Darul Islam in Indonesia* (The Hague: Martinus Nijhoff, 1981).

18  William R. Roff, *The Origins of Malay Nationalism*, 2nd edn (Oxford: Oxford University Press, 1994).

19  On affirmative action programs for Malays, see R.S. Milne and Diane K. Mauzy, *Malaysian Politics Under Mahathir* (New York: Routledge, 1999), 50–79; on the new Malay middle class, see Abdul R. Embong, *State-Led Modernization and the New Middle Class in Malaysia* (New York: Palgrave, 2002).

20  On the impact of the resurgence in Malaysia, see Virginia Hooker and Norani Othman, eds., *Malaysia: Islam, Society and Politics* (Singapore: Institute of Southeast Asian Studies, 2003); and Michael G. Peletz, *Islamic Modern: Religious Courts and Cultural Politics in Malaysia* (Princeton, NJ: Princeton University Press, 2002).

21  For an overview of recent trends, see "Southern Philippines Backgrounder: Terrorism and the Peace Process," ICG Asia Report, no. 80, International Crisis Group, July 13, 2004.

22  Ibid., 2.

23  "Indonesia: The Search for Peace in Maluku," ICG Asia Report, no. 31, International Crisis Group, February 8, 2002, 8.

24  For overviews of the Jemaah Islamiyah in Southeast Asia, see "Al-Qaeda in Southeast Asia: The Case of the 'Ngruki Network' in Indonesia," ICG Indonesia Briefing, International Crisis Group, August 8, 2002; and "Indonesia Backgrounder: How the *Jemaah Islamiyah* Terrorist Network Operates," ICG Asia Report, no. 43, International Crisis Group, December 11, 2002. On the financing of JI operations, see Zachary Abuza, "Funding Terrorism in Southeast Asia: The Financial Network of Al Qaeda and Jemaah Islamiyah," *NBR Analysis* 14, no. 5 (December 2003).

25  "Southern Philippines Backgrounder," 13.

26  Ibid., 17.

27 Author and research assistant's interview with Abu Bakar Ba'asyir, August 2003.
28 On the radical Islamist trope of purgative violence, see John Calvert, "The Mythic Foundations of Radical Islam," *Orbis* 48 (Winter 2004): 29–41; on the religiously-sanctioned violence in comparative context, see Emmanuel Sivan, "The Enclave Culture," in *Fundamentalisms Comprehended*, ed. Martin E. Marty and R. Scott Appleby (Chicago: University of Chicago Press, 1995), 11–68; and Mark Juergensmeyer, *Terror in the Mind of God: The Global Rise of Religious Violence*, 3rd edn (Berkeley, CA: University of California Press, 2000).
29 A theme developed at greater length in Hefner, "Multiculturalism and Citizenship," 1–58.

# 4

# BUDDHISM, VIOLENCE, AND THE STATE IN BURMA (MYANMAR) AND SRI LANKA

*Juliane Schober*

Much recent public and academic discourse on the intersections of religion with conflict in general, and communal violence in particular, has been limited by generalizations about particular religions and a presumably universal conception of the secular. Such discussions often entail implicit presumptions about the propensities, the "essence" or even the authenticity of particular religious traditions and their practical or doctrinal stance towards violence. By illuminating the place of violence in Buddhism, I hope to dispel the notion that religions embracing a doctrine of nonviolence are necessarily immune to it. Similarly, religious justifications for violence do not necessarily translate into actuality. My intention is instead to point to the ways in which religious discourse, a universal anthropological phenomenon, tends to intersect with other sources of conflict to augment a potential for violence.

A second misconception informing many discussions concerns the often unstated preconception that a Western understanding of the secular and its relation to religion are universally shared. Instead, I treat the notion of secular power as an ethnographic concept that is not universally shared, but rather embedded within particular histories of Western enlightenment and colonialism. Modern interpretations of the secular, and of secular state power, derive from a particular history of European post-enlightenment thought. Moreover, they were shaped by Christian cultures and modern political ideologies in the West. And Western colonialism has been instrumental in circulating interpretations of the secular across cultures in many parts of the globe. Interpretations of secular power in Asian cultures, however, often incorporate different understandings concerning the division of human and divine powers. The failure to underscore the ethnographic and religious valorizations of the secular, particularly the secular power of the modern state, has been limiting discussions on the religio-political histories and colonial legacies in South and Southeast Asia.

By contrast, I presuppose in this essay that religious meaning and the interpretation of symbols in social practice draw on cultural memory and can be employed to authorize violence through religious means. Specifically, I argue that religious discourse plays a special role in ameliorating or exacerbating cultural perceptions about social, economic, and political conditions that are prone to violent conflict. Religion plays a special role in communal violence precisely because it furnishes an ultimate language and symbols that essentialize, otherize, and render in absolute moral terms potential conflicts embedded in social and cultural contexts. In the absence of such religious discourse, potential conflicts are located in relative social contexts. Through generalization and moral abstraction and by creating auras of absolute values and universal righteousness, religious discourse can empower, engender, or disrupt violence.

In the West, popular opinion tends to identify "authentic" Buddhism with nonviolence and many presume that Buddhism rejects all forms of violence.[1] From a doctrinal perspective, Buddhism espouses an ethic of nonviolence, as do other religions. Buddhist Precepts (*sila*) prohibit killing and Buddhist texts speak in detail about the moral consequences, in this and future lives, of killing another sentient being, human or otherwise.[2] One's *karma*, the ethical force that determines the quality of this and future lives, will manifest the results of causing violence which, inevitably, creates suffering for the perpetrator in this and future lives. Even the future Buddha is believed to have endured suffering as a consequence of violent action in previous lives.

Buddhist doctrine explains that the Path to Moral Perfection (*nirvana*) extends over rebirths in countless lives. Its mastery speaks primarily to mental and spiritual accomplishments of the individual. Although pivotal in fostering the social and material conditions for enlightenment, Buddhist communities generally do not unite across national boundaries for a common goal or to combat a religious "other." In contrast to other world religions, Buddhism does not uphold a belief in religious redemption through warfare like the Crusades. Nor does it have a doctrine or history to mobilize religious communities to act violently against unbelievers. And, finally, Buddhists generally do not identify with a global, transnational, or universal brotherhood in order to legitimate local practices. Instead, the Buddha's sacred biography and the cult of his relics justify ritual veneration at sacred centers throughout the Buddhist world that are seen as centers of extraordinary power. That power is understood to embody simultaneously political and religious dimensions that reflect on the status of local Buddhist leaders and define a political and ritual hegemony within their communities.[3]

Seen from the vantage point of history, however, violence has been and continues to be present in Buddhist societies as Buddhists have been both targets and agents of communal violence. And finally, communal rioting and killings have been justified by Buddhist and ethnic motives in a number of Asian societies. One is reminded of the Chinese occupation of Tibet which initiated the exodus of Tibetan monks in 1959. The Fourteenth Dalai Lama, then the religious and political leader of Tibet, led his community into exile to Dharamsala in northern India where the Tibetan government in exile now officially resides. In the course of the Cultural Revolution that raged through Tibet, countless Buddhist monks have been killed and monasteries and libraries as the repositories of centuries of Buddhist learning were destroyed.[4] Cambodia suffered similar mass violence against Buddhists, their traditions and institutions during the Pol Pot regime. In Sri Lanka, violent riots have been promulgated by Buddhist monks and lay people in defense of their vision of a distinctly Buddhist nationalism. At the same time, Sri Lankan Buddhists have been the target of violence unleashed against them by ethnic and religious "others," the Tamil Tigers.[5] In 1973, the Thai monk Kitthiwuttho stated that killing communists did not cause negative *karma* and the Buddhist Precepts were tantamount to national law.[6] In Burma, Theravada Buddhism has just as frequently become a site for resisting the power of state. To help project how these dynamics may play out in future conflicts, we need to examine closely the political roles Buddhist monks, institutions, and symbols have played in various historical trajectories and social contexts. The examples adduced here point to the likely continuation of the significant roles Buddhist elements assume in contexts that precipitate violent conflict.

While cautioning against generalizing about the contemporary intersections of religion and violence, this essay examines such recent conjunctures of Buddhism, violence, and the state in Burma and, by comparison, in Sri Lanka. In particular, I hope to illustrate the complexities of public discourse about ultimate meanings of life and death in the modern history of Buddhism, violence, and the state in Burma. I examine the ways in which the present regime continues to function within a colonial legacy, namely to organize the population for the purposes of extracting resources. In the absence of a national constitution since 1988 that would otherwise empower the official acts of a secular modern state in Burma, the regime has employed Buddhist authority and institutions to legitimate its politics. This essay focuses therefore on recent Burmese national politics and the popular uprising of 1988 in which the sangha facilitated a popular revolt against the state; the anti-Muslim riots of 1997, and the subsequent instigations by the regime to exploit anti-Muslim sentiments among Buddhists; and lastly, the ambush of Aung San Suu Kyi's caravan of cars traveling near Dipeyin, Sagaing Division, where, through deceptive use of Buddhist authority, agents of the state massacred many of her supporters. Although other incidents can be adduced, my choice is to discuss these examples in order to indicate a discursive trajectory in which Buddhist symbols and authority can facilitate violence.

A brief consideration of militant Buddhist monks in Sri Lanka documents that a significant number of monks facilitated, advocated, and perpetrated violence. I also enumerate some salient differences in the political roles Buddhist monks have played in perpetuating violent conflict. The conclusions underscore that religion can serve as a catalyst to pre-empt or promote violent conflict. In other words, our focus is perhaps less well served by examining closely any single religious tradition and its justifications for violence. As scholars, we may unwittingly empower a culture of religious violence by decontextualizing its public discourse from the social conditions that render the unfathomable plausible and meaningful in everyday life. Rather, our intention must be to construct an explanation that draws on a broader investigation into the kinds of social and cultural conditions that foster a religious discourse advocating violence and chart their developments when religion becomes a marked variable and assumes a pivotal role in communal violence.

## The *Sangha* and the state in modern Theravada Buddhism

To give some insight into the culture of politics that characterizes Theravada Buddhism in traditional and many contemporary contexts, a few general remarks are appropriate concerning the legitimation of politics that Buddhist monks and institutions have often provided. In traditional culture, one's social, political, and economic status was indicative of past ethical action (*karma*). Buddhist kings (*dhammaraja*) and lay people who aspired to political power or desired to attain a better rebirth participated in a ritual hegemony in which material support given to monks and religious causes was exchanged for spiritual returns in this and future lives.[7] Monks and monasteries continue to be revered and receive significant donations, and they also harbor a powerful potential to mobilize people and resources. This kind of ritual hierarchy is expressed in a variety of Burmese cultural contexts. In his discussion of traditional Buddhist societies in Southeast Asia, Tambiah describes this exchange of material support for religious merit and social status as a total social fact, an all-encompassing cultural system, in which a cosmological worldview encompasses politics, power, economics, history, and culture.

Contrary to popular perceptions in the west, the sangha is an institution structured by multiple principles of hierarchy. A culture of hierarchy pervades interactions with and among monks as junior monks are expected to obey and respect senior ones. Most basic is the seniority that monks acquire through years spent living a monastic life. In most branches of the tradition, full ordination requires that the monk be at least 20 years of age and his seniority increases with each year of service. The relative seniority of a monk since ordination also determines whether he greets another monk by bowing to him or whether he will receive such homage, although the relative position of two individuals to one another may be less marked. Monastic rank within a monastery further differentiates status among monks, with the abbot receiving unqualified respect from monks residing in his compound. Ordination lineages in the Theravada tradition may also differentiate themselves from other lineages by stressing stricter adherence to the monastic code of conduct (*vinaya*). Respective claims to strict purity in monastic practice also introduce an element of contesting relative hierarchy among monastic communities. Modern reforms of the sangha introduced by the state have sought to institute administrative centralization that links local chapters to regional committees and national leadership. While traditional practice espouses strict adherence to hierarchy within the sangha, such interpretations necessarily also recognize, but may not condone, ways to contest it. Hence, it would be misleading to view the sangha as a monolithic institution since historically, it comprises diverse communities that distinguish themselves through local teachings, practices, language, and ethnic identity.

The traditional legitimation of political power through Buddhist institutions has been challenged, but not abandoned, by modern practices of the state that were largely introduced through the advent of British colonialism in the nineteenth century. Through the British colonization of Burma, modern concepts of secular power and structural venues to achieve secular governance were introduced into a political culture that, until then, did not separate secular power from the cosmological worldviews that encompassed all power. Despite this secularizing trajectory, Buddhism has been identified with Burmese national identity throughout the twentieth century. "To be Burmese is to be Buddhist" is a slogan first coined by the early nationalist movement, the Young Mens' Buddhist Association founded in 1906 when the country was a British colony. Since then, this statement about national identity has been invoked in various contexts and has taken on diverse interpretations. Because of its history of mapping national identity onto a universal religious identity, Burmese Buddhism, its practices and institutions have drawn on a deep emotional reservoir and extensive social memory by which Burmese may interpret events of the present through experiences of a past, including riots and mass violence against the powers of the state.[8]

The Buddhist sangha is the only cultural institution surviving the collapse of the traditional kingdom after the third and final Anglo-Burmese war in 1885. Buddhism has been a rallying point for resistance against the colonial state and its successors since independence in 1948.[9] The sangha has played a critical role in mediating such sentiments. As other-worldly ascetics detached from worldly gains, monks have traditionally enjoyed a position of authority permitting the sangha to speak the "truth" to those in power. Monks agitated against colonial rule in 1886 and again in the 1920s and 1930s. The sangha has also been a steadfast critic of Burmese governments from the democratic administration of U Nu, to Ne Win's Socialist Program Party and its successor regimes under the State Law and Order Restoration Council (SLORC), and, most recently, the State Peace and Development Council (SPDC).

With the exception of the British colonial administration, every Burmese government since independence in 1948 has catered to the sangha for popular support, religious blessing, and political legitimation. By the same token, these governments have also had to contend with the power of the sangha to mobilize people. Governments have used Buddhist ritual to legitimate political power in times of constitutional crisis or in the absence of a national constitution altogether. Governments have used Buddhist authority or "Buddhification" to rally nationalist sentiments among the general population, to foster an ideological Buddhist nationalism, to integrate Christian, animist hill tribes and other ethnic minorities into the administration of the nation-state, and to put pressure on non-Buddhists to convert to Buddhism.[10] Perhaps most significantly, Buddhist nationalist sentiments have been invoked to deflect public attention away from other crises, including agricultural shortages, banking failures, and impending anti-government demonstrations.

The modern state imposed centralizing and standardizing reforms on the Buddhist sangha at several historical junctures. In order to revitalize Buddhist learning and invigorate monastic organization, U Nu convened the Fifth Buddhist Council in 1954–56. U Nu initially gained the support of Buddhist monks and thus enhanced his own charisma and the state's legitimation, but the demise of his government in 1962 was triggered by his inability to resist monastic pressure to establish Buddhism as a state religion. During the 1990s, the SLORC regime sponsored a great many lavish Buddhist rituals to legitimate its power in the absence of a national constitution and other means of legitimating the power of the state.[11] Finally, the state has used the authority of Buddhism to instigate and sanction mass violence to be perpetrated against "enemies of the Burmese nation" and religious and ethnic "others." It is important to note the country's ethnic composition in this regard. Although the Burmese sangha is predominantly Burman, it also recruits significant membership among ethnic minorities, including the Mon, Karen, Arakanese, and Shan. Almost all ethnic Burmans, who make up 65–80 percent of the population, are Buddhist. This brings the total Buddhist population in Burma close to 90 percent.[12] During the twentieth century, military power, religion, ethnicity, and national identity have been influential forces in mobilizing communal violence in this country. Yet none of these factors emerged as a single determinant in the occurrence or outcome of violent encounters and political alliances, however fragile and temporary, routinely cut across these distinctions.

### Buddhist monks as facilitators and victims in the 1988 uprising

The anti-government uprising in 1988 constitutes a tragic watershed in the recent history of a country whose citizens believed themselves to be on the verge of political reforms, only to plunge into the shackles of a military regime that rules by force and exploitation. The type of political and economic reforms which Hefner notes as critical to fostering civil society and democracy in Indonesia were not implemented with sufficient cohesion to build a post-colonial state to serve the Burmese nation.[13] The bloody path from that moment of hope in 1988 to the subsequent decades of fear was paved with the bodies of thousands. These deaths and subsequent purges in education, government, and in the monasteries affected the personal lives of every Burmese family. The absence of a national constitution, the lack of effective political reforms, deeply seated resentment towards the military regime, and widespread social suffering have collectively determined the parameters for Burmese politics since 1988.

In the months prior to the uprisings in March and August of 1988, a failing economy caused reverberations throughout Burmese society. Shortages of food staples such as rice and oil, student unrest at Rangoon Technical Institute and Rangoon University, signs of the imminent resignation of the Burmese Dictator Ne Win, and the promise of a multi-party system further heightened tensions. Sparked by a seemingly minor student encounter with police in a Rangoon coffee shop, the demonstrations spread rapidly to the Rangoon Technical Institute and Rangoon University, but were quenched each time with brutal police force. As the demonstrations turned into riots, the police and military killed scores of students, deaths for which the Burma Socialist Program Party (BSPP) refused to hold its security forces accountable. More and more segments of Burmese society took to the streets of Rangoon, Mandalay, and soon cities throughout the country to demand government reform and accountability. In early August 1988, large segments of the Burmese work force, including professionals, civil servants, customs officials, nurses, doctors, and even soldiers from certain military units went on strike to join mass protests and demand radical political change. Perhaps inspired by the Philippine experience of "people power," there was a prevailing sense in Burma and abroad that real political and economic reforms and a change of government were imminent. The army responded quickly and put a bloody end to the uprising. As thousands of demonstrators were killed by police and military, many, especially students and monks who feared reprisals and mass arrests fled upcountry and eventually crossed the border into Thailand.[14]

Amidst the chaos the Burmese sangha emerged to provide an organizational structure to the popular uprising. Monasteries became sanctuaries, particularly at night when military police arrested student agitators at their homes. Monks organized demonstrations, relayed information through an internal monastic network, and even stepped up to administer some judicial and civil infrastructures in those towns and areas considered "liberated" by the democratic uprising. The yellow robes of the Buddha offered anonymity to those fleeing from government persecution and the monastic network became a conduit for safe travel to the border and into exile. Along with numerous other exile and refugee organizations, the All Burma Monks' Union was formed to speak for the sangha from the relative safety of the Thai border.[15] Burma's monks once again had become a political force, acting as facilitators of widespread anti-government mobilization.[16]

The military's actions against the sangha were swift and severe. Monks soon became victims of the state's reprisals against "enemies of the state" who agitated in the uprising. Senior monks were held accountable for the involvement of younger ones in the riots.[17] Many were forcibly disrobed, demonstrating the military's flagrant disrespect for traditional monastic authority.[18] Hundreds of monks were detained and imprisoned for years to come. Some died in prison due to torture, illness, or lack of medical care.[19] The government subjected monasteries to collective reprisals and retaliated with curfews and other restrictions on monastic participation in public life. It imposed rigid and comprehensive reforms on all religious organizations in Burma, Buddhist, Hindu, Muslim, or Christian alike. Nearly every aspect of monastic administration, education, and the personal lives of individual monks was under close government scrutiny. Most significantly, religious reforms since 1988 have brought the Buddhist sangha under the authority of the modern state. The Ministry of Religious Affairs has been strengthened in many ways and has been given the charge to implement the preservation and propagation of Buddhism in Burma.[20] In sum, in response to popular demands for political reform, the state appropriated the religious authority and institutions of Buddhism, exerting unprecedented control over religion in public life.

Against this background of increasing restrictions on monastic life, the State Law and Order Restoration Council (SLORC), the regime that eventually succeeded Ne Win and his disbanded BSPP government, sought to transform a national community into a ritual community devoted to the veneration of sacred relics of the Buddha, thus minimizing the agency of the sangha. Participation in this Buddhist ritual community also implied participation in a national economic and political network few could afford to ignore. In this manner, the state used Buddhist sacred objects and ritual to enforce a totalizing hold on power.[21] At great expense to the citizens who donated money and labor for lavish religious construction and rituals, SLORC largely succeeded in reinforcing its hegemonic power through its use of religious sources of authority. By the early 1990s, the state had co-opted the senior sangha and the majority of the Buddhist population into acquiescent participation.[22] These programs to silence and police Buddhist and other forms of dissent drove popular protest underground, creating a generalized distrust and fear in private and public spheres of Burmese life in which rumors abound, filtering public events and producing counter-narratives at amazing speeds.[23]

## Causes and catalysts of the anti-Muslim persecution in 1997

Rumors and multiple narratives abound about the causes and cataclysmic events that precipitated the anti-Muslim riots in 1997 and engendered explosive violence amidst this otherwise tightly policed nation.[24] Buddhist and civil groups as well as foreign news media report that the regime sparked the riots in order to deflect public attention away from impending sites of crisis. Just a few weeks before, farmers had staged demonstrations to protest against forced government buy-outs of their harvest. Rumors of food shortages ensued. For several months leading up to the spring of 1997, monks from major Mandalay monasteries had secretly organized an impending human rights strike, demanding the release of 16 monks whom SLORC had previously imprisoned.

In March 1997 and in subsequent incidents, Burmese Muslims became targets of violent rampages by Buddhist monks.[25] Anti-Muslim rioting flared up over a local conflict that is said to have occurred in Mandalay. From there, anti-Muslim riots spread to all major cities in Burma within just a few days. The extent of violence inflicted upon Muslim communities is difficult to ascertain. One measure, however, is the large number of Muslim refugees the riots engendered, especially among Rohingas who fled their native Arakan in Lower Burma primarily to Bangladesh. The attacks caused an unknown number of deaths, the burning of Muslim homes and shops, and the desecration of sacred sites and objects, including the destruction of mosques, scattering of Qurans in the street, and driving pigs through consecrated grounds.

Accounts about these raids do not add up to a coherent master narrative, but fall into separate versions. They include an official version given by government media, accounts by Buddhist monastic organizations, and additional versions based on foreign press reports and first-hand descriptions by Burmese Muslims, Buddhists monks, and other eyewitnesses. Each kind of narrative attributes to entirely different contexts the underlying causes and immediate catalysts for these mob attacks on Burmese Muslim.[26]

According to official state media and newspapers, Buddhist–Muslim rioting broke out in Mandalay on March 17, 1997 over the alleged rape of a Buddhist girl by a Muslim man and quickly turned into a rampage in which Buddhist monks are said to have retaliated by attacking and setting fire to Muslim neighborhoods. Intersecting with this narrative were other rumors that alleged the theft of a hitherto unknown, large ruby embedded in the sacred *Mahamuni* Buddha image. The theft was reported to have left a large hole in the icon that forms the central attraction of a major pilgrimage site in contemporary Burma.[27] Popular opinion blamed pagoda trustees appointed by the SLORC regime and damage to the sacred image was generally understood as weakening of the government's political power. These rumors inevitably agitated popular Burmese Buddhist sentiments evoking a complex cultural history with deep cultural resonance. This incendiary situation by itself might have been sufficient for some Burmese Buddhists to participate in an outbreak of violent frustration and the preceding rumors now focused the target of their frustration on the Muslim community.[28]

Different observers affirmed SLORC's role in instigating the riots. Some observers stated that the monastic attackers, whose identity was mostly hidden by robes draped over their heads, were, in actuality, mere imposters and agitators sent by the regime's grassroots organization the Unity, Solidarity, and Development Association (USDA).[29] Muslims throughout the country received warnings from local officials of impending mob attacks,[30] indicating that the riots were not spontaneous, but planned in advance.[31] The strategy also tended to emphasize the loss of property and buildings and likely reduced the loss of lives. In response to the rioting that spread within days throughout Burma, SLORC imposed martial law, closed all universities, and instituted curfews on monasteries in Mandalay and in other cities. Soldiers surrounded many of the larger monasteries, especially in Mandalay and Rangoon. At the same time, state television aired lengthy and frequent broadcasts depicting the regime's leading generals venerating senior Buddhist monks and making extravagant donations to them.

Organizations like the democratic National Council of the Union of Burma (NCUB) called for restraint among all religious groups. In a statement on March 18, 1997, the All Burma Young Monks' Union (ABYMU), an exile group founded in the aftermath of 1988 explained that monks in Mandalay had planned human rights demonstrations to protest against the government's refusal to reveal the fate of 16 monks who had been previously arrested.[32] Their demands also included easing government restrictions on the sangha. Other senior monks urged calm among the general population, explicitly distancing themselves and the sangha as an institution from violence committed against Muslims. Concurrently, they affirmed their allegiance with Muslim suffering in a common struggle against SLORC's injustice.

It appears from these reports that SLORC instigated the initial attacks against Muslims in Mandalay to contain anti-government activities among Buddhist monks in Mandalay and the threat of renewed demonstrations that public knowledge of their activities would likely bring about. Over the past decades, there have been repeated allegations of such diversionary tactics that create unrest the military *can* contain, while detracting public attention away from impending crises that were seen as a greater threat to the state's stability. At the same time, it is also clear that

Buddhist monks participated in later stages of the anti-Muslim mass rioting. Aung Zaw writes in *The Nation*: "A young monk in Rangoon did not deny that they were involved. 'Yes! We do have a plan to protest against this brutal regime. Our target is SLORC.'"[33] The rationale that anti-government monks adduced to justify attacks against Muslims as actually an attack on SLORC appears convoluted. Such justifications were born out of the popular resentment among Burmese of the support SLORC's bid to join the Association of Southeast Asian Nations (ASEAN) had received at that time from Malaysia's Prime Minister Mahathir Mohamad. In addition, Indonesia's former president Suharto had recently visited Ne Win in Rangoon. The public support from Muslim nations for SLORC was popularly seen as undercutting the movement for democracy in Burma. In the same piece, Aung Zaw reports that "... about 50 monks at Bargaya Road in Rangoon followed by soldiers and riot police went to another mosque, chanting: 'We don't want Muslims' and throwing stones at the mosque. The authorities did not intervene."[34]

The narratives illustrate how violence can be instigated against a religious and ethnic "other" as a means to pre-empt public outcry against the state and, at the same time, place further controls upon the likely facilitators of resistance directed against the state, such as the Buddhist sangha. These accounts show how facilitators of violence spread rumors and exploit complex cultural and religious sentiments to accomplish objectives that emerge from entirely different political configurations. They also speak to a Buddhist collusion with political forces to target Muslims[35] and, lastly, they relate how religious identities had become, at one and the same time, targets and victims of violent recrimination.

## *The Dipeyin ambush and massacre*

The ambush and massacre of National League for Democracy (NLD) supporters in a wooded area near Dipeyin began in the evening of May 30, 2003, a day now known as Black Friday in the democratic movement. The events surrounding this incident are primarily political and not religious in character. They indicate heightened political tensions between Aung San Suu Kyi's National League for Democracy (NLD) and the ruling regime, that, by that time, had been renamed the State Peace and Development Council.[36] It is, however, the state's manipulation of Buddhist symbols of authority in constructing the ambush that qualifies it for inclusion in this discussion.[37]

Traveling in the evening of May 30, 2003, the NDL caravan of some two dozen cars and motorcycles was redirected by a military road block, to a minor road that turned out to be blocked by fallen trees.[38] As they made their way through a wooded area near the village of Dipeyin, the caravan was greeted by a large crowd of villagers. A Buddhist monk approached Aung San Suu Kyi's car and invited her to speak to the crowd. Suu Kyi declined due to the late hour, but the monk persisted until her aide, Htun Zaw Zaw, got out of the car to dissuade him. Once the caravan stopped, USDA members emerged from the near-by woods to attack NLD supporters. Hundreds of police, men dressed as monks, armed soldiers, and prisoners from Mandalay Prison suddenly dismounted from trucks, armed with bamboo spears, guns, iron pipes, and rocks and joined in the attack.[39] In the massacre, more than one hundred supporters of the NLD are said to have been brutally slaughtered. Suu Kyi's car escaped to Dipeyin where she was taken into "pre-emptive" custody.[40] In the following days, dozens of members of the parliament were arrested or disappeared. Since May 2003, Suu Kyi has remained under house arrest. The regime justifies this action by referring to a 1975 provision that permits the pre-emptive arrest for up to five years of persons suspected of committing acts endangering the security of the state. The crackdown on the NLD had resumed once again. The attack was planned and carried out by the USDA and the police, under the command of the northwest regional military commander, Brig-Gen. Soe Naing, who acted in alliance with centrally placed generals in the Rangoon government.[41] The official response initially pointed toward a popular dislike of Suu Kyi and the NLD, an account that is widely considered to lack credibility. Signaling perhaps the most egregious manipulation of Buddhist symbols and authority, the monk's role in stopping the NLD caravan speaks to the tremendous respect individual Buddhist monks as well as the institution of the sangha as whole occupy in contemporary Burmese culture and politics.

## Buddhism and violence in Sri Lanka

Sri Lanka's Buddhist engagement with the modern state has dealt with issues similar to those in the national history of Burma. Both states have experienced protracted civil wars with ethnic minorities. In both countries, just and effective policies to integrate ethnic minorities remain a challenge to the power of the state. While both Burma and Sri Lanka share strong identifications of Buddhism with nationality, their historical trajectories differ in important respects. In Sri Lanka, monks have been able to occupy significant political positions in public life, gaining the right to vote in elections and run for political office. In this regard, the Sinhalese sangha negotiated to a far greater degree a modern re-definition of the normative role of a Buddhist ascetic. Traditional monastic ideals remain normative in Burmese national culture, however, where monks may not vote and are encouraged by the Ministry of Religious Affairs, on grounds of rules governing monastic conduct (*vinaya*), to remain aloof from worldly and political affairs.

At the turn of the twentieth century, Buddhism underwent revitalization and reforms in Sri Lanka that were in large measure the result of efforts by Angitara Dharmapala, the Sri Lankan protégé of Henry Olcott and Helena Blavatsky, prominent founders of the Theosophical Society. This revitalization, modeled largely after Christian organizations and a Buddhist identity in Sri Lanka, became a rallying point against British colonial power. Upon independence, monks claimed the right to vote in elections and hold political office.[42] These facts strengthened their role in the public life and politics of the new nation.

For Sri Lankan nationalists, Buddhism is commensurate with a Sri Lankan identity whose history they believe reaches back to the mythic origins of the island recounted in the sacred *Mahavamsa* (Great Chronicle). Sinhalese monks continued

61

to be activists in the ethnic and political struggles of the early 1980s.[43] Their actions, indeed, their self-proclaimed sacred duty, were to preserve that religio-national legacy for future generations. Monks saw themselves as not merely advisors, but as moral guardians of the Sri Lankan nation and defenders of the Dharma, both threatened by ethnic and religious others. It was their responsibility to pave the way for politicians to safeguard a Sri Lanka where Buddhism would prosper. During the bloody civil wars in the 1980s between Tamil separatists and Sinhala Buddhists, monks were instrumental in organizing and mobilizing people to defend the Sinhala identity.[44] Statements like "There is no Buddhist sangha where there is no Sinhala race"[45] were part of their battle cry to ensure a continuing Sinhalese hegemony. Walpola Rahula, the internationally respected monk and scholar of Buddhism, proclaimed that "The sangha is ready to lay down their lives" over proposed legislation to solve the ethnic conflict.[46] In their view, Buddhist teachings not only justified the prosecution of the war, but war was to be prosecuted to preserve Sri Lanka's Buddhism in the future.[47] Monks strongly criticized the government of Jayewardene for what they considered his failure to safeguard the country in times of national crisis by inviting Indian military intervention. Sri Lankan political discourse labeled Tamil Tigers as "terrorists," while monks who were closely allied with the People's Liberation Front (JVP) were righteous defenders of Sinhala identity and Buddhist nationalism. Monastic militancy even led to the murder of Sri Lanka's Prime Minister, Ranasingha Premadasa, in 1993.

This brief excursion into the political and at times violent roles of Sinhalese Buddhist monks does not do justice to the multi-layered history in the struggle for that country's independence and eventual nationhood. But it can give us a glimpse of the inflammatory discourse in which the Sinhalese sangha conducted and facilitated its political activism in the public sphere. While monks in Burma may use incendiary language, they are less likely to do so in public spheres that lie beyond monastic contexts. By contrast, Sinhalese monks defined for themselves a modern identity that openly claims monastic engagement with the political world. In Sri Lanka, monks are political actors in the public sphere and they see the exercise of that public function as their primary religious obligation.

In his book, *Buddhism Betrayed*, the eminent anthropologist and scholar of Theravada Buddhism, Stanley Tambiah, himself a Sri Lankan Tamil, criticized the political conduct of Sinhalese monks and questioned, on the basis of Buddhist doctrine, the political activism of Buddhist monks in Sri Lanka. His book received much public condemnation by Buddhist parties in this conflict and by some academics. It is presently blacklisted in Sri Lanka. While Tambiah's argument is compelling on ethical grounds and adduces sound textual evidence, his work and the critiques of his detractors nonetheless invite us to examine carefully implicit and explicit definitions of an "authentic" Buddhism. Whose Buddhism is labeled as authentic? And what contextual factors may have helped shape the public discourse about Buddhist legitimacy or ethics at that particular moment of Sri Lankan national history? Abeyeskara rightly cautions us against the view that "violence is the antithesis of a supposedly authentic Buddhism that specifically teaches nonviolence."[48] Authenticity is not defined by religious text and academic interpretation, but by the creed of communities that espouse such religious practice and beliefs.

## Anatomies of religion and conflict

The causes of religiously justified collective violence are likely to be as varied and predictable as any sources of conflict: economic deprivation, social inequity, political exploitation, and so forth. In other words, in the absence of such universal causes of conflict, religious discourse is not likely to spark communal violence. At the same time, even religions that teach nonviolence are not immune to forces that create violent conflict with religious inflections.

How then can we analyze the intersection of conflict and religion? I caution against hastily identifying one with the other. Conflict, even violent conflict, and religion are universal features of society with distinct, though at times intersecting, histories. Not all violent conflict, of course, is religious. And while religions generally seek to instill moral norms in communities, many of them, at one time or another, have been invoked to incite or justify communal violence. Multiple considerations, including questions of identity, religion, power, access to resources, come into consideration. The labels we attach to identify and define categories are themselves products of a discourse that is embedded in wider social contexts. Attributions identifying some religious communities as avowing violence or as practicing nonviolence do not characterize essential qualities of any religious tradition or its communities, but instead refer to specific social and historical conjunctures embedded in multiple trajectories. Although religion provides individuals and communities with a universalizing discourse of ultimate meaning, scholars as well as peace activists must be careful to retain the specificity of the social, economic, and political contexts in which such statements inciting religious violence are made.

Religion, as a phenomenon, however, has the capacity to inflame potential sites of conflict or to amplify pre-existing ones by ascribing to them transcending or ultimate significance. Religious discourse links provocative incidents with concepts, symbols, and events that intensify and legitimate conflict in absolute terms. Incidents are taken out of context and stripped of relativizing particulars to lend greater relevance to such accounts and endow them with an aura of religious or cultural "truth." Religious discourse can accomplish this precisely because it engages believers in multiple realities at the same time, be they social, political, psychological, or sacred. It decontextualizes causes of conflict and lends them authoritative truths, thus precluding successfully negotiating context-based resolutions. Difference expressed between social groups is no longer one of degree, but an absolute difference that cannot be bridged. The rift is explained in terms of essentializing qualities that belong to self-evident religious truths. In that way, the inflammatory religious discourse becomes focused on absolutes: "truth," "justice," and "victory."

Religious discourse taps into sentiments associated with cultural symbols and social memory that powerfully evoke the past. Such speeches may idealize traditions of the past or promise to reestablish them in the future. The possibilities of the present are interlaced with memories of the past and promises of salvific redemption. Such religious discourse brings to bear upon actors realities that transcend the present where social norms constitute a measure for action.[49] The language of warring parties evokes cultural and religious metaphors that resonate at multiple mythic, symbolic and social levels. Speeches to incite and mobilize often claim an appropriate religious authority in order to encourage, entitle, or mobilize perpetrators of violence into action. To minds already agitated with emotions, these are powerful motivators to do the impossible, to prevail against all odds, to fight a holy war. This kind of discourse is totalizing, hegemonic, "other-izing," and de-humanizing.[50] It refers to absolute truths and ultimate realities in constructing the enemy and explicating the justification for violence.

Who are the participants in the religious discourse that justifies violent conflict? In his examination of communal violence in South Asia, Paul Brass identifies three types of participants within a given group. Perpetrating actual violence and performing within the mob are recruits who often have minimal education and whose existence is already marginal. They are readily exploited as foot soldiers and have few options to deal effectively with social and economic sources of conflict. In the context of no opportunities, even a relatively small amount of money can be an excellent wage for a few hours' labor. The acceptance of that kind of employment also speaks of a measure of desperation and powerless alienation from cultural realities that can foster peaceful living.

Strategically placed within organizations controlled by the state or within monastic networks of the sangha are mid-level agitators, or "fire tenders," as Brass refers to them. They facilitate conflict, fan incendiary rumors, and make logistical plans. As leaders of rioting mobs, they have the power to start or call off communal violence. Most violent conflict requires the organization of networks ready to move crowds to action quickly.[51] Brass places ideologues and intellectuals at the pinnacle of organizations likely to incite religiously motivated violence. They construct the discourse that motivates street mobs to act. And they can justify mobilizing violent action in the absolute terms of religious "truths."

The role of religion in violent conflict is not singular, nor is it unique. But it is effective. Religiously inflected conflict offers powerful motivation precisely because it interfaces with other culturally mediated messages and yet seeks to stake universal claims. The most effective disruption of violence may well be to persuade the ranks of ideologues of their self-interests in alternate strategies while, simultaneously, creating alternate economic and cultural opportunities for those making a living at the mercy of exploitation.

## Notes

1 Donald Lopez, *The Story of Buddhism* (San Francisco: HarperSanFrancisco, 2001), offers a useful introduction to this religion in its many, diverse forms. Concerning modern Theravada Buddhism and politics in South and Southeast Asia, readers may also want to consult Donald Swearer, *The Buddhist World of Southeast Asia* (Albany: State University of New York Press, 1995).

2  Primary canonical texts in the Theravada tradition offer abundant evidence for a doctrinal position against violence. Justifications encouraging or condoning communal violence are found primarily in commentaries, local chronicles or semi-canonical texts detailing the rules of good governance and law. At the same time, the Theravada canonical literature recognizes that the predicament of kingship for the performance of its duties necessarily entails conducting wars or inflicting violent punishment on culprits, i.e. acts that bring negative karma to the king's future rebirths. For a discussion of a Buddhist theory of just war, the reader is referred to Tessa Bartholomeusz, *In Defense of Dharma* (New York: RoutledgeCurzon, 2002).

3  For detailed discussions of these complex religious and political processes, the reader is referred to the following essays authored by me, namely "Mapping the Sacred in Theravada Buddhist Southeast Asia," in *Sacred Places and Modern Landscapes: Sacred Geography and Social-Religious Transformations in South and Southeast Asia*, ed. Ronald Bull (Phoenix: Program for Southeast Asian Studies Monograph Series, Arizona State University, 2004), 1–29; "Trajectories in Buddhist Sacred Biography," in *Sacred Biography in the Buddhist Traditions of South and Southeast Asia*, ed. Juliane Schober (Honolulu: University of Hawaii Press, 1997), 1–15; and "Venerating the Buddha's Remains in Burma: From Solitary Practice to the Cultural Hegemony of Communities," *Journal of Burma Studies* 6, (2001): 111–39.

4  For an insightful analysis as to why westerners tend to romanticize feudal Tibetan Buddhism and the geo-political roots of the empathy in US–China relations during the Cold War, see Donald Lopez, "New Age Orientalism: the Case of Tibet," *Tricycle* 3, no. 3 (Spring 1994): 37–43.

5  For a history of ethnically and religiously motivated communal violence in South Asia and theoretical insights into the nature of communal violence, see the excellent book by Stanley J. Tambiah, *Leveling Crowds: Ethnonationalist Conflicts and Collective Violence in South Asia* (Berkeley, CA: University of California Press, 1996).

6  Swearer, *Buddhist World*, 95.

7  See Tambiah's essay on the "Galactic Polity in Southeast Asia," in *Culture, Thought and Social Action* (Cambridge, MA: Harvard University Press, 1985).

8  For a history of Buddhism and politics in Burma, including its role in Burmese resistance against the colonial state, see, among many other sources, Donald E. Smith, *Religion and Politics in Burma* (Princeton, NJ: Princeton University Press, 1965); and, Manuel Sarkisyanz, *Buddhist Backgrounds of the Burmese Revolution* (The Hague: Martinus Nijhoff, 1965).

9  The argument that Burma, the independent state, represents a continuation of the colonial state has, convincingly, been made by anthropologists, historians, and political scientists. Mary Callahan argues in her recent book, *Making Enemies: War and State Building in Burma* (Ithaca, NY: Cornell University Press, 2003), that the current state's rationale is identical to that of the colonial state, i.e. to organize the population to facilitate the extraction of resources. The reader is also referred to Mikael Gravers, *Nationalism as Political Paranoia: an Essay on the Historical Practice of Power* (Richmond, Surrey: Curzon, 1999).

10  For instance, "Indian Rights Group Accuses Myanmar of Forcible Conversion of Christians," Agence France Presse, November 11, 2001, reported that according to the Naga People's Movement for Human Rights (NPMHR), hundreds of Christian Nagas had been forced to convert to Buddhism by the ruling military junta and religious bodies. Those resisting either experienced displacement and persecution or were kept as bonded labourers by the junta and Buddhist monks. Other forced conversions occurred in other tribal areas.

11  See Juliane Schober, "Buddhist Just Rule and Burmese National Culture: State Patronage of the Chinese Tooth Relic in Myanmar," *History of Religions* 36, no. 3 (1997): 218–43.

12 Statistics on Burma's ethnic and religious composition vary. In Bruce Matthews, "Ethnic and Religious Diversity: Myanmar's Unfolding Nemesis," Visiting Research Series, no. 3, Institute for Southeast Asian Studies, 2001, 1–18, it is reported that ethnic Burmans, nearly all of them Buddhist, make up 65 percent of the country's population of 50 million people. The combined Buddhist population comprises an 80–90 percent majority, 4 percent Christians, 4 percent Muslim, and about 2 percent Hindu. Other accounts place the Muslim population closer to 8 percent. The above breakdown also does not account for a percentage of tribal, animist groups. According to "The Alms Bowl Remains Overturned: A Report on SLORC's Abuses of Buddhism in Burma," Buddhist Relief Mission, February 1997, http://www.brelief.org/articles3. htm, the current sangha in Burma comprises approximately 400,000 monks.

13 See Robert W. Hefner, *Civil Islam: Muslims and Democratization in Indonesia* (Princeton, NJ: Princeton University Press, 2000).

14 The estimates of the death toll of the 1988 uprising range from 3,000 to 10,000. It states that 600 monks were among the dead in "The Alms Bowl," 7.

15 The parameters of this chapter do not permit this discussion to focus on other secular resistance organizations, including the Burmese Government in exile, the National League for democracy (NLD) and a great many others in and outside of Burma. I simply want to mention them here to underscore that the focus of this chapter does not intend to convey a monolithic presence of Buddhism in the anti-government struggle, though clearly it is a major force contesting the hegemonic powers of the regime. Moreover, as the tensions extended into decades, some monks have successfully circumvented the policing structures of the state through selective collaboration with their efforts and by accepting "taxation," especially on the foreign donations they receive.

16 Although the role of the sangha in organizing the anti-government demonstrations in 1988 and giving logistical support to its victims is well known and significant in any study of modern Burmese Buddhism, scholarly analyses of these and subsequent political action in the sangha has not been possible to date. However, first-hand accounts of the monastic role in these events are found in news media reports, in Bertil Lintner, *Outrage: Burma's Struggle for Democracy* (Hong Kong: Review Publishing, 1989); and in reports by the Buddhist Relief Mission. The regime refers to "the tragic disturbances of August 1988" as the work of communists, especially the Burmese Communist Party (BCP) and other "enemies of the state," including "foreign imperialists" and their agents with whom they are in "collusion." This entirely mythic attack is a diversionary strategy to detract from the actual crises that reappears frequently in the regime's rhetoric. While it may give insight into the ways in which the junta thinks, it has no factual value. See, for instance, Maung Maung, *The 1988 Uprising in Burma* (New Haven, CT: Yale Southeast Asia Monograph, 1999), where the role of the sangha is never mentioned.

17 See "The Alms Bowl" for the names and monastic affiliations of several dozen monks who had been detained.

18 While Buddhist kings (*dhammaraja*) were expected to convene and promote monastic reforms, Buddhist law (*vinaya*) stipulates that monastic ordination removes an individual from civil jurisdiction. Upon becoming a member of the sangha, Theravada monks assume new names and social identities. They also give up all property and are no longer subject to civil authority.

19 Among the monks arrested were prominent leaders, some of them recipients of exalted titles they had received from the government.

20 In an open letter commemorating the fifteenth anniversary of these riots, the All Burma Young Monks' Union (ABYMU) made the following statement: "Since 1988, the Buddhist monks of Burma have been imprisoned, forcibly disrobed, used as porters in military operations, sent to labor camps, prohibited from freely practicing their religion, and forced to move out of the monasteries in which they reside by the leaders

of present military regime. For these cruel acts, there are now some monks who have already passed away in prison. Among the detained monks were many prominent and senior monks, including a well-known Tipitakadhara monk. These leading monks are well respected by lay devotees for their efforts in Dharmma and Vinaya. The regime has a long history of oppressing revered Buddhist figures." ABYMU, "Statement of the All Burma Young Monk's Union Regarding the Demonstrations by Buddhist Monks in Mandalay on March 17, 1997," *BurmaNet News*, no. 672, March 20, 1997, http://www.burmanet.org/bnn_archives/1997.

21 For a more detailed description of the ways in which SLORC used Buddhist symbolism and ritual to legitimate its power, see Schober, "Presence of Buddha." While I focus on religious aspects in popular dissent against the state, I do not imply that SLORC's ability to project a Buddhist identity would be successful without its use of military and other sources of control. Clearly, this was not the case. See also Bruce Matthews, "The Present Fortune of Tradition-Bound Authoritarianism in Myanmar," *Pacific Affairs* 7, no. 1 (1998).

22 Silence, therefore, became one form of resistance; retreat into Buddhist meditation was another. Meditation as a means to promote democracy in Burma is the main theme of the book by Gustaaf Houtman, *Mental Culture in the Burmese Political Crisis* (Tokyo: Institute for the Study of Languages and Cultures of Asia and Africa, 1999).

23 Among several significant events, I am omitting from this discussion a monastic purge in October 1990 in Mandalay, in which 350 monasteries were raided and 3,000 monks were at least temporarily arrested and accused of offenses like possessing anti-SLORC and pro-NLD literature. Among the arrested were high-ranking monks in the Monks' Union (Sangha Sammagi), according to "The Alms Bowl," 2. The Union's leader, Ven. U Yewata, who was arrested himself, called on monks to refuse acceptance of alms from members of the military and their families on a major religious holiday. This traditional sanction that invalidates the status of Buddhist lay donors is seldom invoked. In the following weeks, the boycott spread throughout the country. Amnesty International reported a prolonged arrest of 75 monks in October and November 1990. The Southeast Asian Information Network (SAIN) reported the death of four senior monks in custody (Ven. U Sandwara, Union Secretary, Weyanbonthai Monastery; Ven. U Vimala, Masoeyin Monastery, Ven. U Weyawdana, Hti Lin Monastery, and Ven. U Oketama, vice-president of the Monks' Union (Sangha Sammgi)). All resided in Mandalay. SAIN further reported death sentences pronounced in cases against the Ven. U Kawiya, a well-known preacher at the famous Mahamuni Monastery in Mandalay (who had also given daily anti-government sermons at Mahamuni in 1988) and other monks.

24 To explore the role of rumors and conflicting narratives about events that led up and occurred during the riots, see Paul R. Brass, *Theft of an Idol: Text and Context in the Representation of Collective Violence* (Princeton, NJ: Princeton University Press, 1997); and Vena Das, "Specificities: Official Narratives, Rumour, and the Social Production of Hate," *Social Identities* 4, no. 1 (1998): 109–30.

25 Anti-Muslim riots have been reported as recently as November 2003. These recent riots were also fueled by long-standing anti-Muslim sentiments in Burma.

26 A detailed and multi-faceted report on the situation for Muslims in Burma was published by *Images Asia* in two parts in March 1997. It provides first-hand accounts by Muslim victims, statements of Muslim and Buddhist organizations reacting to the atrocities, as well as appeals to Muslims nations in Southeast Asia and elsewhere to intercede on behalf of Muslims to bring about regional stability. And lastly, the report gives the names of 16 Buddhist monks who died in prison.

27 For a discussion of the sacred, colossal image of the Buddha know as the Mahamuni and its mytho-history in Burmese Buddhist culture and history, see my essay "In the Presence of the Buddha: Ritual Veneration of the Burmese Mahamuni Image," in

*Sacred Biography in the Buddhist Traditions of South and Southeast Asia*, ed. Julian Schober (Honolulu: University of Hawaii Press, 1997). Although myths abound about the origins of this image, a large ruby had not been mentioned in conjunction with it prior to these riots. Hence, its sudden "theft" was, at least, confounding.

28 In later reports, SLORC attributed the theft to the NLD whom it perpetually painted as the state's enemy number one. The NDL, however, swiftly denied any involvement and denounced the anti-Muslim rampage.

29 USDA is the regime's mass organization with local cells throughout the country. Observers noted that on occasion undergarments for purchase in government-run stores would become visible in the course of the struggle, implying the agitators were not monks as the clothing of actual monks does not contain such items.

30 *The Nation* reports on March 28, 1997: "Lt. Gen. Myo Nyunt, Burma's religious minister went to meet local Muslim leaders and reportedly said: 'Let them [monks] destroy it – don't resist them, the army will compensate you for everything.'"

31 Often, warnings of impending attacks would come from local government officials or army officers urging Muslims not to retaliate or fight back, but to endure the Buddhists' rampage. This allowed many Muslim families to flee to safety, abandoning their homes and mosques to destructive fires set by rampaging crowds.

32 The ABYMU is a major constituent of the NCUB. This statement also contains expressions of allegiance with the NLD, workers, students and all ethnic "nationalities."

33 Aung Zaw, "Rangoon Plays the Muslim Card," *The Nation*, March 28, 1997.

34 Ibid.

35 Anti-Muslim violence has colonial roots in Burma. Anti-Muslim riots have periodically erupted since the late 1930s when the majority of Rangoon's population was of Indian origin and more than one million Indians lived in the Irrawaddy Delta region, making a living as land owners and money lenders.

36 A brief background to the political context is needed. Although the SPDC had been under international pressure to negotiate with the NLD, Senior General Than Shwe, Chairman of the SPDC, who staunchly resisted such negotiations, consolidated his power within the inner circles of the SPDC in April 2003 and again in the fall of 2004. Aung San Suu Kyi, Secretary General and charismatic leader of the NLD had been released from house arrest for nearly a year. Despite repeated interference with her travels in Burma and public speeches, Suu Kyi speaks out publicly about her concern over the lack of progress made in UN negotiations. On May 6, she left Rangoon for a tour to re-energize the membership in the NLD youth groups and the events of the massacre led to her eventual re-arrest and detention since that time.

37 For a discussion of religious and political aspects of Aung San Suu Kyi's charisma and her role in formulating Socially Engaged Buddhism in Burma, see Juliane Schober, "Buddhist Visions of Moral Authority and Civil Society: The Search for the Post-Colonial State in Burma," in *Burma at the Turn of the Twenty-First Century*, ed. M. Skidmore (Honolulu: University of Hawaii Press, 2005).

38 My summary is based on a compilation of news reports and diplomatic statements by the Alternative Asean Network on Burma, no. 03/004, June 24, 2003.

39 US Embassy personnel visited the site days later and concluded in an official statement that the attack had been planned.

40 Reportedly, the windows of her car were broken and she incurred injury to her shoulder and face. Recruiting people to participate in the attack had begun six days prior to it. Payment for the transport and dumping of bodies in remote places amounted to about $40.

41 Brig-Gen. Soe Naing was promoted to the number two position within the government during the fall of 2004, following another political reshuffle. In December 2004, he addressed an international Buddhist summit in Rangoon.

42  See Walpola Rahula, *The Heritage of Monks: A Short History of the Bhikkhu in Educational, Cultural, Social and Political Life* (New York: Grove Press, 1974); and H.L. Seneviratne, *The Work of Kings: The New Buddhism in Sri Lanka* (Chicago: University of Chicago Press, 1999).

43  See Stanley J. Tambiah, *Buddhism Betrayed? Religion, Politics, and Violence in Sri Lanka* (Chicago: University of Chicago Press, 1992); and Anada Abeysekara, *Colors of the Robe: Religion, Identity, and Difference* (Columbia: University of South Carolina Press, 2002).

44  In Sri Lanka, about 75 percent of the population is Buddhist. Tamils constitute a minority that is mostly Muslim, but also includes a significant (18 percent) number of Hindus.

45  Ananda Abeysekara, *Colors of the Robe: Religion, Identity and Difference* (Columbia: University of South Carolina Press, 2002), 211.

46  Ibid.

47  Bartholomeusz, *In Defense of Dharma.*

48  Abeysekara, *Colors of the Robe*, 202.

49  In particular, the reader is referred to Tambiah, *Leveling Crowds* for a productive discussion of ritual in the mobilization of violent crowds.

50  See Bruce Lincoln, *Holy Terrors: Thinking About Religion after September 11* (Chicago: University of Chicago Press, 2003), where he analyses the discourse and structural configurations in society to explain the causes of religious conflict.

51  I suspect that most group acts of religious violence are planned events. Their frequent description as spontaneous uprising likely belongs to the rhetoric of religious violence rather than its factual reality.

# 5

# THE ROOTS OF RELIGIOUS VIOLENCE IN INDIA, PAKISTAN, AND BANGLADESH

*Sumit Ganguly*

## Tracing the sources of conflict

Accounting for the sources of ethno-religious conflict in South Asia is not an easy task. The subject has become politically fraught and frequently not amenable to reasonable debate and discussion. Some scholars have sought to attribute the principal religious conflicts in the region to the consequences of British colonial policies and practices.[1] They contend that much of the religious discord that now wracks the subcontinent can be traced to the administrative practices of British colonial rule. Others argue that the roots of religious conflict have longer historical antecedents.[2] Still others hold that most religious conflict is of recent origin and located in the development and evolution of modern political institutions.[3] It is beyond the scope of this chapter to effectively resolve this highly charged debate. Instead it will focus on how some historical legacies, both colonial and otherwise, have provided the foundations of religious conflict in the region. It will also provide a synoptic account of the more proximate sources of such conflicts. The chapter does not purport to be comprehensive. Instead it will deal with a limited set of cases from South Asia confined to India, Pakistan, and Bangladesh.

Historical legacies alone cannot explain the onset of religious violence in South Asia. If these legacies could initiate conflict of their own accord, the region would be caught in a never-ending cycle of violence. More to the point, such an argument would reify the role of historical inheritances. Accordingly, it makes more sense to argue that some of these inheritances provide the necessary grist for the mills of religious conflict and violence in the region.

At the outset, it is necessary to answer a central question. All three states, India, Pakistan, and Bangladesh, emerged from the dissolution of the British colonial empire in South Asia. What then explains their markedly different political trajectories and accordingly the precipitants of ethno-religious violence in these three states? The overarching argument in this chapter is that they were the products of particular nationalist movements that sought to forge distinctive polities. The Indian nationalist movement was, for the most part, committed to principles of secular, democratic nationalism and sought to create a plural polity.[4] Pakistan's nationalist movement explicitly attempted to create a homeland for the Muslims of South Asia.[5] Finally, Bangladesh, which obtained its independence from Pakistan in 1971, was created as a notionally secular state. However, as will be demonstrated in this chapter, its historical inheritance from Pakistan largely blighted the prospects of both secularism and democracy. One of the underlying assumptions of this chapter is that in polyethnic societies ethno-religious conflict and violence will be more likely when states lack a commitment to ethno-religious pluralism, to the protection of minority rights, and to democratic procedures. Accordingly, it will also show that ethno-religious violence has been most acute when states have shown scant regard for these matters.

To this end the chapter will utilize two key explanatory variables. What was the precise social and political compact that led to the formation of each of these three states? In other words what was the basis of constitutional and political order in the three states? This chapter argues that they were markedly different in India, Pakistan, and Bangladesh. The differences in constitutional orders, in part, explain markedly different outcomes. A second vital explanatory variable is the question of state strength and weakness.[6] The strength and capacity of the states of South Asia to manage, limit, and cope with ethno-religious mobilization is a critical factor in explaining ethno-religious violence. A state may have a professed constitutional order but its ability to realize the goals set out in that dispensation depends to a very large degree on state strength. If the state can implement the civic principles that are embedded in its constitution, then it can hope to maintain a just political order in a polyethnic polity. If, however, these principles are breached because of the penetration by dominant majorities with little regard for ethnic and cultural pluralism, conflict and violence are highly likely. In all three states, whenever religious and cultural majority groups lacking a commitment to a civic polity have penetrated state institutions, they have invariably marginalized minority populations. In turn, they have created conditions conducive to ethnic conflict and violence. Examining the cases of India, Pakistan, and Bangladesh enables one to see significant variation in outcomes.

More specific explanations for particular ethno-religious conflicts will be sought within the overarching theoretical context that has been spelled out above. Perhaps the most vexing and seemingly endemic conflict that has afflicted the region for much of the twentieth century has been the Hindu–Muslim rift in India. It has not only poisoned the Indo-Pakistani relationship but it has also resulted in much recrudescent violence throughout independent India. What explains this apparently intractable spiral of hostility between the two communities? A variety of explanations abound.[7] The longer-term roots of this conflict are almost impossible to disentangle. However, there is little question that at least three factors provide the necessary precipitants for conflict. They are the presence and use of historical legacies, the impact of certain British colonial practices, and the experience of the partition of British India into the independent states of India and Pakistan. None of these factors can explain the outbreak of particular incidents.

However, in conjunction they do constitute predisposing factors for conflict and violence. Each of these three factors merits some discussion.

### *Historical legacies and their import*

Perhaps the most complex historical legacy that afflicts much social interaction in the subcontinent but particularly in India is the record of Hindu–Muslim interactions. Some historiography has sought to portray the relationship between these two communities as fundamentally adversarial. Other scholarship has emphasized the role of British colonialism in promoting Hindu–Muslim discord through the artifacts of the colonial census, the creation of separate electorates, and the promotion of anthropological stereotypes. Both positions are problematic. Hindu–Muslim disharmony certainly did not ensue solely with the advent of British colonialism, nor is there an unbroken record of Hindu–Muslim intransigence. The historical record instead suggests that both antagonism and collaboration characterized Hindu–Muslim relations prior to the arrival of the British in the subcontinent. There is, of course, little question that certain British colonial administrative practices did reinforce and strengthen notions of cultural and religious exclusivity. For example, the British decision to create separate electorates in 1909 under the aegis of the Minto–Morley reforms had pernicious effects for Hindu–Muslim accord and collaboration. First, it undermined the prospects of a common nationalist platform against British rule as it privileged religious identity over other cultural markers. Second, it conceded a long-standing demand of some members of the Muslim intelligentsia who had claimed that the Muslims of the subcontinent constituted a distinct, discrete primordial nation. It thereby provided a foundation for Muslim separatism and ignored the many differences within the Muslim communities of India.[8]

The origins of Muslim separatism can be traced to the latter part of the nineteenth century. It was during this period that British imperialism was at its apogee in South Asia. The spread of British colonial power across the subcontinent along with concomitant changes in social, cultural and religious mores spawned a series of revivalist movements. Some were explicitly religious, such as the emergence of the Arya Samaj under the tutelage of Swami Dayanand Saraswati in Punjab, which sought to purify Hinduism and return it to its Vedic roots. Others were more acculturative, such as the Brahmo Samaj in Bengal under the aegis of Ram Mohan Roy.[9] Finally, some movements had a more distinct political agenda. Sir Syed Ahmed Khan, a Muslim intellectual from the United Provinces, was the principal exponent of the movement for Muslim separatism. Khan's attempts to mobilize and create solidarity amongst the Muslims of South Asia stemmed from two distinct sources. At one level, he was increasingly dismayed with the growth of Hindu revivalist movements in India. At another, he had deep misgivings about the erosive effects on the Muslim intelligentsia and culture of the growth of British secular education. Finally, he was opposed to the creation of representative and participatory political institutions on the basis of the demographic composition of the empire. His opposition stemmed from the belief that such institutions would place the Muslims of South Asia at a permanent and structural disadvantage. The Hindu community, by the sheer weight of numbers, would wield a dominant role in these institutions and Muslims would be relegated to a status of endemic inferiority. Ironically, Sir Syed had little in common with the vast majority of the Muslims of the region who were deeply divided along lines of social class, educational attainment, and sectarian practice. His own upper-class origins notwithstanding, he became one of the most ardent exponents of the view that the Muslims of British India constituted a distinctive, primordial nation whose interests would be ill-served with the growth and development of representative political institutions. The British colonial authorities found much merit in Sir Syed's remonstrations, and eventually his demands played a critical role in the creation of separate electorates. The creation of this myth of the existence of a primordial Muslim nation in turn contributed to Muslim separatism.

Nevertheless, attempts at Hindu–Muslim unity emerged in the early part of the twentieth century, the most prominent of which was the Khilafat movement. This movement centered on widespread Muslim discontent against the abolition of the Turkish Caliphate in the aftermath of World War I. Mohandas Gandhi, one of the principal exponents of Indian nationalism, spearheaded this enterprise in 1920 along with two key Muslim notables. This attempt at Hindu–Muslim unity, however, proved to be mostly fleeting. Once again, during the inter-war years, the Congress Party had sought to enlist Muslim support through the famous "mass contact" campaign. Despite these two ventures, which were both well-meaning and politically significant, other factors undermined Congress's ability to fully reassure Muslims that their rights and privileges would be guaranteed in an independent India.

This failure of Congress, the dominant, secular Indian nationalist organization, to provide explicit guarantees to protect the rights of India's Muslim population in the aftermath of British rule, also helped bolster these separatist proclivities.[10] Two factors, in turn, explain Congress's failure to extend these guarantees. At one level, the exigencies of electoral politics necessitated making compromises with local notables to garner the popular vote.[11] At another level, key individuals within the party did not wholeheartedly embrace Congress's commitment to secularism. Of course, Congress's actions alone do not constitute a complete version of the historical record. The Congress, its organizational limitations notwithstanding, represented the dominant, democratic, and secular impulses of the Indian nationalist movement.

However, another strand of the nationalist movement was explicitly anti-secular, pro-Hindu, and, arguably, even anti-democratic. This was the Hindu nationalist dimension of the anti-colonial movement whose principal political manifestation was the Hindu Mahasabha.[12] Despite the political dominance of the Congress, the existence of the Hindu Mahasabha and its popularity in certain parts of India were of understandable concern to the Muslim minority. The Muslim League, which represented a crucial segment of Indian Muslim opinion, embellished these fears and misgivings to generate support for the creation of Pakistan. The success of the Muslim League in creating a separate state of Pakistan embittered significant numbers of Indians. To them the creation of Pakistan, on the basis of religious affiliation, was tantamount to the breaking up of an existing, natural entity and homeland. The veracity of their beliefs is of little significance.

The haphazard, clumsy, and disorganized process of partition and its consequent horrors simply reinforced and adumbrated these beliefs. The British, unable to forge some last-minute accord between the Congress and the Muslim League, agreed to partition the subcontinent. However, the arrangements for the transfer of power to the two emergent political entities of India and Pakistan were inadequate and hasty.[13] The human and material costs of the partition of British India were incalculable. At least ten million individuals moved across newly demarcated borders and at least a million lost their lives in the communal carnage that accompanied the process of partition.[14] No community, in particular, displayed much compassion for the members of other communities, though individual acts of heroism and decency did exist. The memories of the experience of partition scarred individuals and groups in both India and Pakistan.[15] They also had a profound impact on the future course of Indo–Pakistani relations.[16] Individuals who lived through the searing experience of partition found it exceedingly difficult to reconcile themselves to the new political order in South Asia. Their sentiments were almost uniformly partisan. These nascent citizens of both India and Pakistan viewed their counterparts across the border as intransigent, untrustworthy, and deceitful. These images of each other converged on the critical and yet unresolved question of the final status of the disputed state of Jammu and Kashmir.

### *The question of Kashmir: The Intersection of Domestic and International Politics*

Few issues stemming from the partition of India have proved to be as vexing and intractable as the Indo-Pakistan dispute over the former princely state of Jammu and Kashmir. This state has been the site of three Indo-Pakistani wars (1947–8, 1965, and 1999), several crises and a brutal, sanguinary, ethno-religious insurgency since 1989.[17] Why have India and Pakistan been engaged in such an unrelenting struggle over this state and expended so much blood and treasure in the process? The sources of the Kashmir dispute, unlike other inter-state disputes, do not involve vital strategic commodities or a region of great geopolitical significance. Instead the underlying source of this dispute can be traced to the markedly different conceptions of state-construction in South Asia. India, as a state committed to secular nationalism, sought to incorporate this predominantly Muslim state in an attempt to demonstrate its secular credentials. The argument ran as follows: if a Muslim-majority region could thrive within the confines of a predominantly Hindu polity, India's commitment to secularism would be beyond question. For Pakistan, it was equally important to incorporate Kashmir into its realm. As the professed homeland of the Muslims of South Asia, its leaders argued with equal force that without Kashmir their nation was incomplete.[18] In effect, Pakistan's claim to Kashmir was irredentist.[19]

After the collapse of Pakistan in 1971 following the brutal civil war in East Pakistan and the emergence of Bangladesh, Pakistan's moral claim to Kashmir became hollow. If religion alone could not serve as the basis of Pakistan's unity and territorial integrity, it could not legitimately claim Kashmir on the basis of its Muslim-majority status. Simultaneously, with India's flagging practical commitment to secularism in the 1980s, India's claim to Kashmir on the basis of secularism also lost ground. Today, grand moral and ethical claims notwithstanding, both states claim Kashmir on the basis of statecraft and little else: neither is willing to concede territory that it deems an integral part of its nationhood.

The internal dimensions of the Kashmir problem are inseparable from its external features. Following its highly contested accession to the Indian Union after the first Kashmir war, India worked out a complex federal arrangement with the state recognizing its unique status under the Indian constitution. This was codified under the terms of the Delhi Agreement between Prime Minister Jawaharlal Nehru and Sheikh Mohammed Abdullah, the leader of the largest, popular and secular political party in the state, the Jammu and Kashmir National Conference. Under the terms of this agreement, the government of India would limit its writ in Kashmir to questions of defense, foreign affairs, currency, and communications.[20] The Delhi Accord, however, proved to be quite short-lived. Abdullah was dismissed from the prime ministership of the state in 1953 when Indian intelligence agencies alleged that he was planning on declaring independence. Following Abdullah's dismissal, New Delhi propped up a series of governments of dubious legitimacy in Kashmir. As long as these regimes did not raise the secessionist bogey, national governments in New Delhi granted them considerable latitude in matters of governance. As a consequence, unlike in the rest of India, the National Conference was allowed to freely engage in various forms of political malfeasance including the intimidation of political opponents, electoral corruption, and raiding of the public exchequer. Simultaneously, New Delhi, in an attempt to win the sympathies of the Kashmiris, poured enormous developmental assistance into the state. These two contrary processes would amount to a potent and corrosive amalgam in the future. As political institutions were stultified, New Delhi's economic largess contributed to the growth of political mobilization within the state as a new generation of better-educated and politically conscious Kashmiris emerged. By the 1980s, unlike previous politically quiescent generations, this new cohort found New Delhi's political machinations to be intolerable. Lacking an alternative model for social protest and finding the existing institutional channels for political dissent blocked, they turned to violence.[21] Once the uprising started, Pakistan, which for all practical purposes had abandoned any hope of wresting Kashmir from India through the use of force, quickly entered the fray.[22] Pakistan's deep involvement in the Kashmir insurgency has broadened its scope, increased its lethality, and undermined the Indian state's efforts to restore order if not law in the state.

## Pakistan: Muslim sanctuary or Islamic state?

The principal stated purpose of the creation of Pakistan was to provide a homeland for the Muslims of South Asia. Had the Congress or the British been able to make a credible commitment to the protection of the Muslim minority in South Asia in the waning days of British colonial rule, the state of Pakistan may never have materialized.[23] Two key historical legacies have shaped questions of ethno-religious violence in Pakistan. First, the Indian nationalist movement which the Indian National Congress had dominated, was transformed by Mohandas Gandhi in the 1920s from an elitist, upper-middle class, and predominantly Hindu entity, into a mass-based political party seeking to represent all segments of Indian society regardless of cultural background, religious orientation, or class origins.[24] The principal vehicle for the movement for Pakistan, the Muslim League, however, failed to develop a similar grass-roots organization. As British colonial withdrawal approached, the leaders of the League resorted to populist mobilizational strategies to widen its political base. Unlike Congress, however, it did not develop institutional mechanisms for political representation within the party. Consequently, intra-party democracy, which was a hallmark of Congress, simply did not exist within the Muslim League. Until the time of the transfer of power the principal support base of the Muslim League remained confined to the upper-class Muslim gentry of the United Provinces.[25] This lack of intra-party democracy and the failure to develop robust institutional structures would soon be mirrored in the new state's attempts to develop institutional structures for governance.

The second factor that profoundly influenced the course of events relating to ethno-religious conflict in Pakistan was the searing effect of partition. British planning was woefully inadequate and carried out in a most haphazard and slapdash fashion. As noted above, close to a million individuals perished at the time of independence and partition, and another ten to twelve million were displaced, though no accurate figures can be adduced. There was mass violence as Hindus, Muslims, and Sikhs all preyed on vulnerable segments of one another's communities. This tragic episode must be considered one of the most sanguinary partitions of the twentieth century.

The memories of partition came to haunt elites and masses to varying degrees on both sides of the border. In Pakistan, the effects were even more acute. It was a far smaller state, it was bifurcated by several hundred miles of Indian territory, and it was a fragment of the erstwhile British empire in India. Since it started its independent existence as a secessionist state, it had to forge a distinct national identity, a task that proved exceedingly difficult.[26] Though Islam was one binding factor, other differences of sect, language, region, and social class soon came to the fore.

Pakistan's short history illustrates an extreme case of predatory nationalism coupled with weak political institutions contributing to a climate of intolerance and repression of ethnic and religious minorities. Ironically, few remember today that the country at its founding was declared a secular republic; one of founder

Mohammad Ali Jinnah's first speeches insisted that citizens of the new country were "free … to practice your religion" whether that religion was Islam, Hinduism, Zoroastrianism, Sikhism, Christianity, or anything else.[27] Yet it proved difficult to maintain the idea of a secular republic in the face of powerful religiously motivated groups. From the very outset they insisted that the Islamic character of the state should be reflected in the country's constitution. Indeed, the first constitution of Pakistan, which was tabled in 1954, ensured that the sentiments of religious leaders and parties were suitably addressed.[28]

The relationship between the nation and Islam has formed the central political debate in Pakistan since its birth.[29] Islamist leaders, who had never supported the Pakistan Movement under the rationale that Muslims should not seek a state of political sovereignty but rather an *ummah* in which sovereignty would reside with God, began political agitations as early as the 1950s, demanding that the state intervene in matters of religion.[30] This debate would coalesce around the definition of who is a Muslim, and its first victims of violence would be the Ahmadiyya community. The weakness of Pakistan's political institutions, ranging from its judicial system to its press, provided permissive conditions for the persecution of this hapless minority.

### The Ahmadis

The Ahmadiyya, or Ahmadi, community (also known as Qaidianis) are the followers of a late nineteenth century religious reformer named Mirza Ghulam Ahmad (1835–1908), who was a resident of Qaidian, now in Indian Punjab. In theological terms, Islamic orthodoxy objects to the Ahmadis because Ghulam Ahmad declared himself to be the second messiah, considered a blasphemous statement by those who believe in the finality of prophethood claimed by Muhammad. Yet Ahmadis were not persecuted in a widespread way or with state sanction, either in pre-independence India, including the territories now comprising Pakistan, or in Pakistan immediately following independence. One must acknowledge that the theological complaint of Ahmadiyya blasphemy appeared to gain sociopolitical ground only from 1949 onward. Indeed, Pakistan's first foreign minister was a member of the Ahmadiyya community.[31] But the new state of Pakistan had a tenuous foothold on the ideological ground of secularism. It would take only two years before members of Sunni Islamist movements began to focus on steering the Pakistani state toward implementation of a version of Islamic practice acceptable to them – abandoning their earlier position that the creation of Pakistan itself had no legitimacy in Islamic jurisprudence.

In 1953 the Jamaat-I-Islami led the Punjab riots, riots which targeted the Ahmadiyya. Apart from the violence which accompanied Partition, this was the first instance of violence against a community in independent Pakistan justified by its perpetrators on religious grounds. While the Pakistani state initiated an inquiry into the riots, the political effect would be to force the Pakistani state towards a closer legal imbrication with Islamic law – for no one wanted to appear against Islam.

Popular understandings of Pakistan's political trajectory tend to attribute the country's Islamization to the dictatorial rule of General Zia ul-Haq (1977–88), but in fact it was under the democratically-elected regime of Zulfiqar Ali Bhutto (1972–77) that formal changes to Pakistan's constitution were introduced, as well as new education policies which began to narrow the nation's ideological framework. In the wake of another series of anti-Ahmadi riots in 1974, an amendment to the constitution was introduced which explicitly defined a category of non-Muslim citizens, and included Ahmadis among the list. Four years later, General Zia would use the list of non-Muslims to generate separate electorates, a situation of outright discrimination although one not necessarily indicative of sanctioned violence against religious minorities. However, it signaled the closing opportunities for religious minorities to participate as full citizens. In 1984 Zia again amended the constitution in such a way as to accord Islamic law supremacy over national jurisprudence. Zia also included amendments which specifically targeted the Ahmadi community, and created legal grounds to prosecute any person "posing" as a Muslim or professing faith in the Ahmadiyya religion openly. These grounds for prosecution would take place under laws against blasphemy, offenses punishable with life in prison if not death. Perpetrators of violence against Ahmadis are never prosecuted, and Ahmadis can theoretically be jailed or executed for carrying a Quran or uttering the Islamic confession of faith. In this sense a political climate against a religious minority forced the state to craft laws which sanction violence against this targeted group.

## *The rise of sectarian conflict and Pakistan's Shia community*

If the case of the Ahmadiyya represents the first wave of targeted religious violence in Pakistan, the Shia are surely the second. Over the course of the past twenty-some years, a serious deterioration in the security situation for Shia citizens of Pakistan has occurred. Anti-Shia violence is carried out with seeming impunity by Sunni militias, who castigated Shia Muslims for being "infidels" and therefore acceptable targets for execution. Within this ideological climate, it is hard to remember that Jinnah himself was a Shia of the Bohra community.

This account can be located in the changed climate of state policies, related to arms supply as well as ideology, instituted during the Afghan War. This narrative underscores yet again the difficulties of any attempt to discuss religious violence using only a national framework – for the macroframework in which the rise of sectarian conflict has occurred in Pakistan has a great deal to do with transnational flows during the Afghan War, which lasted officially from 1979–89, but which continues to exercise its effects on Pakistan.

Specifically, by employing holy warriors against the Soviets, and supporting them financially as well as with arms, the US in partnership with Pakistan (and Saudi Arabia) created a new class of monied Sunni mercenaries. It is hard to overstate the destabilizing effects this has had on the region. The CIA, in order to provide cover of plausible deniability to its activities, arranged for the arms supplied via Pakistan to be those of Soviet make, delivered through unofficial networks, and coordinated by Pakistan as the front actor.[32] The Kalashnikov, a powerful and efficient assault rifle, thus became a visible part of life first in the regions bordering Afghanistan, and now, after more than two decades of continued smuggling, a routine presence throughout much of Pakistan.[33] Its proliferation in the country has contributed to a severe decline in law and order, and to what Pakistanis themselves refer to as the "Kalashnikov culture," about which there is rising public concern. An initiative of 2001 to reduce the flood of small arms throughout the country has to date been ineffectual.[34]

What explains the Pakistani state's seeming unwillingness and obvious inability to protect these two vulnerable minority communities? To answer this question it is necessary to return to the central argument sketched out at the beginning of this chapter. Pakistan's political institutions, from the outset, have faced a fundamental crisis of legitimacy. It took Pakistan's leaders seven years after independence to forge a new constitution.[35] From the outset, there was significant opposition to this constitution from a variety of quarters. The most important dissenters were Hindu politicians from East Pakistan who considered the constitution to be Islamic. The constitution that had taken so long to draft proved to be stillborn, as a constitutional coup took place with the aid of the army in 1954. The army, key elements of the elitist Civil Service of Pakistan, and some West Pakistani politicians had deemed the constitution to be too democratic for their liking and preferred a more centralized polity. Consequently, from the outset, Pakistan's political institutions proved to be both unrepresentative and lacking in political legitimacy. It was precisely these two features of its polity which would create conducive conditions for unscrupulous politicians and military dictators to pander to religious extremists throughout Pakistan's subsequent history. The debility of the nation's political institutions gave them considerable latitude for scapegoating and marginalizing minorities in an effort to bolster their own dubious and tenuous political standing.[36]

## Bangladesh: schizophrenic identity

The state of Bangladesh emerged in 1971 from the break-up of Pakistan following a particularly vicious civil war. India, the principal neighbor of East Pakistan, became embroiled in the civil war because of the flight of several million refugees from East Pakistan in the aftermath of the brutal Pakistani military crackdown. The origins of the civil war have been examined in some detail elsewhere.[37] Suffice it to say that its roots can be traced to the grossly inequitable social and economic policies that the West Pakistanis had pursued toward their eastern counterpart.

Bangladesh started its independent existence as an avowedly secular state. Its founder, Sheikh Mujibur Rehman, significantly beholden to India because of its role in the creation of Bangladesh, could have hardly chosen to have drafted a non-secular constitution. More to the point, for much of the Bengali-speaking Muslim world there existed an intriguing tension in their social identities. On the one hand, their identities were distinctly Islamic; on the other hand, their initial quarrel with the Pakistani state had emerged from the imposition of an alien language, Urdu, as the national language of Pakistan in 1952. There was no gainsaying their attachment to a distinctive linguistic identity along with all its cultural accoutrements.[38]

Finally, Islam had entered Bengal through a most intriguing route. Contrary to popular belief it had not proven attractive to the population of Bengal because of its egalitarian ideology in contrast to the presence of caste hierarchies in Hinduism. Nor had it spread through coercive forms of proselytization. Instead, as Richard Eaton's magisterial work shows, it was primarily because Muslim entrepreneurs introduced new agricultural techniques into the region.[39] Conversion to Islam in Bengal was gradual, subtle, and extended. Not surprisingly, the practice of Islam in Bengal, barring its core elements, shared little in common with those of its adherents in West Pakistan. Indeed, many West Pakistanis viewed their fellow Bengali Muslim brethren with a mixture of disdain and distrust.[40]

Bangladesh has faced seemingly impossible odds in its short existence. Between 1947 and 1971, Bangladesh was the eastern province of the Pakistani state. During this span of time it was treated as a virtual internal colony of Pakistan.[41] The bulk of foreign assistance was utilized in West Pakistan, few investments went into East Pakistan, and representation in the powerful Civil Service of Pakistan (CSP), not to mention the armed forces, was fundamentally lopsided. Most galling to East Pakistanis, however, was the imposition of Urdu as the national language of Pakistan, denying Bengali, their language, national status. Ultimately, the accumulated grievances drove the growth of Bengali sub-nationalism, which in turn led to civil war. Indian intervention in this civil war ultimately contributed to the creation of Bangladesh. The Bangladesh Liberation War of 1971 resulted in the deaths of between one and three million people. Of late, increasing attention (in India) has been given to the selective violence employed by the Pakistani Army during 1971, which disproportionately targeted the province's Hindu minority. As is the case with Partition in 1947, a complete mapping of what happened in 1971 has never been done; the question of essentially religious violence targeting the Hindus of East Bengal has to date been taken up primarily by Hindu nationalists, which has added a veneer of political ideology to such research.

Sadly, the nascent state started its political existence with a number of important institutional handicaps. Sheikh Mujibur Rehman was notionally committed to the creation of a democratic, egalitarian and secular polity. In practice, however, Sheikh Mujib, as he was popularly known, did little or nothing to foster an institutional legacy to promote those ends. As political instability mounted and the government's ability to maintain public order declined, Mujib increasingly resorted to authoritarian measures. He declared a state of emergency in 1975 and dispensed with the parliamentary form of government, declaring himself to be the president of Bangladesh.[42]

In fairness to Mujib it also needs to be stated that the tasks he confronted were daunting. To begin with he had to contend with creating a state out of a breakaway province. Additionally, he had to deal with a segment of the Bangladeshi military that remained unreconciled to the breakup of Pakistan and still harbored pro-Pakistani sentiments. Also, he faced the intransigence of the radical Islamist

Jamaat-I-Islami, a political party fundamentally opposed to the creation of a separate, independent state of Bangladesh. Finally, his administration had to contend with the simple but compelling matter of curbing the powers of local condottierri who had emerged in the wake of the civil war. All these factors undermined the stability of his regime, and he was assassinated along with most members of his immediate family in a sanguinary military coup in 1975.

The military regime led by General Zia ur-Rehman justified its takeover on the usual grounds: the previous government had failed to curb growing lawlessness, had been involved in corruption, and had failed to address a number of pressing social and economic needs. To some small degree Zia's regime did indeed deliver on his promises as economic development did take place, some of the cronyism of the Mujib years was curbed and efforts to limit population growth, a bane of Bangladeshi society, were put into place. Yet civil liberties and personal rights were squelched and the Zia regime displayed scant regard for the rights of the substantial Hindu minority (approximately 10 percent of the population). The formal commitment to a secular state which promised equality before the law for all citizens, regardless of religious affiliation, evaporated under General Zia's military dictatorship.

## Conclusions

A key problem that confronts all three states can be summed easily: they are all characterized by strong societies and weak states.[43] Societal forces frequently challenge and overwhelm weak political institutions. More to the point, as political institutions command questionable degrees of legitimacy, political leaders in all three states feel compelled to make sectarian appeals to bolster their shaky standing. Not surprisingly, such appeals inevitably corrode institutional norms, routinized political processes, and state neutrality. The state all too often privileges majority ethnic and religious groups at the inevitable cost of marginalized minorities.

In India, much ethno-religious violence has stemmed from the departure of the state from the norms and practices that should characterize a secular and civic polity. When the state has attempted to resolve ethno-religious disputes within an institutional context, it has managed to stave off violence. On the other hand, when it has failed to utilize such channels and allowed political entrepreneurs to arouse populist and sectarian passions, violence has erupted. In Pakistan and Bangladesh, the chronic debility of political institutions has permitted the abuse of historical inheritances to a far greater degree. Neither state, despite a series of fitful attempts, has been able to institutionalize and embed democratic and civic principles. Consequently, political entrepreneurs in both states have been able, with considerable impunity, to engage in sectarian appeals, to subvert the rule of law and to promote ethno-religious discord in the quest for short-term political advantage. Despite its obviously flawed record, the possibilities of ethno-religious accord remain greatest in India. Its political institutions, though hardly free of taint, nevertheless function with some efficacy. More to the point, certain key features of democracy have become ingrained in India's political culture. Free and open elections, the independence of the judiciary, the freedom of the press, and respect for personal rights and civil liberties are the norm. Though all of these principles have, on occasion, been breached, these breaches are correctly seen as aberrations.[44] Until Bangladesh and Pakistan can emulate India's example of building viable political institutions and promoting norms of civic nationalism and cultural pluralism, their ability to contain ethno-religious violence will prove elusive.

## Notes

1  See for example G. Pandey, *The Construction of Communalism in Colonial North India* (New Delhi: Oxford University Press, 1990).
2  See the essay by Christopher A. Bayly, "The Pre-history of 'Communalism'? Religious Conflict in India, 1700–1860," in *The Origins of Nationality in South Asia: Patriotism and Ethical Government in the Making of Modern India* (New York: Oxford University Press, 1998).
3  See for example the discussion of the role of electoral politics in fomenting religious violence in India in Steven I. Wilkinson, *Votes and Violence: Electoral Competition and Ethnic Riots in India* (Cambridge: Cambridge University Press, 2004).
4  Donald E. Smith, *India as a Secular State* (Princeton, NJ: Princeton University Press, 1963); also see Granville Austin, *Working a Democratic Constitution: the Indian Experience* (New Delhi: Oxford University Press, 2000).
5  For two contrasting accounts see Christophe Jaffrelot, ed., *A History of Pakistan and Its Origins* (London: Anthem Press, 2002); and Akbar S. Ahmed, *Jinnah, Pakistan and Islamic Identity: the Search for Saladin* (London: Routledge, 1977).
6  For one of the earliest and most important statements on this subject, see Samuel P. Huntington, *Political Order in Changing Societies* (New Haven, CT: Yale University Press, 1968).
7  Two of the most important and competing accounts are Paul R. Brass, *The Production of Hindu–Muslim Violence in India* (Seattle: University of Washington Press, 2004); and Ashutosh Varshney, *Ethnic Conflict and Civic Life: Hindus and Muslims in India* (New Haven, CT: Yale University Press, 2002).
8  On the myth of a unified, primordial Muslim nation, see Mushirul Hasan, "The Myth of Muslim Unity: Colonial and Nationalist Narratives," in *Legacy of a Divided Nation: India's Muslims since Independence* (New Delhi: Oxford University Press, 1997).
9  One of the finest treatments of the origins and rise of these movements can be found in Kenneth W. Jones, *Socio-Religious Reform Movements in British India* (Cambridge: Cambridge University Press, 1989).
10  On Congress's shortcomings see Francis Robinson, *Separatism Among the Indian Muslims: The Politics of the United Provinces 1860–1923* (Delhi: Oxford University Press, 1993).
11  On this subject, see Peter Hardy, *The Muslims of British India* (London: Cambridge University Press, 1972).
12  For a discussion of the origins of the Hindu Mahasabha and its progeny, see Bruce D. Graham, *Hindu Nationalism and Indian Politics: the Origins and Development of the Bharatiya Jana Sangh* (Cambridge: Cambridge University Press, 1990).
13  On this point see Leonard O. Mosley, *The Last Days of the British Raj* (London: Weidenfeld and Nicolson, 1961); and Sir Penderel Moon, *Divide and Quit: An Eyewitness Account of the Partition of India* (Berkeley, CA: University of California Press, 1962).
14  For a succinct discussion see Radha Kumar, "The Troubled History of Partition," *Foreign Affairs* 76, no. 1 (January/February 1997): 114–30.

15  For a thoughtful set of perspectives, see Suvir Kaul, ed., *The Partitions of Memory: the Afterlife of the Division of India* (Delhi: Permanent Black, 2001).

16  One of the most important accounts is Sisir Gupta, *Kashmir: A Study in India–Pakistan Relations* (Bombay: Asia Publishing House, 1966).

17  The literature on the Indo-Pakistani dispute is simply voluminous. A working sample includes: Sumit Ganguly, *Conflict Unending: India–Pakistan Tensions Since 1947* (New York: Columbia University Press, 2001); Russell Brines, *The Indo-Pakistani Conflict* (New York: Pall Mall, 1968); J.N. Dixit, *India–Pakistan in War and Peace* (New Delhi: Books Today, 2002).

18  Zulfiquar A. Bhutto, *The Myth of Independence* (London: Oxford University Press, 1969).

19  Naomi Chazan, *Irredentism and International Politics* (Boulder, CO: Lynne Rienner, 1991).

20  Jyoti B. Das Gupta, *Jammu and Kashmir* (The Hague: Martinus Nijhoff, 1968).

21  For a complete account of the origins of the 1989 insurgency in Kashmir, see Sumit Ganguly, *The Crisis in Kashmir: Portents of War, Hopes of Peace* (New York: Cambridge University Press, 1997).

22  For evidence of Pakistan's involvement in the Kashmir insurgency refer to Victoria Schofield, *Kashmir in Conflict: India, Pakistan and the Unfinished War* (London: I.B. Tauris, 2000).

23  On the concept of a "credible commitment" see James D. Fearon, "Commitment Problems and the Spread of Ethnic Conflict," in *The International Spread of Ethnic Conflict*, ed. David A. Lake and Donald Rothschild (Princeton, NJ: Princeton University Press, 1998).

24  Barbara D. Metcalf and Thomas R. Metcalf, *A Concise History of India* (Cambridge: Cambridge University Press, 2002).

25  Paul R. Brass, *Language, Religion and Politics in North India* (Cambridge: Cambridge University Press, 1974).

26  See the discussions in Christophe Jaffrelot, ed., *Pakistan: Nationalism Without a Nation?* (New Delhi: Manohar, 2002).

27  Mohammad A. Jinnah, *Quaid-i-Azam Mahomed Ali Jinnah: Speeches As Governor-General of Pakistan 1947–1948* (Karachi: Pakistan Publications, 1976).

28  On this point see the trenchant discussion in Allen McGrath, *The Destruction of Pakistan's Democracy* (Karachi: Oxford University Press, 1996).

29  See Leonard Binder, *Religion and Politics in Pakistan* (Berkeley, CA: University of California Press, 1961); and Ayesha Jalal, *The Sole Spokesman: Jinnah, the Muslim League, and the Demand for Pakistan* (Cambridge: Cambridge University Press, 1985).

30  For the best overview of the Jamaat-I-Islami and their changing political activities in Pakistan, see Seyyed V. Nasr, *The Vanguard of the Islamic Revolution: the Jama`at-i-Islami of Pakistan* (Berkeley, CA: University of California Press, 1994).

31  See Amjad M. Khan, "Persecution of the Ahmadiyya Community in Pakistan: An Analysis Under International Law and International Relations," *Harvard Human Rights Journal* 16, (2003): 222–3.

32  Several recent books have illumined how this process worked. See Ahmed Rashid, *Taliban: Militant Islam, Oil and Fundamentalism in Central Asia* (New Haven, CT: Yale University Press, 2000); see also Steve Coll, *Ghost Wars: The Secret History of the CIA, Afghanistan and bin Laden From the Soviet Invasion to September 10, 2001* (New York: Penguin Books, 2004); and for a short article, see also Milton Bearden, "Afghanistan, Graveyard of Empires," *Foreign Affairs* 80, no. 6 (November/December 2001): 17–30.

33  Small arms and their easy availability have changed the complexion of violence and conflict in societies worldwide. See the special issue of *Bulletin of the Atomic Scientists*

on the effects of small arms on conflict: "Small Arms, Big Problems," *Bulletin of the Atomic Scientists* 55, no.1 (1999).

34 See "18 Million Illegal Weapons in Country: Small Arms Survey 2002," *Dawn*, January 13, 2003.

35 McGrath, *Destruction of Pakistan's Democracy*, 1996.

36 On the question of scapegoating, see the treatment in Stuart Kaufman, *Modern Hatreds: The Symbolic Politics of Ethnic War* (Ithaca, NY: Cornell University Press, 2001).

37 One of the earliest and best treatments of the subject remains Robert Jackson, *South Asian Crisis* (New York: Praeger, 1975).

38 Amena Mohsin, "Language, Identity and the State in Bangladesh," in *Fighting Words: Language Policy and Ethnic Relations in Asia*, ed. Michael E. Brown and Sumit Ganguly (Cambridge, MA: MIT Press, 2003).

39 Richard Eaton, *The Rise of Islam and the Bengal Frontier* (Berkeley, CA: University of California Press, 1993).

40 See for example the discussion of the Bengalis of East Pakistan in Mohammed A. Khan, *Friends, Not Masters: A Political Autobiography* (Oxford: Oxford University Press, 1967).

41 One of the best treatments remains Raonaq Jahan, *Pakistan: Failure in National Integration* (New York: Columbia University Press, 1972).

42 Tanzeen M. Murshid, "Democracy in Bangladesh: Illusion or Reality," *Contemporary South Asia* 4, no. 2 (1995).

43 Joel Migdal, *Strong Societies and Weak States: State–Society Relations and State Capabilities in the Third World* (Princeton, NJ: Princeton University Press, 1988).

44 Sumit Ganguly, "India's Multiple Revolutions," *Journal of Democracy* 13, no. 1 (2002).

# 6

# RELIGIOUS CONFLICT AND THE GLOBALIZATION OF KNOWLEDGE IN INDONESIAN HISTORY

*Mark Woodward*

This paper explores relationships between the globalization of knowledge and religiously inspired or justified conflict in Indonesia. It builds on theoretical approaches to the study of religious extremism and collective violence developed by Juergensmeyer, Lawrence, Tambiah, and Herman.[1] Juergensmeyer describes acts of terror as "symbolic empowerment" of marginal men.[2] Tambiah's observations about collective violence in South Asia are equally applicable to Indonesia. The first is that collective violence is often used as a tool by political elites. Second, the targets are frequently symbols of collective identity and third, rumors, often grotesque ones, play a major role in fomenting violence.[3] Lawrence shows that most religious extremists are "secondary elites" most of whom have modern, primarily secular educations, but with little chance of attaining their social and economic goals.[4] In an afterword to her classic study of psychological trauma, *Trauma and Recovery*, Herman extends her discussion of the psychological consequences of violence to social groups victimized by civil war and ethnic cleansing. These analyses provide valuable insight into the social psychology of today's Indonesia.

Religion was a major source of conflict and in the first two decades of Indonesian history, a country that established independence from the Dutch in 1945. From the earliest days of the republic there has been a debate about whether Indonesia should be an Islamic state or a nation based on belief in "The One True God." This reflects a basic religious distinction between orthoprax Muslims know locally as *santri* and others who practice a form of folk Sufism (Islamic mysticism) in which veneration of local saints is held to be more important than *shariah*.[5] The latter group is known in Java as *kejawen*. In 1945 *santri* politicians wanted to include the phrase: "with the obligation for Muslims to abide by *shariah* law" to the section of the constitution describing Indonesia as a nation based on devotion to God.[6] This would have established Indonesia as a *de facto* Islamic state. While it went underground for much of the Suharto period (1965–98) this debate never really ceased. With the fall of Suharto it surfaced as a major source of political and religious conflict.

## Religion, conflict, and New Order Indonesia

The government of Indonesia's second president Suharto (ruled 1965–98) was known as the New Order to distinguish it from that of the former president Sukarno. The New Order began and ended with outbreaks of collective violence that appear to have been orchestrated by elements of the military.

Throughout the Sukarno period (1945–65) party politics was based largely on religious affiliation. The Nationalist and Communist parties were made up primarily of nominal or *kejawen* Muslims. Conservative Muslims were represented by different, explicitly, Islamic parties. In 1965, in the wake of an abortive coup, hundreds of thousands of supporters of the Communist party (PKI) were murdered. In central Java and Bali most of the killing was conducted by conservative factions of the Nationalist Party, who opposed the communists for economic reasons. In east Java most of the killing was done by Ansor, the youth wing of Nhadlatul Ulama, the then-conservative traditionalist Muslim party, who accused PKI members of being apostates. It was orchestrated by the organization's senior leadership.[7] The military did nothing to stop the killings and often provided logistical support.[8]

Indonesians who can remember the slaughter often speak of headless and/or limbless corpses floating in streams and the stench of decaying, unburied bodies. This is a powerful symbolic statement to Muslims because of the requirement that corpses be ritually purified and buried quickly. The desecration of corpses robs them of their Muslim identity. It suggests that victims were apostates deserving of death. It also denied the families of the victims the ability to perform pilgrimage to the grave at the end of Ramadan. This is an important element of the folk Islam practiced by most of the victims. The killings were, in a perverse way, religious acts. Denying victims proper funerals was a ritual of negation. Many Javanese affirm this negation by avoiding sites associated with the killings in fear that victims have become dangerous ghosts. Some of the victim's families attempt to negate the negation by describing the dead as martyrs.

This orgy of violence led to the establishment of the "New Order," a military-dominated, managerial state focused on development and political stability. Despite the undemocratic character of the regime, its accomplishments in economic development and education were remarkable. While friends and relatives of the president and ranking officials made huge fortunes, it is clear that ordinary Indonesians were much better off in 1995 than they were in 1965.[9]

The New Order was as concerned with the management of ideology and religion as it was with that of the economy.[10] This, combined with the *kejawen* orientation of the elite, led to the impression that the regime was anti-Islamic. Some criticism of the regime's management of religion emerged in discussions of bills introduced in parliament. More virulent criticism circulated in the form of rumors. What follows is an account of orthodox Islamic grievances against the New Order.

- The modernist Islamic political party Masyumi was banned and its leaders imprisoned by Sukarno for supporting a rebellion in south Sulawesi. Many modernist Muslims expected that because of their roles in the destruction of the Communist party Masyumi would be rehabilitated. Suharto refused.[11] The party reorganized as a foundation, Dewan Dakwah Islamiyah Indonesia (Indonesian Council for the Propagation of Islam).[12]
- Christians were disproportionately represented in the New Order government, particularly in the early years. This led to widespread speculation that Suharto and/or his wife had secretly converted to Christianity.
- Chinese Indonesians are a small minority but control vast segments of the nation's economy, ranging from giant conglomerates to small businesses. There is widespread resentment of the Chinese in most segments of Indonesian society. The fact that many Chinese are Christian exacerbates this resentment.
- In the 1970s and 1980s the government introduced a series of bills in the legislature that observant Muslims found deeply offensive. One would have allowed secular marriages.[13] A second would have afforded recognition to *aliran kebatin* – Javanese mystical groups – which *santri* Muslims consider to be heretical. A third required that social organizations adopt *Pancasila*, the national creed which, in part, pledges belief in a non-denominational God, as their "sole organizing principle."[14] Muslim organizations maintained that these bills promoted adultery and apostasy. The government ultimately compromised on secular marriage and the *aliran kepercayaan.* It would not budge on *Pancasila.*[15]

The components of *Pancasila* are:

- *Ketuhanan Maha Esa* – Devotion to God
- *Kemanusiaan yand adil dan berahad* – Human society which is just and characterized by mutual respect
- *Persatuan Indonesia* – The unity of Indonesia
- *Kerakyatan yang dipimpin oleh hikmat kebijaksanaan dalam bermusyawararan/perwakilan* – Society governed with wise justice in the context of mutual consultation and assistance
- *Keadilan social baga seluruh rakyat Indonesia* – Social justice for all of the people of Indonesia.

The government took the position that only the *Pancasilaization* of society could ensure stability and development. The social organizations act allowed the government to disband any organization that did not "accept" *Pancasila.* Indonesia's two largest Muslim organizations, Nahdlatul Ulama and Muhammadiyah, seriously considered active resistance but concluded that the cost in human life would be too high and that the probability of success was minimal.

## Managing violence

Collective violence was a routine part of Indonesian politics throughout the New Order period. It was most common during election campaigns. Most frequently outbreaks were triggered by campaign marches colliding.[16] There were also periodic student demonstrations that sometimes sparked violent incidents. The degree to which these incidents were provoked and by whom are difficult to determine. Many people speak of mysterious provocateurs that incited violence and of powerful figures known as *kambing hitam* (black goat) or *dalang* (puppeteer) that arranged and financed it. Opinions about who or what group provoked any given event depend almost entirely on the political and religious orientations of the individual in question.

Tambiah has argued that collective violence can become an institutionalized and indeed ritualized aspect of election campaigns.[17] In the South Asian elections he considered there was at least some question about which party would emerge victorious. In Indonesia the question was whether or not Golangan Karya (commonly known as Golkar), the government party, would attain the size of majority it desired. This raises the question of what purpose organized political violence could serve. Many Indonesian observers maintain that organized violence was the only way that opposition to government policy could be expressed.

Between 1965 and 2004 the state's reaction to collective violence varied greatly. In some instances it employed deadly force at the slightest provocation to make clear that dissent would not be tolerated. In other cases, including the massive riots that proceeded the fall of Suharto in 1998, it helped to provoke violence. In most instances violence was successfully managed. Both the number of incidents and loss of life were limited and the long-term consequences were minimal. Two exceptions were the Malari affair of 1974 and the Tanjung Priok incident of 1984.[18]

The Malari affair began as a protest by students and intellectuals against the visit of Japanese Prime Minister Tanaka to Indonesia. It came at a time when Muslim leaders had been angered by the proposed secular marriage bill and of heightened anti-Chinese feeling resulting from an economic recession. Students protested against corruption and the increasing role of foreign corporations in the Indonesian economy for several months. They had broad support from intellectuals, some military officers, and a large segment of the press. There were rumors that Suharto intended to sell the national oil company Pertamina to Japanese investors. On January 15 as many as one hundred thousand demonstrators gathered in central Jakarta. The crowd was dispersed by security forces. Subsequently, groups of young men roamed the streets burning Japanese cars. One of Jakarta's central markets was looted and burned. At least eight people were killed by security forces.

The government blamed the protests and riots on leaders of two outlawed political parties: Masyumi and the Indonesian socialist party, both supported by many intellectuals. Some were imprisoned. Much stricter press regulations were imposed and tight restrictions placed on student organizations. The Malari affair also motivated a Pancasila indoctrination campaign that eventually required all students and civil servants to pass exams on Pancasila principles and ethics. Most intellectuals regarded it as ridiculous. Many *santri* Muslims regarded it as the promotion of unbelief.

"Alumnae" of the Malari affair maintain that they had no part in the riots of 1974 and that the looting and arson had been carried out by gangs recruited by the security forces in an attempt to discredit the opposition. Many that I interviewed in the late 1990s continued to hold informal discussion groups. Some are academics; others hold significant positions in business or government. They freely admitted that the goal of the movement was to bring about regime change. When the economic crisis of 1997 began and a younger generation took to the streets, Malari "alumnae" helped to organize and finance the demonstrations. They supplied student "command posts" with food, bottled water, medical supplies, phone cards, and banners. Underground newspapers were produced in safe houses in upper-class neighborhoods with material and editorial assistance from a leading English language daily.

The Malari protests grew out of a sense of moral outrage, but were not explicitly religious.[19] The Tanjung Priok affair grew from Islamist outrage about the *asas tunggal* policy, which stipulated that only Pancasila was permissible as a foundation for social organizations. Tanjung Priok, Jakarta's port district, is known for fervent, though unschooled, Muslim piety. In August and September of 1984 preachers delivered vitriolic sermons against the government's Pancasila campaign. There were also denunciations of Christians, and the Chinese and Muslims who associated with them. Muslims with ties to Chinese were described as "no better than dogs." This is an extremely insulting statement because for Muslims, dogs, like swine, are defiled creatures. Several encouraged the population to struggle against the government to the point of martyrdom. What follows is a segment of a prayer offered in a sermon by Syarifin Maloko:

> Bring down your curses on those who will not confess that this earth is your creation, oh Allah. Shut the mouths who say that this earth is the creation of the *Pancasila* eagle.[20] Inspire us to rise up all together in protest against those tyrannical people Allah. If we rise up in protest, it will no longer be through words, but we will go to them with our daggers and cutlasses, oh Allah.[21]

On September 8, two security officers wearing boots entered a *musholla* (prayer room) and used gutter water to blacken posters advertising a rally/prayer meeting.[22] Wearing foot coverings in mosques violates Islamic law. In Tanjung Priok gutter water is raw sewage. As Kolstadt observes, both of these acts defiled the *musholla*, rendering prayers performed there invalid.[23] These events triggered acts of open defiance. Four men attacked a security officer and burned his motorcycle. They were arrested and allegedly tortured.

This triggered a far more serious outbreak on September 12, about which there are conflicting accounts of the incident. This much is clear. At approximately 11:00 pm approximately 1,500 unarmed people marched from a mosque to the police station demanding that the detainees be released. They were confronted by soldiers who opened fire with automatic weapons. Some of the demonstrators were detained and subsequently tried for subversion. Government accounts minimized the death toll. They state that 14 people died. Armed Forces chief Moerdani emphasized the fanatical and threatening character of the crowd. Critics describe the crowd as peaceful and claim that approximately 400 people died and that many bodies were dumped in the ocean. Any such victims were denied Muslim burials. The Tanjung Priok incident prompted protests, arsons, and bombings. In many cases Chinese interests and/or associates of the Suharto regime were targeted. Churches were burned on Christmas Eve. The most symbolically charged act of violence was the January 22, 1985 bombing of the eighth-century Buddhist monument Borobudur. This structure is regarded by many Javanese as a symbol of the glory of Indonesia's past. It is also the most important pilgrimage site for Indonesia's Buddhist community which is overwhelmingly Chinese. The symbolic significance of this incident resembles that of the destruction of the Babri Mosque in India by Hindu Nationalists.[24] In both instances a blow was struck at a religious community by attacking one its most sacred shrines. The bombing of Borobudur provoked the same sort of outrage among Buddhists and Javanists that the defilement of the Tanjung Priok Mosque did among *santri* Muslims.

In early 1985 Indonesia was deeply polarized. Many *santri* Muslims believed that Suharto intended to declare Pancasila the state religion. Others maintained that he and his top official Moerdani were promoting Christianity. Moerdani's repeated statements that he was a loyal official who happened to be Christian were greeted with scorn. Javanists, Christians, and Chinese feared an Islamic Revolution. Suharto stated that he would "wipe out terrorism before it becomes a national disaster."[25] Indonesians on both sides feared a return to the anarchy and violence of the early New Order. The struggle appeared to many to be a zero sum game, just as party politics was in the 1950s.

The conflict not withstanding, the Pancasila legislation had remarkably few consequences. Pancasila did not become a religion. Muslim organizations remained as they were. The feared Christianization campaign did not take place and there was never a serious threat of Islamic revolution. The fears and predictions of Muslim leaders proved to be unfounded. In the late 1980s and 1990s Indonesian society, the government, and even the armed forces became much more self-consciously Islamic. Attendance at Friday prayers and the percentage of people fasting during the month of Ramadan increased dramatically. Thousands of mosques were built, some with support from a foundation sponsored by the Suharto family.[26] By the end of the 1980s overflow crowds praying in the streets were a common sight on Fridays. Suharto went on the haj. His daughter Hardiyanti Rukmana, who clearly had political aspirations, began to wear the *jilbab* (head covering) as did many other Indonesian women. Islamic publishing flourished. Suharto endorsed the founding of the Association of Muslim Intellectuals and the establishment of an Islamic bank in 1990.[27]

The armed forces split into "Green" (Islamic) and "Red and White" (Nationalist) factions.[28] In the early days of the republic there were very few *santri* officers because few had the necessary level of education.[29] By the mid-1970s significant numbers of *santri* educated in government schools or those run by the modernist Muslim organization Muhammadiyah began to enter the officer corps. Some, including Suharto's son-in-law Prabowo Subianto exhibited strong sympathy for Islamist causes.[30]

This was also an era of rapid globalization, both of the economy and of Islam. In the late 1970s the politics of Islam was locally focused. During the 1980s the increasing number of Indonesians educated in Egypt and Saudi Arabia and improvements in print and electronic communications vastly increased Indonesians' knowledge of the larger Muslim world. Today events in Bosnia, Iraq, Palestine, and Afghanistan figure significantly in Indonesian discourse. Thousands of Indonesians fought in the war against the Soviets in Afghanistan where they acquired religious indoctrination as well as military experience. Taken together these factors led to the radicalization of segments of the Indonesian Muslim community. These Islamists are part of a globalized system of knowledge and discourse that defines *world* politics as a zero-sum game pitting beleaguered Muslims against an alliance of Christians and Jews. Conflicts within Indonesia are defined as elements of this larger global struggle.

## Religion, conflict, and the end of the New Order

The legitimacy of the New Order regime was contingent upon rapid economic growth. In the summer of 1997 the Indonesian economy collapsed in the wake of the Asian currency crisis. This sparked demonstrations demanding Suharto's resignation. Collectively they were known as *Reformasi* (Reformation). There were also serious outbreaks of ethnic and religious violence. The rhetoric surrounding these events was as much religious as it was political and economic.

On May 12, 1998 security forces opened fire on students at Jakarta's elite Trisakti University. They were proclaimed *Pahlawan Reformasi* (Heroes of the Reformation) by the press and the public. The term *pahlawan* is the same one used to describe those who died in the revolution and is strongly associated with the Islamic concept of martyrdom. Their deaths galvanized the opposition. Faculty and administrators at universities throughout the country joined the students in their call for Suharto's resignation.

Security forces stood by as large segments of Jakarta burned.[31] Tens of thousands roamed the street looting and burning Chinese businesses and those identified with the Suharto family. The homes of several prominent Chinese businessmen with ties to the government were burned. The primary aims of most of the participants were economic. Supermarkets, banks, ATM machines, and appliance and electronics stores were particularly hard hit. The poor used the opportunity to grab anything they could carry and burned what they could not. More than a thousand people were killed, most of them looters unable to escape from fires that other, more sinister elements in the crowds set.

Some of the worst violence occurred in the oldest portion of Jakarta known as Kota. This area has been among Jakarta's Chinatowns for centuries. Many of the rioters were residents of the ethnically mixed, impoverished neighborhoods located along the harbor near the Chinese community. These people felt – and have been – betrayed by the Indonesian government and the local economic elite. The inflation caused by the monetary crisis made life nearly impossible. People who once could barely afford to send their children to school could barely afford rice. It is tragic that the Trisakti incident led them to erupt in violence. It is also not surprising. There were no winners in the days of rioting and looting – only losers. Grabbing bags of rice as one runs through a burning building does not change the fundamental conditions of poverty that motivate such desperate acts. Denouncing "Muslim violence," as some Chinese Christians have done, does nothing to change the fundamental economic conditions which drove the poor to violence.

While most of the rioters were motivated by the desire for short-term economic gain, others were organized gangs intent on terrorizing the Chinese community. Accounts of the riots describe provocateurs yelling anti-Chinese, anti-student, and anti-opposition party slogans and posting signs reading "destroy Chinese property."[32] The Chinese were denounced as "pigs, lice and dogs," suggesting that they are defiled beings. There were reports that military vehicles were used to transport these gangs and that some of the buildings looted and burned were tear-gassed to disable security guards.

More insidious are the numerous, well-documented accounts of gang rapes of Chinese women by men yelling "Allah Akbar" (God is great). *Asia Week* reported that at least 468 women were raped.[33] The total was probably higher because victims are often reluctant to discuss abuse.[34] Many more were publicly stripped and humiliated. Many were assaulted in front of their families. Some of the victims were as young as ten years old. An unknown number were murdered, some beheaded or burned alive. Many of the bodies were mutilated. Some of the victims suffered such shame that they committed suicide. Others were hospitalized for psychological trauma as well as physical injuries. While riots and looting occurred in many parts of the city, almost all of the rapes occurred in Chinese neighborhoods.[35]

What follows are statements by Chinese Indonesian victims. They combine shock, anger disbelief and the generalized sense of numbness characteristic of victims of violence and clearly implicate the government.[36]

> GOD, please help them ... the innocent people. Pray for them. ... those idiots were looting and burning everything in sight while the military doesn't do anything just to protect people ...

Another wrote:

> Armed with sledge hammers and steel bars, the Muslim masses pried off the protective steel roll-doors shouting "Allah Akbar" (Allah is great). ... The Chinese have worked hard all their lives from before dawn to late at night. Now Chinese families sit on the ground near the smoldering ruins, some weeping, others staring, saying nothing.

The following is a statement by one of the rape victims:

> ... a huge crowd had gathered around the apartment. They screamed, "Let's butcher the Chinese!", "Let's eat pigs!", "Let's have a party!" ... We were all very frightened. In our fright, we prayed and left everything in God's hands. ... We hurried into the room and locked the door tight. At that time, we heard them knock the other rooms' doors loudly, and there were screams from women and girls. The room was filled with fear. We realized that they would come to us. So we spread throughout the room and hid in corners. Inside, we could hear girls, whose age around 10–12, screaming, "Mommy ... Mommy ...", "Mom ... Mom ..., it hurts."
>
> I saw a woman in her 20s being raped by four men. She tried to fight, but she was held tight. ... We tried to rescue her, but we had to give up. There were around 60 of them. They tied us – I, my father, my mother, Veny, Dony, Uncle Dodi, Aunt Vera –with ripped sheets. They led us to a room. Uncle Dodi asked what they wanted, but they didn't answer. They cast an evil and savage look. One of them grabbed Veny rudely and dragged her to a sofa. At that time, I knew that she was in danger. I screamed loudly, and one of the mob slapped me. My father who also screamed was hit by a wooden block, and he fainted. My mother had fainted when Veny was dragged to the sofa. I could only pray and pray that the disaster would not befall us ... There were about five people who raped Veny, and before beginning, everyone always said, "Allah Akbar." They were ferocious, brutal. Not long afterward, around nine men came to the room and dragged me. I instantly fainted and everything was blank. I became conscious at around 5 or 6 in the afternoon. My head was in pain, and then I realized that I had no clothes on my body. I cried. I was very depressed. I realized that my family was still there, and obscurely I saw my father hugged my mother and Doni. I also saw that Uncle Dodi was lying on the floor, and Uncle Vera was crying over his body. I felt so weak and fainted again.[37]

These were "leveling crowds." Their purpose was to destroy property, lives and honor. While the riots and the rapes were certainly planned, the ability of provocateurs to organize such extreme violence speaks to the intensity of tension between Chinese and "indigenous" (*pribumi*) Indonesians. Ethnic, economic and religious factors all contribute to this tension. One of the consequences was a great incidence of emotional trauma. In the long run the trauma inflicted on Indonesian Chinese may have done more damage to the Indonesian economy than the looting and arson. Buildings can be reconstructed and shops refilled. It is far more difficult to rebuild trust and confidence in those who have come to be known as perpetrators of physical and symbolic assault.[38] Herman has argued that for victims of violence – be it war, rape, or domestic assault – to find healing they must first find safety. For many of the victims of the 1998 riots, Indonesia will never again feel safe. Many Chinese business people fled the country, taking their money and their business acumen with them. Some may eventually return. Others will not because they equate Islam with arson, pillage, and rape.

On the basis of an extensive survey, Daihani and Purnomo determined that riots broke out in many locations simultaneously.[39] This suggests careful planning. The question is not if, but by whom they were orchestrated. Many believe that Suharto's son-in-law, General Prabowo, was responsible. Prabowo was among the leaders of the "green" segment of the military and had linked to Islamist paramilitary groups. *Asia Week* explained that as commander of the strategic reserve forces he had both the motive and the opportunity to foster civil discord. One theory is that he orchestrated the riots to show that only he could save the nation. Another is that he wanted to redirect the focus of the people's anger from Suharto to the Chinese. The fact that for several weeks before the riots officials and military officers had made thinly veiled references to disloyal groups intent on wreaking economic havoc supports this contention. Everyone denied involvement. Military officers stated that they did not have sufficient forces to quell the riots. They also denied that any women had been raped. These denials did nothing to quell rumors, charges and counter-charges, and the search for a "black goat."

The official response to the killings was an expression of condolence to the families and the promise of an investigation. Almost no one was satisfied. Suharto appears to have been shaken and deeply troubled by the bloodshed. He had long believed that he was a divinely chosen leader. These events appear to have convinced him that Allah had withdrawn the *wahyu* – a Javanese term for divine appointment. He gave a rambling speech in which he stated that he was prepared to "*lengser keprabon*" (renounce the throne). Suharto was speaking not in Indonesian, the language of politics, but in Javanese, the language of mysticism. He explained it was not a problem for him to do this if the people no longer believed in him. He was prepared to step aside, to become a sage and grow close to Allah, encourage children to become responsible citizens, and give advice to the nation. In the same speech he denied that he or his family had great wealth and explained that they had given most of what they had acquired to the people through a variety of foundations.[40]

No one took Suharto's claim of poverty seriously. The words *lengser keprabon* became the slogan of the day. Many in the opposition movement did not believe that Suharto meant what he said and found the notions that he could grow close to Allah or that he had any reasonable advice to give the nation absurd. The military, speaking through General Wiranto, claimed that the president had been misunderstood and that he did not intend to step down. Cooler heads seized the opportunity to hold him to his word.

On May 18, after meeting with a group of Islamic scholars for over two hours, Suharto announced that he would "reshuffle the cabinet" and establish a reform commission. The Muslim leaders refused to participate. Other opposition leaders followed their example. Fourteen ministers resigned the next day. When informed by the Minister of Religion that the liberal Muslim intellectual Nurcholish Madjid would not serve as chair of the reform commission, Suharto reportedly stated that if Cak Nur (Madjid), a supposedly moderate man, was not willing to serve on the commission, then there was no alternative but for him to resign as president.

The crisis that brought the New Order to a close was not originally religious. It began as an economic crisis. It became a religious crisis because Indonesians believe that religion and politics cannot be separated. Most maintain that there are inherent relationships between moral standing and the ability to govern. The local political crisis acquired global connections in several ways. Protests were organized by people of Chinese descent in North America, Europe, Australia, and Taiwan. The Fellowship of Indonesian Christians in America engaged in lobbying efforts and publicized the atrocities on its Web page. Evangelical Christian organizations, including the Christian News Service, Operation Christian Concern, Project Open Book, and others published graphic accounts of the "persecution" and "martyrdom" of Indonesian Christians. These and other publications depict a global struggle between Christianity and Islam in which Christians are innocent victims and Muslims are seen as bloodthirsty aggressors.

## Laskar Jihad and the rise of Islamism

Laskar Jihad was founded in 2000 by Jafar Umar Thalib in response to a rising tide of Christian/Muslim violence.[41] The violence began in Ambon and spread to other islands, especially Sulawesi and Halmahera. Christians and Muslims both claim to be the victims.[42] The root causes of the violence were demographic change resulting in an increased number of Muslims from other parts of Indonesia in the area and economic collapse. Elements of the military intervened on both sides. Discourse about the conflict was largely religious. Christians attempted to link Laskar Jihad with Osama bin Laden and called for UN intervention. Laskar Jihad linked its own, armed struggle with the global war against "Crusaders and Jews."

Jafar is an Indonesian of Yemeni descent.[43] He was educated in Saudi-sponsored schools in Indonesia, the Islamist Maududi Institute, and the Peshawar *madrasahs* in Pakistan.[44] There he became acquainted with the works of Sayyid Qutb. Sayyid Qutb was the father of the virulent anti-Westernism of contemporary Muslim radicals.[45] He termed Arab as well as Western nationalisms unbelief. He characterized the values and institutions of the Muslim world as those of *jahiliyya*, an Arabic term translated as "ignorance" and refers to the culture of the pre-Islamic Arabs. It suggests that the leaders of Muslim societies are guilty of the sin of *shirk* or associating other beings or powers with God. This is among the most serious sins a Muslim can commit.[46] In the early 1990s Jafar studied with the Islamist Sheikh Muqbil bin Hadi al-Wad'i in Yemen. Al-Wad'i taught that democracy is un-Islamic because it allows people to choose among moral systems. Freedom of religion is unacceptable because it legitimizes apostasy. Despite this he is considered to be a moderate Islamist because of his understanding of the conditions required for the conduct of jihad. He maintained that while jihad will be necessary to restore the purity of the Muslim community, that time has not yet come because there are too few committed Muslims. His position was that jihad is permissible only in cases such as Bosnia and Afghanistan in which the Muslim community is attacked. Al-Wad'i also wrote a fatwa (legal opinion) authorizing jihad in eastern Indonesia.

Jafar traveled to Afghanistan were he received military training and fought with the Taliban. In 1993 he returned to Indonesia and founded a *pesantren* (boarding school). Among the texts he taught were those of Ibn Taimiyah, a fourteenth-century jurist known for his denunciations of *bidah* (religious innovation) and mysticism, and Abdul Wahab, the founder of the Wahhabi sect. Wahhabi texts are not normally studied in Indonesia but are part of the core curriculum at Islamist schools throughout the world. Jafar's goal is the establishment of an Indonesian Islamic state. His program for the establishment of *shariah* includes stoning adulterers and cutting off the hands of thieves.

Jafar declared the Christians of eastern Indonesia to be *kafir harbi* – unbelievers who have declared war on Islam. Consequently, it is an individual religious obligation for the Muslims of the region and a collective obligation for other Indonesian Muslims to take up arms against them. The following statements were included in a speech he delivered calling for resistance to government efforts to disarm his forces:

> In the name of Allah! If one Muslim is killed by the security personnel, then Kudamati and Passo Christian areas of Ambon will become a sea of fire.
>
> Therefore I order all members of *Laskar Jihad* of *Ahlussunnah Wal Jamaah* to write their will and testament and prepare themselves to take up the position of martyrs. Get all the weaponry out.
>
> Listen you accomplices of the United States. Listen you accomplices of the World Church Council. Listen you accomplices of Zionist Evangelists. Listen you Jews and Christians: We Muslims are inviting the US military to prove its power in Maluku. Let us fight to the finish.[47]

Laskar Jihad dispatched at least 10,000 volunteers to Ambon and Sulawesi. Some recruits were drawn from the youth of the Jakarta slums, but many I spoke with were educated middle class youths from throughout the country. Some were affiliated with Dewan Dakwah Islamiyah Indonesia and with Islamic political parties linked to the old Masyumi. I was present at a recruitment rally held at the Dewan Dakwah Islamiyah Indonesia office. Potential recruits were shown photographs of burned-out mosques and Muslims killed by Ambonese Christians. Volunteers were asked to come forward. Those who did were questioned concerning their piety, dedication to jihad and were roughed up as a test of physical endurance. Those selected received rudimentary training at a camp in west Java. They were issued white Arab-style robes and headgear – symbols of Muslim identity.

The emergence of Laskar Jihad is an example of what Tambiah terms the "nationalization" of violence. At least four factors contributed to the nationalization and subsequent globalization of conflict in Indonesia. The communications revolution ensured that national and international attention was drawn to the conflict. The Jakarta riots, despite being primarily economic and ethnic conflicts, were reimagined as religious ones. Because of the communications revolution, Indonesians were aware of conflicts between Christians and Muslims in other parts of the world. Both Christians and Muslims understood violence in eastern Indonesia as an element of a global struggle. In this respect the civil war in Maluku was a parochialization of an imagined global conflict. This imagined reality developed as Muslims saw a pattern in the ethnic cleansing and civil wars that followed the collapse of the Soviet Union. Afghanistan, Bosnia, Kosovo, Chechnya, the southern Philippines, and Palestine can all be understood as local battles in a global crusade to destroy Islam if one assumes that there is a Christian–Zionist alliance bent on world domination. If one believes that the persecution of Christians is a sign of the coming of the "End Time," violence in Jakarta and Ambon can be linked with the killing of Christians in the Sudan, Protestants in Latin America, and the suppression of the house church movement in China.[48] Finally, Christian and Muslim representations of the conflict became elements of a "virtual conflict" or propaganda war conducted largely on the internet but reaching into churches and mosques throughout the world.

Rumors, projection, and denial figure prominently in this discourse, as do stereotypical depictions of grotesque forms of violence, arson, and rape. Communal violence serves to dehumanize and destroy the symbolic identity markers of the "other." Depiction of such violence demonizes the "other" in national and global contexts. The language of dehumanization is extreme. People are not killed. They are brutally slaughtered. Participants in these discourse systems seek out or imagine the archetypes of evil and brutality. These are used to characterize social and religious communities as well as individuals.

Consider the following statement found on a UK-based Islamist website, the IslamicAwakening.com.

> IMAGINE now a land where Muslims have been brutally murdered by the thousands. Not only murdered and beheaded etc. but afterwards mutilated, hearts cut out and eaten or pounded to make a gunpowder mix for ammunition.
>
> IMAGINE a land where Muslims are burnt alive whilst performing *Salaat ut-Taraweh* last Ramadan.
>
> IMAGINE women being raped in mosques by savages including priests who afterwards pass comments like the flesh of the *Muslimahs* were delicious in front of their families who await their turn for death.
>
> IMAGINE an *imam* being killed and buried only to be exhumed later, crucified, his genitals chopped off and stuffed in his mouth with pieces of raw pork. The earth shook and only that act of Almighty Allah stopped them from going further.
>
> IMAGINE the sick and the wounded treated on the floors of mosques and make do areas with compound fractures held together with external fixtures made of bicycle spokes ... wounds covered with honey and cloth. (By Allah's will, the wounds healed and the union of the bones occurred.)
>
> IMAGINE Christian doctors who for the past few years have made it their mission to snuff out newborn Muslim babies or doing caesarian hysterectomies in an attempt to curb the growth of the Muslim community.

If these allegations were correct, few Muslims would question the call for jihad. It is likely that the circulation of rumors of this sort contributed to the reluctance of Muslim leaders to demand that strong measures be taken against Laskar Jihad. This text speaks of God's blessing and power even during times of terror. References to pork are a uniquely Muslim element. Christians are depicted as cannibals, supposedly celibate priests, as rapists. The fact that murders are carried out in mosques during one of the most sacred days in the Muslim year can be understood as a symbolic representation of the destruction of the Muslim community. Infanticide and the involuntary sterilization of Muslim women convey a similar message. The use of Muslim bodies to make weapons with which Muslims will be killed adds an element of reflexivity to the discourse of terror. Muslims are the source of their own destruction. Finally, the image of families watching wives and daughters being raped while waiting to die speaks of the powerlessness of Muslims in the face of evil. The discourse of terror is mitigated only by God's intervention to halt the most horrible of desecrations and to miraculously heal survivors.

Christian texts are equally polemical. They portray saintly Christians killed and abused by Muslim fanatics. The following are extracts from an account of a journey to Ambon posted on a New Zealand Evangelical website and reports from the Christian Broadcasting Network and Christian Solidarity Worldwide.[49]

> Cries come out from the mosque whipping the Muslims into frenzy and calling upon the military and the police to join them in a fight to defend the religion of Allah and to wipe out the Christians. ... once they have sufficient people through they then attack the Christian positions, killing, maiming, burning and looting.
>
> The Christians do not attack, they just defend their positions, and while under attack sing some of the most beautiful worship hymns of history to praise and glorify Jesus Christ even as they are under siege. I wept every time I heard them singing so worshipful and yet in some ways it was like a surrender to an inevitable death and mourning ...
>
> One of the Christians went behind Muslim lines and took graphic footage going in and out among *jihad* warriors. They must have thought he was a Muslim or maybe the Lord just made him invisible to them ...
>
> All along the way people would stop and ask me, "Are the UN coming?"
>
> Here are letters addressed to the Secretary General of the United Nations: "Mr Secretary General of the UN, we children of Ambon are very frightened of the *jihad* soldiers and the army. They murder, loot and burn our homes, and chase us away. They also rape the women they catch ...

The following account is from the Christian Broadcast Network:

> An elderly couple was burned to death in their house. Bullet holes still riddle what's left of buildings. But, in the midst of all this devastation, a Christian left handwritten messages behind on the walls of their ruined home: "I love Jesus" and "Jesus is my Life."

Forced conversions and circumcision are common themes in Christian narratives.

> Women and children, as well as men, have been made to convert to Islam on penalty of death. Rites of circumcision with a razor blade are then carried out to complete the process – without anesthetic. The same blade is used over and over again.
>
> One victim, 32-year-old Christina Sagat told *The Sydney Morning Herald*: "I feel like I'm no longer complete, both as a person and a woman."
>
> More than 600 believers were given the choice of death or Islam on the Islands of Kesui and Teor alone. Some who refused to recite the Islamic declaration of faith were killed. In Kesui, Muslims paraded the severed head of a Christian as a warning.
>
> Another woman, Alwina, and her family were attacked while in church. *Jihad* warriors killed her husband while he held their 4-year-old son in his arms. Today, she says her son is terrified of anyone in Islamic clothing.
>
> The Muslims then tried to force Alwina to convert to Islam. "They wanted me to make a ritual to convert me. They ordered me to take off my Christian clothes and put on Muslim clothes."

Another account speaks of Muslim treachery.

> Berthy and the others were escorted to a Muslim village where Indonesian troops were waiting for them. Then they were forced to change their religion by signing a statement that they had turned from Christianity to Islam. After a ritual purification, they were brought before the Imam and taught to say the *sahadat* (Confession of Faith). ... Next they were escorted to the mosque where the Muslim religious leader said, "You have now returned to the right path and abandoned the wayward road." But after a few days they were told that all the former Christians would be killed to avenge the deaths of Muslims who had died during the *jihad*.

Christian accounts echo those of Muslims, portraying themselves as devout, innocent victims of brutality at the hands of evil fanatics. Like their Islamic counterparts, they often make indirect reference to central themes in Christian symbolism and theology.

Hammond speaks of the gradual Muslim encroachment on Christian territory and the "frenzy" of Muslim "warriors." These are virtual archetypes in Christian anti-Muslim discourse. He speaks of the near inevitability of defeat and of the great piety of Christians speaking of their love for Jesus at the moment of death. This is an account of the destruction of a community as well as the deaths of individuals. His text makes references to Biblical miracles and calls on God for assistance. The intended audience is clearly the Western world.

He describes the terror and fear of children and old women, of brutal killings. The account of a father killed by a soldier while holding his young son is particularly telling. It speaks of the betrayal of Christians by the government, the inhuman brutality of the Muslims and the trauma inflicted on innocent Christians.[50] Like the Muslim accounts these narratives speak of the mutilation of corpses and the beheading of victims. Just as Muslims are described being killed in mosques it is stated that Christians were killed at church. The underlying theme is the same, the desecration of bodies and of sacred time and space.

The narratives concerning forced conversions are unique to Christian accounts of the struggle. They emphasize the abandonment of symbols of Christian identity and the assumption of symbols of Muslim identity: circumcision wearing Muslim instead of Christian clothing and the receiving of Muslim names.[51] In these narratives there are tropes of the Christian myth that conversion by the sword was the primary means by which Islam was spread.

It is impossible to determine the veracity of these accounts. If any of them are true they are serious crimes against humanity. In another sense it does not matter because Christians and Muslims in Indonesia and elsewhere believe them to be true. The future of Muslim–Christian relations in Indonesia will be influenced by these beliefs for decades, if not generations to come. In Maluku, Muslims and Christians were simultaneously victims and perpetrators. Both communities suffer from a combination of denial and trauma. Each community must portray itself as victims and demonize the other to deny their own culpability.

## Conclusions – religions and collective violence – projection and denial

The analysis of collective violence in Indonesia presented in this chapter supports Tambiah's thesis that "leveling crowds" are rarely spontaneous.[52] It does not, however, explain the forms that it takes. In the cases examined here, violence was directed not only at people and property but also against symbols of religious identity. Eliade observed that in traditional societies acts are meaningful only if they replicate cosmic archetypes; in the construction of mythologies historical events are transformed to bring them into accord with these archetypes.[53] The process of demonizing members of an ethnic or religious group projects an archetype of evil upon the "others." The other is transformed, becoming what they most fear while their self-identification is the archetype of virtue and martyrdom. This enables communities to define their own violence as defensive.[54] This cycle of projection and denial combined with the psychological trauma experienced by victims contributes to the ritualization of violence. Those who have endured trauma, if left untreated, relive it, when they come in contact with events, persons, or places associated with traumatic experience. It is likely that the victims of the Jakarta riots and sectarian violence in Maluku will relive their experiences when they encounter individuals that they associate with their perpetrators. It in turn can contribute to the creation of conditions in which new waves of violence and counter-violence transpire.

Tambiah argues that neutral and determined security forces play essential roles in preventing cycles of violence. This is undoubtedly true. At the same time it does little to ameliorate the underlying social, religious, and psychological conditions that create the environment from which violence can emerge. Nor can security forces cure the emotional wounds of the victims. Competent and unbiased security forces are the sociological equivalent of Prozac. They treat the symptoms and not the causes of the disease of communal violence. Their role in the psycho-social healing process is to establish the safety of individuals and communities who have been victimized.

There are a number of additional steps that can be taken to break the cycle of violence.

- Problems of social, economic and political inequality must be addressed.
- Those responsible for orchestrating and perpetrating acts of violence must be held accountable by the state *and by their own ethnic/religious communities.*
- A concerted, public effort to denounce demonizing rumors is also essential. Leaders of ethnic/religious communities must themselves expose the falsehood of rumors and slanderous interpretation of "others."

This is a great deal to ask of any society. Unfortunately it is not clear that Indonesia is capable of establishing the basic security and safety of its citizens, which is essential for further steps in healing the individual and collective wounds of ethno-religious violence. Herman describes reconnection and community building as the final stages in the healing of psychological trauma. For Indonesians, establishing the sense of "Unity in Diversity," the national motto, is a daunting challenge.

## Notes

1 Mark Juergensmeyer, *Terror in the Mind of God: The Global Rise of Religious Violence*, 3rd edition (Berkeley, CA: University of California Press, 2003). Stanley J. Tambiah, *Leveling Crowds: Ethnonationalist Conflicts and Collective Violence in South Asia* (Berkeley, CA: University of California Press, 1996). Judith Herman, *Trauma and Recovery: The Aftermath of Violence from Domestic Abuse to Political Terror* (New York: Basic Books, 1997).
2 Juergensmeyer, *Terror in the Mind of God*, 191.
3 Tambiah, *Leveling Crowds*, 275, 271.
4 Bruce B. Lawrence, *Defenders of God: the Fundamentalist Revolt Against the Modern Age* (San Francisco, CA: Harper and Row, 1989), 100.
5 On this distinction see Mark Woodward, *Islam in Java: Normative Piety and Mysticism in the Sultanate of Yogyakarta* (Tucson: University of Arizona Press, 1989).
6 L. Suryadinata, *Interpreting Indonesian Politics* (Singapore: Times Academic Press, 1999), 29–48.
7 There is an extensive and controversial literature on the coup of 1965. Some scholars, particularly Anderson and McVey, maintain that it was an internal military feud and that the communists were not directly involved. Benedict R. Anderson and Ruth T. McVey, *A Preliminary Analysis of the October 1, 1965, Coup in Indonesia* (Ithaca, NY: Cornell University Modern Indonesia Project, 1971). For the present purpose what is significant is not who was ultimately responsible for the attempted coup and the death of a group of generals, but simply the scale and ferocity of the killings. An English translation of the Indonesian government's account of the coup is *The*

*September 30th Movement, the Attempted Coup by the Indonesian Communist Party: Its Background, Actions and Eradication* (Jakarta: State Secretariat of the Republic of Indonesia, 1995). For a detailed account of the east Java killings, see H. Sulistyo, "The Forgotten Years: The Missing History of Indonesia's Mass Slaughter (Jobang-Kediri 1965–1966)" (unpublished dissertation, Arizona State University, 1997).

8  John Bresnan, *Managing Indonesia: The Modern Political Economy* (New York: Columbia University Press, 1993), 7–28.

9  My first experience in Indonesia was in 1979. I have visited the *kampung* (neighborhood) in which I lived in the city of Yogyakarta on a regular basis for twenty-five years. The changes are nothing short of remarkable. Friends who in 1979 lived in bamboo houses with thatched roofs now live in brick houses with tile roofs. Motorcycles have replaced bicycles as the most common mode of transportation.

10  On the centrality of management in New Order politics, see Bresnan, *Managing Indonesia*, 293–5.

11  See K. Ward, *The Foundation of the Partai Muslim in Indonesia* (Ithaca, NY: Cornell University Modern Indonesia Project, 1970).

12  Juergensmeyer has argued that participation in terrorist acts is a form of symbolic empowerment for the marginalized. It would appear that Masyumi patricians expected genuine empowerment as a reward for participating in state-sponsored terror.

13  The secularization of family law provokes strong and often violent resistance throughout the Muslim world. For comparative studies of Islamic family law, see the Emory University/Ford Foundation project at http://www.law.emory.edu/IFL/.

14  President Suharto announced this policy initiative in a speech delivered on August 16, 1982. For a critique by a leading conservative Muslim scholar see D. Noer, *Islam Pancasila Dan Asas Tunggal* (Jakarta: Yayasan Perkhidmatan, 1983).

15  See Mark Woodward, "Textual Exegesis as Social Commentary: Religious, Social and Political Meanings of Indonesian Translations of Arabic Hadith Texts," *Journal of Asian Studies* 52, no. 3 (1993): 565–83 for further discussion of this controversy and for Indonesian language references, and Donald E. Weatherbee, "Indonesia in 1984: Pancasila, Politics, and Power," *Asian Survey* 25, no. 2 (February 1985): 190.

16  On election-related violence see Kees van Dijk, *A Country in Despair: Indonesia Between 1997 and 2000* (Leiden: KITLV, 2001); and Bresnan, *Managing Indonesia*, 236.

17  Bresnan, *Managing Indonesia*, 230.

18  On the Malari affair see Harold A. Crouch, *The Army and Politics in Indonesia* (Ithaca, NY: Cornell University Press, 1978); and Bresnan, *Managing Indonesia*, 135–63.

19  On the *Tanjung Priok* incident see Bresnan, *Managing Indonesia*, 218–84; and K. Kolstad, "Enemy Others and Violence in Jakarta: An Islamic Rhetorical of Discontent," in *Toward a New Paradigm: Recent Developments in Indonesian Islamic Thought*, ed. Mark Woodward (Tempe: Program for Southeast Asian Studies, Arizona State University, 1996), 357–80.

20  The Indonesian coat of arms includes an eagle with a shield emblazoned with the text of *Pancasila* covering its chest.

21  Translation from *Indonesia Mirror*, no. 5, March 1987. Tapes of many of these sermons continue to circulate in Indonesia twenty years after the events.

22  A *musholla* is a room or small building used for prayers other than the Friday noon congregational prayer that must be performed in a mosque.

23  Kolstadt, "Enemy Others," 363.

24  See Tambiah, *Leveling Crowds*, 244–65.

25  Cited in Bresnan, *Managing Indonesia*, 230.

26  *Yayasan Amal Bhakti Pancasila*. Mosques constructed by the foundation have a unique architectural style featuring the traditional three-tiered tile roof capped by a silver-colored dome. They are instantly recognizable.

27  See Robert W. Hefner, "Islam, State, and Civil Society: ICMI and the Struggle for the Indonesian Middle Class," *Indonesia* 56, (October 1993): 1–3; and Robert W. Hefner, "Islamizing Capitalism: On the Founding of Indonesia's First Islamic Bank," in *Toward a New Paradigm: Recent Developments in Indonesian Islamic Thought*, ed. Mark Woodward (Tempe: Program for Southeast Asian Studies, Arizona State University, 1996), 291–322.

28  Red and white are the colors of the Indonesian national flag.

29  Most *santri* were, at that time, educated in *pesantren*, traditional religious schools that resemble Middle Eastern and South Asian *madrasah*.

30  On the rise of radical Islamism in Indonesia, see Zachary Abuza, "Muslims, Politics, and Violence in Indonesia: An Emerging Jihadist–Islamist Nexus?" *NBR Analysis* 15, no. 3 (September 2004).

31  This portion of this chapter is based on sources which must remain confidential to safeguard informants and correspondents and on ethnographic research conducted in Jakarta over the past decade.

32  See "Ethnic Chinese Tell of Mass Rapes," *BBC News Online*, June 23, 1998, http://news.bbc.co.uk/ 1/hi/events/indonesia/special_report/118576.stm; and "The Rapes in the Series of Riots: The Climax of an Uncivilized Act of the Nation Life," *Tim Relawan Untuk Kemanusiaan* (Volunteers Team for Humanity), Jakarta, July 13, 1998, http://www.huaren.com/Indo/atrocities.html.

33  *Asia Week*, July 24, 1998.

34  Herman, *Trauma and Recovery*, 67, observes that many rape victims have difficulty even naming their experience.

35  See "Rapes in the Series of Riots."

36  On the psychological conditions suffered by victims see Herman, *Trauma and Recovery*.

37  For full account see the website Jakarta Black May, http://www.siamweb.org/news_culture/jakarta_riot/.

38  For an account of the psychological trauma suffered by victims, see *Asia Week* June 19, 1998.

39  D. Daihani and A. Purnomo, *Lansekap Berbagai Kerusuhan da Potensi Disintegras* (Jakarta: Lembaga Penelitian Universitas Trisakti, 2000).

40  *Kompas*, May 16, 1998.

41  See "Profile: Jafar Umar Thalib," *BBC News Online*, January 30, 2003, http://news.bbc.co.uk/1/hi/ world/asia-pacific/1975345.stm; and *Inside Indonesia*, no. 67 (July–September 2001).

42  For a Christian perspective, see Ambon Berdarah Online (Bloody Ambon), http://www.geocities.com/ ambon67/noframe/photoy2knf.htm. For an academic discussion of the conflict, see K. Schulze, "Laskar Jihad and the Conflict in Ambon," *Brown Journal of World Affairs* 9, no. 1 (Spring 2002): 57–69.

43  On relations between Yemen and Indonesia, see Michael F. Laffan, *Islamic Nationhood and Colonial Indonesia: the Umma Below the Winds* (London: RoutlegeCurzon, 2003). For Jafar's biography, see *Tokoh Indonesia* (Indonesian Leaders), http://www.tokohindonesia.com/ensiklopedi/j/jafar-umar-thalib/ index. shtml.

44  The Madudi Institute teaches a combination of secular and religious subjects. It is affiliated with the Islamist organization Jamaat-I-Islam, known for its support of the Taliban and of the Muslim insurgency in Kashmir. See "Maududi Institute has no Link with Militants: Omer," *Daily Star*, August 23, 2004, http://www.dailytimes.com.pk/default.asp?page=story_23-8-2004_pg7_14.

45  For an overview of the history of Muslim radicalism, see W. Montgomery Watt, *Islamic Fundamentalism and Modernity* (London: Routledge, 1988).

46  Qutb stated that many so-called Muslim societies "bestow characteristics that belong exclusively to the Divinity upon others beside God." quoted in Gilles Kepel, *Muslim*

*Extremism in Egypt: The Prophet and the Pharoah*, trans. from French by Jon Rothschild (Berkeley, CA: University of California Press, 1985), 47.

47  See Ambon Information Website, http://www.websitesrcg.com/ambon/documents/laskar-jihad-010502.htm.

48  On this view of the persecution of Christians, see Persecuted Church, http://www.geocities.com/Heartland/Hills/5977/suffer/suffer.html; and World Evangelical Alliance, http://www. worldevangelical.org/persec.html.

49  See Jeff Hammond, "Indonesia – Ambon Report," *Across Pacific Online*, July 26, 2000, http://across.co.nz/AmbonReport-Jly2000.htm.

50  Like their Muslim counterparts, Christian websites include graphic images of burned and mutilated corpses.

51  It is ironic that changes of clothing were used to help women escape from rape during the Jakarta riots and as means of symbolic domination in Maluku.

52  Tambiah, *Leveling Crowds*, 332–4.

53  Mircea Eliade, *The Myth of Eternal Return: or, Cosmos and History* (Princeton, NJ: Princeton University Press), 39.

54  Some Muslim responses to the tragedy of September 11, 2001 are clear examples of this. Many Muslims, especially those who saw themselves as victims of Western aggression, found it impossible to believe that fellow Muslims could have committed such acts. Many projected their fear and hatred of Israeli security forces and the CIA onto the hijackers, and genuinely believed rumors concerning their supposed role in the attacks.

# 7

# RELIGIOUS VIOLENCE BEYOND BORDERS

## Reframing South Asian cases

*Alyssa Ayres*

As a general practice, analyses of religious violence in South Asia – or anywhere else, for that matter – take the nation as their primary optic. In the world of the modern nation-state, such a focus on the nation should come as no surprise; however, as a framing device, the nation can obscure some connections as much as it can illuminate others. This chapter discusses religious violence in South Asia with an explicit focus on its transnational dimensions, in the process providing a different kind of purchase on the cross-border flows of ideas, peoples, and the basic capital of violence (arms and money). This is an interpretive essay, one concerned primarily with identifying how a framework incorporating a transnational analysis of religious violence in the region might lead to durable solutions.

I will first flag the interrelationship among the three major countries of South Asia (India, Pakistan, and Bangladesh), which despite independent existence remain bound by memories of violence. I will then discuss the presence of Pakistan (and of late, Bangladesh as well) as a constant memory haunting Hindu–Muslim relations within India, lending a peculiar transnational cast to one of India's important social cleavages. Turning to the most prominent case of religious violence in India – Kashmir from the 1990s forward – I discuss the relationship between internal insurgency, cross-border involvement of Pakistan, and the iconic replication of Hindu–Muslim conflict onto what had once been a demand for autonomy. Then, turning to the cases of Punjab in the 1980s and more recent violence against Christians, I point to the documented role of the transnational diasporas in supporting certain kinds of beliefs, with significant effects "back home."

The chapter then turns to look at Pakistan, an unstable country facing internal problems with religious violence quite distinct from, although with repercussions on, its imbrications in conflict with India. Pakistan's troubles with religious violence, transnational and internal all at the same time, will be delineated, with a brief recap of the deep penetration of other states in Afghanistan and Pakistan.

Finally, I will give some attention to Bangladesh. The concluding section draws upon the preceding narrative to make several policy recommendations.

## The persistence of memory

Sumit Ganguly's chapter outlines the historical sources of religious conflict in South Asia and explains the unique relationship of India, Pakistan, and Bangladesh as stemming from the Partition of India in 1947. The moment of independence for India and Pakistan (Bangladesh was then East Pakistan) was both one of freedom from colonial rule and one of genocide. The months leading up to and following Partition witnessed appalling violence – rioting, targeted murder, pillaging, and violence against women, including abduction and rape. Estimates on Partition locate the numbers killed at approximately one million, and the number displaced (forcibly as well as voluntarily) at 12–18 million, making it the largest migration in human history. Punjab and Bengal, the two provinces divided up between India and Pakistan, felt the worst of the violence. The city of Lahore was emptied of nearly all its Hindu and Sikh residents, and Muslims from regions that became Indian Punjab fled to Pakistan. We do not know the extent of religious violence taking place in spaces that were both national and transnational at the same moment; a social scientific mapping of the violence of Partition awaits the writing.[1] But the genealogical links between India, Pakistan, and Bangladesh have ensured that religious violence in the region has taken place at local, national, and indeed transnational levels, structured by the constant memory of Partition – the revenge of the past.[2]

If, for much of the West, collective memory seems to take World War II as a point of inauguration, Partition occupies the same structural role for India and South Asia. Partition was an outcome of two very different political theories of nation, one which embraced a multi-ethnic, multi-religious but secular state, and another which argued that Hindus and Muslims were (primordially) two separate nations and could not co-exist. Scholars continue to debate the extent to which the "two nations theory," as it came to be known, represented the Muslim League and Mohammad Ali Jinnah's true beliefs,[3] and cannot be resolved here. Important to note, however, is that the notion of Partition as a process in which a secular nationalist front battled Islamic nationalism obscures the fact that there has long been a powerful nationalism that conceptualizes India as Hindu. In this line of reasoning, Indian Muslims are the descendents of invaders, invaders whose holy lands lie outside the territory of the Indian nation.

Against this backdrop, it is important to remember that to this day, India has a significant Muslim minority population (approximately 12 percent); most of whom are the descendents of Muslim families who elected to cast their futures with India in 1947 instead of migrating to Pakistan. Viewed from this angle, the decision to stay in India would appear to underscore a sense of deep patriotism towards India – yet the very fact of Pakistan's creation has often served instead as evidence of the insufficient patriotism of Muslims to India as a homeland. One measure of this relationship lies in the not uncommon accusations of Indian

Muslims as a "fifth column" more loyal to Pakistan than to India, or as defective citizens who must prove their patriotism rather than having it an assumed starting point. Typical measures of this kind of insufficient patriotism include the widely circulated yet apocryphal story that Indian Muslims will cheer for Pakistan during cricket matches that pit India against its neighbor.[4] Or that Indian Muslims can be taunted with "Jāo Pākistān" (go to Pakistan).[5] These two examples highlight the structural relationship in which Hindu–Muslim relations *within India* are always pregnant with the memory of Partition, and as a result, incidences of religious violence at the local levels simultaneously draw upon the ever-looming historical memory of Partition. Thus a transnational relationship of two sovereign states recurrently "implodes" into the local.[6] This tendency to conflate being Muslim as *prima facie* evidence of loyalty to Pakistan, even if by assumption or accusation rather than fact, would seem to undermine the overt design of the Indian state as a secular, democratic republic – yet this logical fallacy is not uncommon.

Not surprisingly, from a vantage point within Pakistan, Hindu–Muslim violence in India can never be taken at face value. Incidences of Hindu–Muslim violence in India are closely watched in Pakistan, for the unstated yet readily apparent implication of such conflict is to justify Pakistan's creation. The pogrom in Gujarat (India) in 2002 – which resulted in the deaths of some 2,000 Muslims – for example, was front page headlines for weeks in Pakistan. These kinds of transnational sympathies, imputed as well as real, create a different conceptual matrix for religious violence in the region, one that perennially links these countries in a kind of symbiosis that renders national borders too limited a container for the full measure of affect.

## Kashmir – recursiveness of an opposition

The conflict in Kashmir, about to enter its sixteenth year of violence, is the most obvious example of religious violence with transnational dimensions in the region. This takes place at two levels: one, the conceptual basis of the nation-states of India and Pakistan – referring us again to Partition – and two, the role of "cross-border" terrorism permitted if not outright engineered by Pakistan.

As scholars have noted, and as Sumit Ganguly explains in greater detail in this volume, the *territorial* quality of the Kashmir dispute between India and Pakistan – which we will distinguish from the sanguinary insurgency of the past fifteen-plus years – is, of course, a direct result of the messiness of Partition. Pakistan claims the entire former princely state (the "K" of Pakistan's coined name) as an integral part of its claim to the contiguous Muslim majority areas of what had been British India and the princely states. India, of course, points to the legal accession of the state to India in 1947 as sufficient to prove that Kashmir exists integrally within India. At this level, at what some have termed the "real estate" problem of Kashmir, it is quite clearly a transnational dilemma.

But the Kashmir dispute unfortunately has not remained an abstract point of contention between India and Pakistan. The insurgency which began in the Kashmir valley in 1989 and continues through today has arisen in a complicated relationship to both India and Pakistan, and is also something more than what each country claims. Its eruption in 1989 has been discussed at length elsewhere,[7] and its complexity cannot be fully traced here. The important point is the way in which the demand for autonomy in Kashmir was in its early days a mobilized political response to repression by the Indian state,[8] and its initial demands were for autonomy. In its early years, much of the insurgency's energy came from the pro-autonomy Jammu and Kashmir Liberation Front (JKLF). But with the involvement of Pakistan in supporting demands for autonomy, as investigative journalists have noted, came a marked preference for more Islamic organizations, known as *tanzeems*, and the movement acquired the cast of a religiously-pitched battle rather than a quest for political autonomy.

The effects have been catastrophic for Kashmir, not the least of which has been the forced expulsion of the valley's Hindu minority, which has now held refugee status (in makeshift camps primarily in Jammu and Delhi) for some fourteen years. This expulsion and the subsequent reimagination of the valley as an Islamic region have been wearing away at the concept of *kashmiriyat* (local culture) with unclear implications for the future. The effects have also been felt on women's freedoms, with calls for women to veil in public, and even the decapitation of three young women in the Rajouri district, Jammu region, carried out by Islamic militants in late 2002.[9] The JKLF as an organization exists now as a shadow of its former vanguard status, and a variety of *tanzeems* committed to accession to Pakistan and an Islamic Kashmir have become, since 1996–97, much more active in the region.

While one could hardly defend the Indian government's record of human rights abuses in Kashmir, and certainly not the record of rigging elections prior to the outbreak of insurgency, the gradual co-optation of this insurgency to resemble an Islamic movement is directly correlated with Pakistan's involvement. Most observers attribute the change to the rising presence of foreign militants changing the complexion of the militancy. If, in the early years, Pakistan's support for this cause entailed training Kashmir youth who would cross the border and then re-infiltrate, by the latter part of the 1990s it had become clear that non-Kashmiris were playing a much greater role. Their presence is difficult to measure, but according to Indian Army statistics, foreign militants comprised 62 percent of those killed in 2002 compared with 0.2 percent in 1991.[10] Pakistan is the primary source of support for these militants – a fact denied by Pakistan but openly claimed by the groups themselves, as confessionals and recruitment ads published on the Web readily attest.[11] Thus, an insurgency previously framed in terms of independence and self-rule has undergone something of a "Talibanization," which represents a significant shift in the ideological terms of debate, although the shift to simplify complicated political arguments into simple oppositions is a characteristic feature of nationalist discourse. For Kashmir, the effect is that larger Hindu–Muslim conflict within India, now more than ever before, has become projected onto the Kashmir crisis. This illustrates a recursive process by which a dominant opposition (here, the idea of Hindu–Muslim conflict) is applied to other, perhaps not entirely analogous situations, collapsing complicated particulars into simple parallels.[12]

108

## Beyond Kashmir: conflicts exacerbated by diasporas

Kashmir has not been the only religious cleavage in India's independent existence. During the 1980s, a violent secessionist movement unfolded in Punjab which sought to create a homeland for Sikhs, a "Khalistan." The struggle for Khalistan, long quashed, with its only remaining adherents in diaspora, had two key transnational dimensions worth remarking upon: first, the unclear role of Pakistan in providing support (moral, diplomatic, or otherwise) for pro-Khalistan militants, and second, the importance of the Punjabi Sikh diaspora in maintaining the demand, indeed in one scholar's account, creating a new vision of a homeland.

It is difficult to say much about the Pakistani role in exacerbating the Khalistan issue during the 1980s. That role, widely assumed by many in India, has been rather more difficult to pinpoint in any systematic way; there is plenty of circumstantial evidence which points to Pakistan's role in providing arms and training facilities to Khalistani militants, but which nonetheless falls far short of proving an organized state policy.[13] In a recent essay making a strong argument that Punjab was a "test case" for what became Pakistan's proxy war in Kashmir, Praveen Swami concedes that Western scholarship on the phenomenon does not focus on the Pakistan dimension, and Indian scholarship depicts Pakistan's involvement to varying degrees.[14] Given the difficult nature of providing indisputable evidence of a cross-border dimension of this conflict, it is perhaps best to simply acknowledge its existence as the subject of discussion and speculation, to which there is no doubt merit.

But also worth noting, with direct relevance for the increasingly dispersed – indeed, *disseminated* – natures of populations worldwide, has been the increasingly important role that the global Sikh diaspora has apparently played in defining the terms of the Khalistan demand in the latter part of the 1980s and its waning years in the early 1990s. One anthropologist, Brian Axel, has studied the Sikh diaspora in great detail, with the provocative conclusion that the diaspora has been as important in defining its terms of a homeland as a homeland has been in defining the diaspora. Through a look at sites of exchange and gathering in the United Kingdom, and the electronic circulation of images of torture and violence, Axel's work argues for an understanding of diaspora as fundamentally constitutive of their territories of origin.[15] This insight draws attention to the diffuse yet important role of transnational diasporas and their impact back home.[16]

Closer to these shores, a recent report has linked elements of the US-based Hindu diaspora to religious violence in India, specifically through organizations tied to Hindu extremists. A 2002 report prepared by Sabrang Communications and the South Asia Citizens Web has implicated funding networks in the United States, specifically, the India Development and Relief Fund (IDRF), to India-based institutions engaged in organized violence against Christians. The report also suggests that IDRF-funded organizations played a role in the 2002 anti-Muslim pogrom in Gujarat.[17] The evidentiary basis for this accusation lies in the publication's tracking of transnational aid dollars to organizations in Gujarat seeking to bring tribal groups who had converted to Christianity back into the fold of Hinduism. Such reconversions have at times been violent, and certainly from 1998 forward incidences of violence against Christians in India were serious enough to gain the attention of Human Rights Watch and the US State Department, and of course the US Commission on International Religious Freedom.[18]

The Sabrang Communications report, by implication, touches briefly upon the proposition that tribal activists – who played an unprecedented role in the 2002 Gujarat violence – can similarly be linked back to the same US funding sources. The evidence for that claim is entirely circumstantial, but the linkages are worth considering.

While the IDRF issued a counter-report denying the accusations, the "Foreign Exchange of Hate" report sounds a warning bell for an undeniable phenomenon: transnational networks of ideological affiliation are easily able to circulate messages, ideas, and capital. The US presence of the Hindu Swayamsevak Sangh, the analogue of the Indian organization, Rashtriya Swayamsevak Sangh (RSS), which has a network of voluntary weekend programs and summer schools, community service projects, and like-minded affiliates maintains strong linkages with the RSS in India.[19] That the RSS's "official spokesman" went on a brief speaking tour in the US during the fall of 2004 suggests that the organization takes seriously its US-based constituency. The more difficult dilemma lies in being able to draw causal connections between funding mechanisms and their deployment for violent uses.

## Pakistan

What constitutes the framework for discussing the transnational dimensions of religious violence in Pakistan? The regions comprising today's Pakistan at one time had sizeable Hindu populations in cities like Karachi and Lahore. That is no longer the case. In a very real sense, more than fifty years after Partition, this land has eliminated the composite nature of society. The idea of minority religions in Pakistan now connotes Christianity (2 percent, mainly in Punjab) and Shia Islam (20 percent according to the CIA World Factbook), and the rarer still Zoroastrianism. While it is certainly the case that Pakistan's Christian minority have been the victims of religious violence – indeed, during 2002 attacks on Christians and churches increased – the primary cleavage of religious violence in Pakistan has become an intra-Islam schism: Sunni versus Shia. Generally referred to as the problem of "sectarian violence," this cleavage has been exacerbated by a combination of transnational penetrations alongside internal processes of recursion that seek to remake the country into what it has imagined it has always been.

By now only scholars and esoteric journalists recall that Pakistan's first months were, at least in the words of the country's founder, not intended to be religiously discriminatory. Despite the religious nationalist sentiment driving the Pakistan Movement, Mohammad Ali Jinnah argued that the new country should provide a free space for its citizens to practice their religion, whatever it may be.[20] Conceptually, however, the narrowed cultural framework providing the basis for popular nationalism in the Pakistan Movement focused less on political theory – such as protecting minority rights – than on the idea of a people united in Islam. This distinction matters greatly, for it marks the difference between a rights-based rationale for political existence versus the cultural exclusion of a powerful nationalism, necessary for any demarcation of a "US" that lays claim to a nation-state. Pakistan as a political concept thus easily became synonymous with the confession of the Islamic faith. Indeed, a core slogan employed during the Pakistan Movement's agitations prior to independence, often invoked today, stems from a two-line couplet by the poet Asghar "Saudai" Sialkot: *"Pakistan ka matlab kya? La ilaha illilah"* ("What is the meaning of Pakistan? There is but one God, Allah").[21] If the political claim of the Pakistan Movement was that a separate nation-state was necessary to safeguard the interests of the Muslim minority in an India, in which, under any democratic dispensation Hindu interests could outvote Muslims by nearly four to one, it, then, appears that the constitutional-legal focus has been long forgotten in favor of a reinterpretation of the country's existential role as an instrument of God.

One result has been the struggle over what role Islam should play in Pakistan's political life, and what kind of Islamic person a Pakistani should be. Sunni clerics whose pre-Partition opinions had been to *oppose* the creation of the country, soon after independence sought to wrest the nation away from a secular republic path in the hopes of instead forging an Islamic state.[22] This would of course require that the state take on a more activist role in adjudicating acceptable forms of religious practice, such as establishing the cultural basis of the nation-state.

The logic of recursion discussed previously in the case of Kashmir, whereby one set of oppositions is applied to another level, has operated here as well, with very negative effects in Pakistan. By this I mean that the collapse of the *concept* of Pakistan into one of religious exclusivism has provided the ground upon which citizens whose faith falls outside that defined as the national culture (or national religion), are transformed into a threat to the existence of South Asian Islam, this parallels what the "two nations theory" posited for Hindu dominance prior to Partition. A small reformist Muslim sect, the Ahmadiyya, thus became the focus of early Islamist agitations quite early in Pakistan's existence, agitations led by an elite Sunni clerical. The state, instead of responding with vigorous statements of protection for any minority religion, elected to declare this sect "non-Muslim" thus rendering the community vulnerable to persecution.[23] The next extension of this philosophy of exclusion would be to Shias, a process that has been under way in Pakistan and has been accompanied by great violence. Sunni–Shia clashes mark what have become known as "sectarian conflict" in Pakistan, and although this cleavage has been exacerbated by developments well beyond Pakistan's borders, the conceptual logic through which Shia represents not fellow citizens of a related faith but persons outside of faith altogether helps explain the deep antipathies driving anti-Shia violence in Pakistan.

## Shia as the internal enemy: sectarian conflict in Pakistan

How has it come to pass that Shia Pakistanis are the targets of violence? For a country founded to provide a safe homeland for the Muslims of South Asia, today's sectarian violence would appear to utterly undermine its founding rationale. In fact, the security situation for Pakistani Shias has been declining so precipitously over the past decade that now some Sunni militias have declared Shias to be infidels, justifying execution. Sectarian conflict in Pakistan takes place within a conceptual matrix discussed above, but exacerbated by the transnational circulations relating to the Afghan War. Pakistan has been at the center of more than two decades of international engagement that have, on balance, had catastrophic effects on the country. Multiple stakeholders (the US, Saudi Arabia, and Iran, for example) directed funds and arms to further their own national interests, but the end result has not been to Pakistan's benefit. Briefly, and discussed in greater detail in Sumit Ganguly's chapter in this volume, the combination of US and Saudi support for the *mujahidin* to fight the Soviets empowered a *mullah* warrior class to the great detriment of secular nationalists, and flooded the region with weapons, including semi-automatic machine guns that appear to be everywhere.[24]

If the presence of these weapons in the country is the direct result of international *realpolitik*, the growing divide between Sunni and Shia Pakistanis has been its malignant offshoot. As mentioned above, Pakistan's involvement as the staging ground for the Afghan War allowed the US to exercise plausible deniability; with the US operating at arm's length from this conflict, Pakistan was free to choose its own favored sons from among the many groups of *mujahidin* in the region. This is where General Zia ul-Haq was able to leverage his Islamization policies, to provide a stronger national glue for the realities of a Pakistan reduced to half its size after the 1971 war and the secession of Bangladesh and within which ethnic nationalisms appeared to be rising from all corners. With the infusion of resources brought by dollars and riyals, the Pakistani state was able to strengthen the most conservative Sunni elements and cast them as heroic patriots.

A second result was that internally, the Inter-Services Intelligence agency (ISI) created to manage the Afghan War began to meddle in domestic political intrigues. The extent of the ISI's involvement in abetting Sunni–Shia violence is unmapped yet widely assumed, for they became kingmakers in local sectarian disputes by providing aid and a well-oiled political machine of support to radical Sunni elements.[25] Also assumed is the involvement of the Iranian state in channeling funds to support Shia religious education in Pakistan, as well as Iranian financial and political support for the creation of the Shia sectarian militia, the Tehrik-e-Jafriya, in Jhang in 1979. Jhang, a district in southern Punjab, would become the crucible of sectarian violence in Pakistan from the mid-1980s forward, but Karachi would carry the mantle beginning in 1994.

Anti-Shia sentiment first mobilized into a formal militia in southern Punjab, with the creation of the Sipah-e-Sahaba Pakistan in 1985 in Jhang. Some analysts attribute the rise of anti-Shia sectarianism to economic inequality and Sunni resentment of landed Shia; indeed, it is certainly true that the Jhang region has a Shia landlord class vastly wealthier than the impoverished masses. Yet the comparative absence of anti-Shia violence prior to the mid-1980s suggests the insufficiency of this explanation. The gradually narrowing framework for who constitutes an acceptable Muslim citizen in the eyes of the state, as described above, operated alongside the growing patronage of radical Sunni groups in the Afghan War. It is difficult to pinpoint the precise levels and effects of this sort of transnational involvement, but that it took place is undeniable.

By the early 1990s anti-Shia violence was becoming a fact of Pakistani life. Violence which initially targeted Shias in mosques or in their homes in Punjab soon made its way to Karachi, which had become perhaps the world's most dangerous city by the mid-1990s.[26] To be sure, Karachi's rampant violence in the 1990s was also a product of Sindhi separatism, Mohajir nationalism epitomized by a militia-cum-political party, the Muttahida Quami Movement (MQM), and the unfortunate nexus of criminal smuggling networks, including drug trade from beleaguered Afghanistan.[27]

But the violence unleashed upon Shias has been severe. Indeed, since the post-September 11, 2001 war against terrorism brought Pakistan back within the ambit of a partnership with the United States, internal security for Pakistani Shias has declined. This is, once again, related to the complicated linkages between Sunni militias and their internal as well as international actions; the widespread explanation for the more recent rise in anti-Shia violence has been that post-September 11, Pakistan struck something of a devil's bargain with the Sunni militias it had patronized over the years, and which have been linked with Pakistan's support of the Taliban. In exchange for withdrawing official support from the Taliban and its network of Sunni supporters, observers say that the government agreed to go lightly on activities relating to jihad in Kashmir and against Pakistani Shia. An illustrative example of this sleight-of-hand can be seen in the case of Maulana Tariq Azam, former leader of the anti-Shia militia Sipah-e-Sahaba. While in jail, Azam was allowed to stand for election in late 2002, and won his contested seat. He was then released despite his record, and despite the official ban on his militia – which changed its name and kept on functioning – and went on to support Musharraf's coalition before being gunned down in broad daylight in 2003.[28]

Azam's story is a microcosm of the problem: the transnational network of extremist groups linked to the Afghan War and its aftermath are not held accountable for "internal" actions of religiously-motivated violence. The security situation for Pakistani Christians has severely declined, but the worst hit has been Pakistani Shias. Since September 11, a number of Shia mosques have been suicide bombed, and gunmen on motorcycles have on several recent occasions carried out "drive-by" shootings targeting Shias. Mosque and car bombings, as well as targeted assassinations during 2004 took place prominently in Karachi, Quetta, Lahore, Sialkot, and Multan. The phenomenon has received international attention, and Human Rights Watch is now tracking violence against Shias. One clear result has been that in addition to the incidences of mass murder, Shia professionals have become the targets of a low-intensity assassination campaign centered in Karachi.

The campaign is designed to intimidate them to leave the country entirely – a sorry state of affairs for a country created to protect the interests of the Muslim minority of the Indian subcontinent.

## Bangladesh

Bangladesh literally means the land of Bengalis – Bangla- or "Bengali," and -desh, "land of." Between 1947 and 1971, the territory comprising today's Bangladesh was East Pakistan, with all of today's Pakistani territory some 1,000 miles away as West Pakistan. A country split into two pieces, separated by a less than friendly neighbor, would have posed formidable challenges of governance even in the most optimistic of circumstances, but the intellectual and political leadership of Pakistan never took Bengal seriously as an integral part of the new nation – and treated it as such. Political power, economic benefit, and cultural hegemony were all hoarded by West Pakistan. The details of Bengali nationalism and the intricacies of this political history have been well documented by scholars; for our purposes, the important point is that Pakistan in its two-winged form was not sustainable as a nation-state.[29] Bangladesh came into existence in 1971 following a bloody war in which some one to three million were killed – a genocide in which documentation is now coming to light that focuses on the targeting of Bengali Hindus.[30] This civil war, which began with the deployment of Pakistani Army soldiers to quash a secessionist rebellion in the eastern province, grew into an international engagement when the Indian Army intervened following an outpouring of Bengali refugees into Indian Bengal. To this day, a widespread opinion in Pakistan blames the loss of its eastern wing to "Indian intervention" rather than on repression and misgovernance within Pakistan itself.

There are two key transnational aspects to religious violence in Bangladesh today. The first is related to the umbilical cord of Partition which, as with the India–Pakistan relationship, has ensured that Bangladesh and India exist in a sort of negative symbiosis. The second relates to the increase over the past decade in transnational Islamic groups and their activities in the country.

Bangladesh has a higher proportion of Hindu citizens than does Pakistan and again – as with the conflict in Kashmir, but in reverse – this Hindu minority by the very fact of their religion have been iconicized as the "enemy" within. Bangladeshi Hindus are a religious minority persecuted with state sanction through the 1972 Enemy/Vested Property Acts, which permitted the seizure of Hindu citizens' property with impunity until its repeal in 2001. Human rights organizations have sounded the alarm about the dramatic decrease in the population of Hindus in Bangladesh, which appears to be correlated with emigration to India, a flow of refugees which rights groups attribute to persecution within Bangladesh. An estimated 30 percent of Bangladesh's Hindu population has been affected by the law. The Bangladeshi Association for Land Reform and Development (a non-governmental organization), which correlated the use of the Vested Property Act with Bangladesh's declining Hindu population, has asserted that it "would not be an exaggeration to conclude that the Enemy/Vested Property Acts functioned as an effective tool for the extermination of Hindu minorities from their motherland."[31] Indeed, according to one estimate, the Hindu population has shrunk from some 13 percent of the country at independence to now about 9 percent.[32] The act was repealed in 2001, but the government has not made significant progress to reinstate property to those from whom it had been seized.[33]

Seizure of property is not the only kind of persecution the Hindu minority faces; riots targeting Hindus have taken place periodically in Bangladesh. Following the logic of iconicity, and the logic of implosions discussed above, whereby larger conceptual political frameworks implode down into the local, events that affect India's Muslim minority can be mobilized as a rationale for reprisal persecutions of Bangladesh's Hindu minority. The most vivid example – and one which further underscores the complicated transnational relationships affecting religious violence in South Asia – took place in 1992–93. Following the Hindu nationalist destruction of a mosque (the Babri Masjid) in northern India in December 1992, anti-Hindu riots erupted throughout the country, resulting in the destruction and looting of Hindu property, rape of Hindu women, and dozens of deaths. It resulted in yet greater refugee outflows of Hindus into India.

It has been difficult for internal debate within the country to address the violence against and harassment of the country's Hindu minority – largely because the broader public opinion continues to conflate Hindu with India, and thus view Hindus as the oppressors. A measure of the inability to even speak of this topic was the 1994 publication of a novel, *Lajja* (*Shame*), by Taslima Nasreen.[34] Nasreen chronicled the shame of her country's slide from independence and a commitment to secularism to a growingly illiberal Islamic state that persecutes its Hindu minority. The novel was almost immediately banned, and a Bangladeshi cleric issued a fatwa against Nasreen. She now lives in exile, and has been sentenced in absentia under Bangladeshi law to one year imprisonment for offending the sensibilities of Muslims.

The second transnational dimension of religious violence in Bangladesh can be linked to the rise of Islamist movements in the country. This landscape has not been fully mapped, and there appears to be great unwillingness in Bangladesh to discuss the phenomenon. A 2002 story in the *Far Eastern Economic Review* resulted in accusations that the reporter had written a "motivated story" to harm Bangladesh's image, and had done so under false pretenses.[35] Nonetheless, it does appear that the country has undergone significant transformation since its founding as a secular democratic republic. Under the first government of General Zia (the father of the current prime minister) in the 1980s, Islam was declared the state religion, taking the country a significant step away from its secular foundation. For a country which has long been seen as a model for a "moderate Muslim state," reports over the last half-decade which have come to question that assessment mark quite a change. Citing the "mushrooming" of Islamic *madrasah* institutions to some 64,000, Bertil Lintner's *Far Eastern Economic Review* story suggested that Islamic extremist networks in the country are benefiting from Saudi charity networks and possible links to Osama bin Laden – with chilling implications for the country's future. Bangladesh has reportedly become an under-the-radar-screen transit route for transnational Islamic networks, and it has been cited particularly as part of a path for those operating within Southeast Asia.[36] Certainly the political role of Islamic parties in the country has never been greater; it was only in the elections of 2001, as part of a coalition, that two Islamic parties gained power and a political voice.

Events following that election signal potential further problems for religious minorities. Reports emerged that Hindu families were attacked, beaten, robbed, and in some cases murdered – under the allegation that Hindus had supported the opposition Awami League.[37] Recalling the ease with which the Hindu minority can be isolated for attack in ghost reprisals for events in India, it is no leap to link the Islamist attacks on Hindus as scapegoating this internal "enemy" for their supposed alliance with the forces of secularism. The year 2001 was a terrible one for this kind of persecution in Bangladesh; by one account, close to 100,000 Bangladeshi Hindus fled to India. The Bangladeshi government, however, denies that such out-migration has taken place.[38]

## Policy rescriptions

In her influential book, *Losing Control? Sovereignty in an Age of Globalization,* sociologist Saskia Sassen issued a call for a broader framework of analysis which would require "policymakers [to] attach migration impact statements to various policies having to do with overseas activities, from foreign direct investment to military aid."[39] Her rationale was that globalization was eroding state sovereignty in economic matters, while migration regimes – although intrinsically related and impacted by economic regimes – remained the sole provenance of the state. This call for an expanded framework of analysis to avoid "unintended impacts" has relevance for our discussion here.

This chapter has delineated key ways in which religious violence, in India, Pakistan, and Bangladesh, has transnational components which are not simply add-ons, or external factors, but are part of deeper conceptual matrix of social relationships. When Hindu extremists in India carry out attacks targeting Muslims, they are channeling nationalist sentiments from the time of Partition to justify their notion that Muslims should "go to Pakistan," even when the presence of Indian Muslims is evidence of a clear choice *not to have gone to Pakistan* when presented the option. After Indian Hindu extremists brought down the Babri Mosque in 1992, reprisals against Hindus took place in Bangladesh and Pakistan (where mobs attacked Hindus symbolically, bringing down an old Hindu temple in Lahore). After state policies instituted to defeat the Soviets in Afghanistan mobilized Sunni militias precisely because of their adherence to Islamist beliefs – and willingness to fight to the end – Pakistan's internal security order began a sharp decline, with increasing attacks on Shia Muslims back home. These actions operate under a recursive logic of similarity that takes transnational relationships of enmity and creates iconic relationships at home. Viewed in this way, the field of vision cannot be confined to the nation-state, for that framework will forever be too narrow to accommodate events beyond it that nonetheless have direct impact.

It is also important to acknowledge that the very problem that Partition of 1947 was supposed to solve, that is the Hindu–Muslim conflict, has remained, and even replicated both across national borders and also internally with newer oppositions. As a policy solution, then, it would appear that forced separations and partitions should not necessarily be viewed as workable policy solutions for seemingly intractable conflicts.[40] The result, at least with the South Asian cases here, has been to absolutize oppositional dichotomies – such as Hindu/Muslim – such that they dominate the matrix of social relations and restrict scope for negotiated solutions. This is particularly true for the three post-Partition states discussed here, for the still-recent memories of violence provide ready history to justify rationales of grievance, even enmity, and even across national boundaries. Territorial partitions reify ideas of ethnicity and religious incompatibility – indeed, it is the central *goal* of any nationalist movement to achieve perfect isomorphism between territory and national peoples.

In terms of policy solutions for the problem of religious violence, the necessity of specifying, or mapping, transnational frameworks with greater precision, and well in advance, would appear to be of significant value. This should include historical as well as sociological frameworks in addition to the more traditional security analysis that has privileged political science as a discipline. But a mapping of implications can only go so far. Durable solutions for problems of religious violence in the region will also require strength and political will on the part of governments to hold actors – even those who may be politically useful – accountable for actions of violence. This is, of course, the taller order.

Of the three countries discussed here, there are greater reasons to be optimistic about India. For one, the May 2004 parliamentary elections which dealt the coalition led by Hindu nationalists a drubbing, have reminded politicians that their seats of power are indeed dependent upon the people. Early analyses of the election outcomes have suggested that voters may have been responding both to insufficient attention to rural development along with a rejection of religious violence such as what took place in Gujarat in 2002.[41] Thanks to a free and aggressive press, at times even muckraking, and an Election Commission which has long demonstrated its independence from political influence, the mechanisms of democracy *do work* in India. As important, strong traditions of political as well as intellectual dissent have meant that lively, vigorous, and often bitter debates take place in India over ideas and their solutions – but in general, people are not persecuted on the basis of ideology.

There are more reasons to worry about Pakistan and Bangladesh. Bangladesh has by far more promising indicators: a healthy non-governmental sector responsible for mobilizing communities to be self-sufficient; traditions of learning and more equitable access to education for women; and a press that, as with India, is by all accounts a vigilant watchdog. Yet the reasons for concern delineated above remain. In addition to reports of declining governance, and the rise of political Islam within the polity, the core question is this: If Bangladesh, founded as the homeland for *Bengalis*, irrespective of religion, cannot undo the narrowed framework of citizenship which has squeezed Bengali Hindus from full participation, rendering them vulnerable to abuse and violence, will it be able to safeguard their continued existence in that state? This situation would inevitably produce further migration into India, with unclear implications for an Indian governmental response.

There are few reasons to be optimistic about the state of religious violence in Pakistan. Under General Musharraf's watch, security for religious minorities has precipitously declined. The country, despite the façade of parliamentary elections, remains in the grip of the military, which means that politicians cannot be held accountable for policies because they are essentially powerless. The constitution has been promiscuously amended such that the president holds virtually all power, and the courts are adjudicated by judges who have kept their positions by swearing an oath of allegiance to General Musharraf. Militia leaders with a record of sectarian violence are not barred from contesting elections, and sectarian militias are banned but allowed to continue operations under new names. Militias known for recruiting young boys to perpetrate jihad across the border in Kashmir, under the slogan of "fighting Hindus," remain in operation despite a nominal ban on such activities. They also continue to publish recruitment literature, not to mention lively and opinionated websites.[42] Investigative agencies and police, which in tandem should be pursuing the perpetrators of the past several years' attacks and bombings of religious minorities, appear unable to do so. With political will so utterly absent, it is difficult to think of any policy solutions which might help this troubled country steer itself back on course.

## Notes

1  Two recent historical efforts are pushing the boundaries on memory of violence at Partition. See Urvashi Butalia, *The Other Side of Silence: Voices from the Partition of India*, US edition (Durham, NC: Duke University Press, 2000); and Gyanendra Pandey, ed., *Remembering Partition: Violence, Nationalism, and History in India* (Cambridge: Cambridge University Press, 2001). Modern literature provides contemporary clues about the issue. See, for example, Sa'adat Hasan Manto, *Khol Do* and *Thanda Ghost*; Khushwant Singh, *Train to Pakistan*; Amrita Pritam, *Ajj Akkhan Waris Shah Nu*. I am unfamiliar with the Bengali literature, for which I apologize.

2  This formulation references the work of historian Ronald Suny on nationalism and the Soviet Union. See Ronald G. Suny, *The Revenge of the Past: Nationalism, Revolution, and the Collapse of the Soviet Union* (Stanford, CA: Stanford University Press, 1993).

3  For the best argument that Jinnah was using the idea of Pakistan as a bargaining chip, not as a desired goal, see Ayesha Jalal, *The Sole Spokesman: Jinnah, the Muslim League, and the Demand for Pakistan* (Cambridge: Cambridge University Press, 1985).

4  For a refutation of this story see Samar Halarnkar, "Cheers from Mohammad Ali Road," *Indian Express*, March 6, 2003.

5  Editorial, "A Flawed Formulation," *Indian Express*, April 4, 2004.

6  Here I am relying on Arjun Appadurai's formulation of "ethnic implosions," for the feedback loop of the global and the local is what pushes Partition and the transnational relationship of India and Pakistan into Hindu–Muslim relations in India. See Arjun Appadurai, *Modernity at Large: Cultural Dimensions of Globalization* (Minneapolis: University of Minnesota Press, 1996), 149–56. Regarding "transvaluation," see also

Stanley J. Tambiah, *Leveling Crowds: Ethnonationalist Conflicts and Collective Violence in South Asia* (Berkeley, CA: University of California Press, 1996).

7 There is a huge body of literature on the Kashmir conflict. For good overviews, see Sumit Ganguly, *The Conflict in Kashmir: Portents of War, Hopes of Peace* (Washington DC: Woodrow Wilson Center, 1996); and Sumit Ganguly, *Conflict Unending: India– Pakistan Tensions Since 1947 (New York: Columbia University Press, 2002)*.

8 Ibid.

9 See Praveen Swami, "Through the Valley of the Shadow of Death," *Asia Times*, January 9, 2003, http:// www.atimes.com/atimes/South_Asia/EA09Df02.html.

10 Rajat Pandit, "Army Bracing for Spurt in Infiltration," *Economic Times*, April 14, 2003. Pandit quotes Indian Army sources as saying that in 1991 only two of 844 militants killed were foreign; in 2002, 1,063 of 1,707 killed were foreign. This statistical measure is itself problematic; however, given that from the outbreak of the insurgency the Government of India has long laid primary blame on Pakistan, the data point that only 0.2 percent of total militants killed in 1991 were foreign is something of a revelation.

11 See, for example, the *Lashkar-e-Tayyaba* publication which openly details the story of a mujahid who crosses into Indian Kashmir. See the publication's website http://www. jamatuddawa.org/English2/ index.htm. Also note that the above story is in English but this publication contains countless stories of jihad written in Urdu, which presumably are directed at a different audience.

12 On the logic of recursivity in social differentiation, see Susan Gal, "Bartok's Funeral: Representations of Europe in Hungarian Political Rhetoric," *American Ethnologist* 18, no. 3 (1991); and Susan Gal and Judith T. Irvine, "The Boundaries of Languages and Disciplines: How Ideologies Construct Difference," *Social Research* 62, no. 1 (1995).

13 See, for example, the recent memoir of a retired Indian administrator, Sarab J. Singh, *Operation Black Thunder: An Eyewitness Account of Terrorism in the Punjab* (New Delhi: Sage Publications, 2002).

14 Praveen Swami, "Failed Threats and Flawed Fences: India's Military Responses to Pakistan's Proxy War," *India Review* 3, no. 2 (2004).

15 Brian K. Axel, *The Nation's Tortured Body: Violence, Representation, and the Formation of a Sikh "Diaspora"* (Durham, NC: Duke University Press, 2001).

16 In the Sri Lankan context, the Liberation Tigers of Tamil Eelam (the LTTE or "Tamil Tigers") are said to raise great sums through their overseas networks, particularly in Canada. This case would appear to support the argument for a global- and diasporically-integrated analysis of violence; I am not considering it in this chapter, however, because the conflict in Sri Lanka is only remotely linked to religion.

17 See "The Foreign Exchange of Hate: IDRF and the American Funding of Hindutva," Sabrang Communications, November 20, 2002, Mumbai, http://stopfundinghate.org/ sacw/downloads/sabrang_ sacw.pdf.

18 Human Rights Watch published a report specifically on violence against Christians in 1999; see Smita Narula, "INDIA Politics By Other Means: Attacks Against Christians in India," Human Rights Watch 11, no. 6, September 1999. The US State Department Annual Human Rights Report has closely tracked this issue since 1999, and each of these annual reports notes anti-Christian violence. For the annual reports see http:// www.state.gov/g/drl/hr/c1470.htm.

19 See Sadanand Dhume, "India: No Place Like Home: Hindu Nationalism Draws Strength from US Supporters," *Far Eastern Economic Review*, February 25, 1999.

20 Mohammad A. Jinnah, *Quaid-i-Azam Mahomed Ali Jinnah: Speeches As Governor-General of Pakistan 1947–1948* (Karachi: Pakistan Publications, 1976).

21 Note that "La ilaha illilah" is the *kalima*, or the confession of faith in Islam. For an enlightening autobiographical meditation (Urdu language), see Qudratullah Shahab, *Shahabnama* (Lahore: Sang-e-Meel, 1987), 289–93.

119

22  For the best overview of the Jamaat-I-Islami and their changing political activities in Pakistan, see Seyyed V. Nasr, *The Vanguard of the Islamic Revolution: the Jama`at-i-Islami of Pakistan* (Berkeley, CA: University of California Press, 1994).

23  An excellent overview is provided by Amjad M. Khan, "Persecution of the Ahmadiyya Community in Pakistan: An Analysis Under International Law and International Relations," *Harvard Human Rights Journal* 16, (2003): 222–3.

24  Several recent books on the Afghan War are recommended: Barnett Rubin, *The Fragmentation of Afghanistan*, 2nd edition (New Haven, CT: Yale University Press, 2002); Larry Goodson, *Afghanistan's Endless War* (Seattle: University of Washington Press, 2001); Ahmed Rashid, *Taliban: Militant Islam, Oil, and Fundamentalism in Central Asia* (New Haven, CT: Yale University Press, 2000); Steve Coll, *Ghost Wars: the Secret History of the CIA, Afghanistan, and bin Laden, from the Soviet Invasion to September 10, 2001* (New York: Penguin Press, 2004); for a short article, see also Milton Bearden, "Afghanistan, Graveyard of Empires," *Foreign Affairs* 80, no. 6 (November/December 2001): 17–30.

25  See, for example, Ahmed Rashid's journalism from the early 1990s, for example: Ahmed Rashid, "Islam – the Great Divide: Sunnis and Shias Battle it out in Pakistan," *Far Eastern Economic Review*, March 9, 1995.

26  See the chapter on Karachi in Tambiah, *Leveling Crowds*.

27  According to BBC News, more than 4,000 people have been killed in Shia–Sunni violence in Pakistan since 1990; see Zafar Abbas, "Pakistan's Schisms Spill Into Present," *BBC News*, October 7, 2004, http:// news.bbc.co.uk/1/hi/world/south_asia/3724082.stm.

28  See Barry Bearak's profile, "Pakistan Is," *The New York Times Magazine*, December 7, 2003.

29  See Rounaq Jahan, *Pakistan: Failure in National Integration* (Dhaka: Oxford University Press, 1973). See also the more recent three-volume series tracking the history, culture, and politics of Bangladesh: S.R. Chakravarty and Virendra Narain, eds., *Bangladesh* (New Delhi: South Asian Publishers, 1986).

30  Following the 1971 war, the government of Pakistan commissioned an inquiry into allegations of Pakistani Army misconduct. The report, named after its chief investigator, Justice Hamoodur Rahman, was never published after its formal submission to the government in 1974, presumably because its contents were not believed to showcase Pakistan in the most flattering light. It was said that all copies of this document were destroyed. This all changed when, in August 2000, an Indian magazine, *India Today*, somehow got hold of the report and published it on its website. Within a week, a top Pakistani daily, *Dawn*, had mirrored some of the report's content on its own site. The report contains damning admissions that the Army had been acting under verbal as well as written "instructions to eliminate Hindus."

31  See "The Hindu Minority in Bangladesh: Legally Identified Enemies," Human Rights Features Fortnightly, South Asia Human Rights Documentation Centre, New Delhi, January 11, 2000, http://www. hrdc.net/sahrdc/hrfeatures/HRF13.htm.

32  Jaideep Saikia, "Terror Sans Frontiers: Islamic Militancy in North East India," ACDIS Occasional Paper, University of Illinois, Urbana-Champaign, IL, July 2003, Appendix 5, http://www.acdis.uiuc.edu/ Research/OPs/Saikia/contents/appendix_5.html.

33  See "Bangladesh – The Vested Properties Return Act 2001," Human Rights Features Fortnightly, South Asia Human Rights Documentation Centre, New Delhi, April 18, 2001, http://www.hrdc.net/sahrdc/ hrfeatures/HRF35.htm.

34  For the English translation of the Bengali original, see Taslima Nasreen, *Lajja* [Shame] (New Delhi: Penguin India, 1994).

35  Bertil Lintner, "In Bangladesh, as in Pakistan, a Worrisome Rise in Islamic Extremism," *Far Eastern Economic Review*, April 4, 2002.

36  See also Shahriyar Hussain and Teresita Schaffer, "Bangladesh: Trouble Below the Radar Screen," *South Asia Monitor*, Center for Strategic and International Studies, Washington DC, November 1, 2004.

37  See "Bangladesh: Attacks on Members of the Hindu Minority," Amnesty Report, Amnesty International, December 1, 2001.

38  See Moazzam Hosain, "Bangladesh Hindus 'Will Not Go Back,'" *BBC News*, November 22, 2001.

39  See Saskia Sassen, "Chapter 3: Immigration Tests the New Order," in *Losing Control? Sovereignty in an Age of Globalization* (New York: Columbia University Press, 1996).

40  As the international community begins to discuss options for Iraq, a partition-like solution periodically reappears which would, in its ideal-type vision, create three new states: one for Kurds, one for Shia, and one for Sunnis. The South Asian experience may provide some guidance here.

41  See Niraja G. Jayal, "A Malevolent Embrace? The BJP and Muslims in the Parliamentary Election of 2004," *India Review* 3, no. 3 (2004).

42  See Alyssa Ayres, "Jihad.org," *Wall Street Journal*, May 12, 2003.

# 8

# THE (PSYCHIC) ROOTS OF RELIGIOUS VIOLENCE IN SOUTH AND SOUTHEAST ASIA

*Kumar Ramakrishna[1]*

In their admirable chapters, Sumit Ganguly and Alyssa Ayres argue that the roots of religious violence in South Asia are traceable ultimately to "British colonization" and the ensuing "production of Hindu–Muslim differentiation and violence." The focus of their chapters, however, is on the legacy of the more recent past, i.e. the Partition of British India in 1947, an event that in their view, signified the incommensurability of the Indian freedom movement's notion of a secular, multi-religious nation-state with the Pakistan movement's claim that only in a Muslim-majority political entity could the interests of Muslims be protected. While they note India's relatively greater institutional capacity to contain ethno-religious conflict, they concede that Indian secularism has always had its limitations. In addition, today influential Hindu fundamentalist opinion leaders are publicly calling for an end to concessions to minority communities such as the Muslims. In sum, Ganguly and Ayres contend that India needs to strengthen and deepen its democratic institutions and uphold its time-honored secular principles. Their net assessment for Pakistan and Bangladesh is bleaker. They feel that governing institutions are failing at the very moment that ethno-religious tensions between Muslim sects in Pakistan and between Muslims and Hindus in Bangladesh are on the increase. Islamabad and Dhaka, they iterate, must stop pursuing policies toward religious and ethnic minorities which could lead to the unraveling of the fabric of their societies. In particular, both states must do a better job of protecting minority rights while stemming the growth of hyper-nationalist histories and religiously chauvinist political parties and organizations.

Mark Woodward shifts the focus to Southeast Asia and offers a theoretically informed, historically grounded, and empirically meaty chapter entitled "Religious Conflict and the Globalization of Knowledge in Indonesian History." He focuses attention on the May 1998 anti-Chinese riots in Jakarta accompanying the fall of the New Order regime as well as the Muslim–Christian violence in the Maluku archipelago in eastern Indonesia in 1999–2000. Woodward argues that both Muslims and Christians, thanks to a propaganda war conducted through the internet, saw the "civil war in Maluku" as a "parochialization of an imagined global conflict" between the two great civilizations. Indonesian Muslims began to see the violence against co-religionists in the former Soviet Union, Afghanistan, Bosnia, Kosovo, Chechnya, the southern Philippines, and Palestine as spearheaded by a "Christian–Zionist alliance bent on world domination." Similarly, violence against Christians in Jakarta and Ambon were seen as signs of the "Last Days" before the return of the Messiah. A second theme that runs strongly through Woodward's chapter is that the violence in Jakarta and Ambon were anything but spontaneous. Rather they were the work of mobs whose passions had been stoked and manipulated by political elites. Woodward suggests that while "neutral and determined security forces" are important in preserving the order within which minority rights can be respected, they are "the sociological equivalent of Prozac," able only to "treat the symptoms and not the causes of the disease of communal violence." Apart from calling for community leaders to play a bigger role in ameliorating ethno-religious tensions, Woodward's basic prescription is that the "underlying social, religious, and psychological conditions that create the environment from which violence can emerge," must be dealt with.

## Social psychology, religion, and ideology[2]

While Ganguly and Ayres suggest that deepening and strengthening democratic institutions is perhaps the stock remedy for dealing with ethno-religious conflict, Woodward arguably is closer to the mark when he talks about the need for a greater focus on the "underlying" social and psychological conditions that breed ethno-religious conflict. Gordon Allport observed in his landmark *The Nature of Prejudice* that "it is only within the nexus of the personality that we find the effective operation of historical, cultural and economic factors," for after all it is in the end *"individuals* who can feel antagonism." This is why he placed a "heavy and convergent emphasis upon psychological factors."[3] The present chapter accordingly proceeds from the premise that a social psychological perspective is needed to shed light on the ways in which the ethno-religious tensions described by Ganguly/Ayres and Woodward boil over into actual violence. To this end the chapter is divided into four sections. In the present section the overriding importance of a social psychological perspective in analyzing religious violence is emphasized, and the relationship between religion and ideology is explored. The following section makes the argument that the root of ethno-religious violence is neither structural democratic nor economic deficits but rather what we may call "mimetic frustration," a social psychological phenomenon. The third section of this chapter examines the ways in which the "haters" within a wider community of prejudice develop the psychological capacity to kill members of the outgroup – and the role of so-called "ideological entrepreneurs" in this regard. The final section examines the unreconstructed nature of religious fundamentalism in general and argues that it is the incipient *will to power* displayed by many religious fundamentalists that is a major cause of ethno-religious violence.

It is well accepted today that the human mind "groups people, as well as objects, into categories" so as to enable individuals to "simplify the present and predict the future more effectively."[4] The problem however is that it is "a small step from categorization" to "stereotyping and favoritism for one's group." In a nutshell, "taken to extremes," ethnocentrism and stereotyping can foster prejudice.[5] J. Harold Ellens bemoans that prejudice is lamentably an all-too-common phenomenon and "a devastating force in our political and social order," that emerges from "a very sick psychology at the center of our souls."[6] Prejudiced individuals tend to be indifferent to the sensibilities and welfare of the less favored outgroup.[7]

On *prima facie* evidence we may shrug along with Ellens and simply concede that prejudice is here to stay. However within a community of prejudiced individuals there is a smaller number, who, following Gaylin, may be considered as *bigots*. Much more so than the simply prejudiced, bigots tend to be "strongly partial to one's own group, religion, race, or politics." Of no small significance, moreover, rather than being passively indifferent, bigots are *actively* "intolerant of those who differ."[8] The bigot, in Gaylin's estimation, would quite happily "support legislation and social conditions" that deprive the disliked outgroup of not merely its "autonomy" but also its basic "right to be respected."[9] Finally, it is from the smaller socio-cultural community of bigots that the *haters* emerge. While a "bigot may feel malevolence whenever he thinks of the despised group," he "is not obsessively preoccupied with them."[10] On the other hand, hatred "requires both passion and a preoccupation with the hated group."[11] In this vein, Aristotle once pointed out that while the "angry man wants the object of his anger to suffer in return; hatred wishes its object not to exist."[12] There could be "significant slippage" between the community of bigots and the smaller pool of haters.[13] Gaylin is surely right in pointing out that it is this prejudice–bigotry–hatred continuum that may well be the irreducible root cause of inter-group conflict:

> Prejudice and bigotry ... facilitate the agendas of a hating population. They take advantage of the passivity of the larger community of bigots, a passivity that is essential for that minority who truly hate to carry out their malicious destruction.[14]

Gaylin proceeds to make the very important additional point that when "everyday bias is supported and legitimated by religion," the "passions of ordinary malcontents will be intensified and focused."[15] By "religion" we mean "an organized system of beliefs and practices designed to embrace and advance spiritual ideals and experiences and their applications in the world."[16] It should be noted that religion is often politicized and "yoked" to "political objectives."[17] It is at this point that a religion may be transmuted from a personal faith into a political ideology – in which power is sought to actualize a desired religious vision of society.[18] The point to be made here is this: religion per se or its derivative political ideologies, do not actually cause inter-group conflict but rather *legitimate* it. As Jerold M. Post famously put it once, the *"cause is not the cause."* Instead, the cause that is encoded within a group's ideological justification for violence becomes merely the "rationale" for the violence the group is *already* "driven to commit."[19] R.S. Ezekiel in this connection offers a pithy description of the actual role of ideological frameworks in explaining and perhaps justifying the hater's violence against members of the outgroup:

> He believes the ideology literally, word for word – there is an Enemy, the Enemy is Evil. He believes that ideology because he wants it: He wants the grounds for radical action. He must have radical action. Violence is the language in which he can speak his message ...[20]

This is why, although Woodward is utterly correct in drawing attention to the ways in which the Maluku fighting was seen by some Indonesians as a local battle-zone in the wider cosmic war against the so-called Jewish–Crusader axis, the "parochialization of an imagined global conflict" argument, while very important, has its limits. Rather than religious ideology per se, ultimately, it is social psychology that holds the greater explanatory power for ethno-religious conflict in Southeast Asia and elsewhere.

## Religion, identity, and mimetic function

In this respect it seems that the element of *frustration* may well be the key to unlocking the puzzle of ethno-religious violence. Gaylin has shown how frustration represents the irreducible link between objective social conditions and subjective states of mind:

> Feeling deprived bears no relationship to the actual amount of comfort or goods that a person may possess. One can be surrounded with all the indulgences of the affluent society and still feel deprived. Contrary to this, we can observe people existing in great poverty, where each expenditure must be measured and considered, every nutrient stored and rationed, who still do not feel deprived.[21]

Gaylin argues that "a sense of deprivation" is a "relative feeling, more closely associated with entitlement than want."[22] Neil Kressel similarly argues that "the *perception* of injustice is not the same as *actual* injustice."[23] Focusing on "relative deprivation," he notes that individuals are "especially likely to feel frustrated" if they have or receive less than what other people similar to themselves receive.[24] Rene Girard, a scholar of French language and civilization, has provided perhaps the best wide-ranging and systematic examination of the mechanics of relative deprivation in his theory of *mimetic desire*. Girard suggests that human beings "desire things because others have them."[25] In his view, humans have both the inborn capacity to learn their desires from others and the concomitant drive to possess what those others possess. This socially learned desire and the drive to possess the object of that desire together constitute mimetic desire. In short, humans desire "objects" – which may be material, like wealth, or metaphysical, like social status or power – because "their possession by others gives them value in our eyes."[26] The point is that when circumstances arise where socially desired objects are for some reason out of reach of certain individuals or constituencies, mimetic desire may precipitate *frustrations* that may ultimately give rise to conflict.[27]

Mimetic desire presupposes a strong ingroup identity and outgroup bias; and this is precisely what religion or a religious ideology fosters. Benjamin Beit-Hallahmi and Michael Argyle point out that religiosity tends to generate ethnocentric, prejudiced, and discriminatory attitudes.[28] Paul N. Anderson concurs and shows that violence is often the byproduct of religiously generated dichotomies:

> An important aspect of religious power is that it creates an "us." It solidifies group identity and appeals to religious certainty, eternal consequences, and principled loyalties. These shape individuals and groups. Indeed, Yahweh's warfare against tribal adversaries in Hebrew Scripture, the dehumanization of infidels in the Qur'an, and the temporal and eternal warnings against the unfaithful in Christian Scripture function to create an us–them mentality common to prejudice and violence.[29]

He adds that in this sense, the "organizing power of religion to create intra-group solidarity" can be a "devastating contributor to inter-group opposition."[30] Contributing to the considerable primordial forces infusing group identity/ membership is the reality that the latter meets critical psychological needs such as "belongingness," "distinctiveness," and "respect."[31] Thus group membership is akin to a large protective "tent" for group members and if the tent – whether "ethnic, religious or national" in nature – is perceived to be under attack by other groups, "shoring up the 'tent' takes precedence over individual identity needs."[32] Moreover, social identity theory informs us that during inter-group conflict, group identity becomes more valued than individual identity; concern with ingroup welfare replaces individual concerns; there is a heightened sense of shared grievances; and importantly, ingroups tend to become aggressive behaviorally and engage in outgroup stereotyping.[33] Very importantly, "an attack or affront" is perceived by ingroup members as "personal when directed not only against one's physical self," but rather the wider ingroup, or one's "collective self."[34] This *identity simplification dynamic*, if you like, is well captured by Croat writer Slavenka Drakulic in her description of the impact of the Serb–Croat war on individual Croats:

> Along with millions of other Croats, I was pinned to the wall of nationhood – not only by outside pressure from Serbia and the Federal Army but by national homogenization within Croatia itself. That is what the war is doing to us, reducing us to one dimension: the Nation.[35]

We may posit therefore that members of a religiously-defined ingroup, confronted with a vast structural power, wealth, and status imbalance in favor of the disliked outgroup, may under certain crisis conditions, experience mimetic frustration. This in turn tends to generate the associated affective states of humiliation and envy. "Humiliation and envy," Perlman informs us, "go together," and are "exceedingly destructive emotions."[36] She explains:

> Being humiliated is like being filled with poison that has to be expelled in order to regain composure. Humiliation carries a narcissistic wound that contains an implicit demand for rectification, often by taking down the humiliator.[37]

Juergensmeyer adds that what is crucial is the "intimacy with which the humiliation is experienced."[38] Following Perlman, we may argue that the "intolerable effects" of individuals who perceive themselves to be humiliated by the outgroup are "projected" onto the outgroup itself – "the powerful, the envied, the humiliators, the privileged ones."[39] Mimetic frustration on the part of Jakarta's poorer Muslim public – and the resulting overwhelming urge to evacuate the intolerable effects generated onto the envied and hated Chinese upper class – seems to be a plausible explanation for the dynamics of the violence in Jakarta in May 1998. As Woodward observes, "Some of the worst violence occurred in the oldest portion of Jakarta known as Kota. This area has been among Jakarta's Chinatowns for centuries." Woodward has observed that many of the rioters were residents of the ethnically mixed neighborhoods along the harbor near the Chinese community; people who felt exploited by their wealthy Chinese neighbors.

In a very real sense, therefore, when there seems to be no way to address power/ status imbalances peacefully, violence may be "a way of transforming victimhood to mastery."[40] It may well be that the rioting Indonesian Muslim mobs wanted to *force* the privileged, envied wealthy Chinese to taste – however momentarily – their powerlessness, their despair, their dark – as Juergensmeyer's puts it – "habitus."[41] The psychoanalyst W.R.D. Fairbairn put it pithily in observing that "people would rather be bad than weak."[42]

## The capacity to kill and the role of ideological entrepreneurs

Even when people feel the overwhelming urge to be bad rather than weak does not in any way imply that killing individual members of the hated outgroup *ipso facto* follows naturally. Social psychologist Albert Bandura has argued that humans in all societies are socialized into accepting socially mandated "self-sanctions" that regulate their behavior. He points out that "to slaughter in cold blood innocent women and children in buses, department stores, and in airports," requires "moral disengagement" of these self-sanctions. This is the only way to "create the capacity to kill innocent human beings."[43] According to Bandura, one powerful way to relax self-sanctions is by "cognitively restructuring the moral value of killing, so that the killing can be done free from self-censuring restraints."[44] In like vein, Donald Horowitz, in an excellent study of ethnic riots, argues that the rioting crowds feel that they are morally justified in engaging in violent actions against members of outgroups. In fact, the rioters often feel that their actions express "more widely shared sentiments about what the targets deserve."[45] In the May 1998 anti-Chinese Jakarta riots, it is certainly clear from Woodward's account that many of the urban, poor Muslims "felt – and have been – betrayed by the Indonesian government and the local economic elite." There was thus a reservoir of simmering resentment which agent provocateurs could tap to generate violence. Cognitive restructuring of the morality of killing certainly took place in the case of Laskar Jihad fighting in the Malukus as well. Jafar's fighters clearly regarded their activities as morally justified, as they saw themselves as defenders of fellow Muslims being "slaughtered" by Christians.

A second mechanism for disengaging the moral self-sanctions against killing is what Bandura calls "euphemistic labeling," which "provides a convenient device for masking reprehensible activities or even conferring a respectable status on them."[46] Certainly Jafar's Laskar Jihad militia, as the name implies, saw themselves as engaged in the divinely sanctioned activity of "jihad" and not genocide in the Malukus. The third moral disengagement technique Bandura discusses is displacement of responsibility. He argues that "people behave in injurious ways they normally repudiate if a legitimate authority accepts responsibility for the consequences of their conduct."[47] In this respect, Woodward makes the important point that the well-known Yemeni cleric Muqbil bin Hadi al-Wad'i, who acted as Jafar's mentor of sorts, "wrote a fatwa authorizing jihad in eastern Indonesia." Similarly, several Malaysian and Singaporean Jemaah Islamiyah (JI) terrorists have mentioned Osama bin Laden's February 1998 fatwa declaring jihad on the Jewish–Crusader alliance as justification for their own terror activities.

A fourth and final mechanism of disengaging self-sanctions against killing is dehumanization. In other words, self-sanctions against "cruel conduct can be disengaged or blunted by divesting people of human qualities." Bandura observes:

> Once dehumanized, the potential victims are no longer viewed as persons with feelings, hopes, and concerns but as subhuman objects. They are portrayed as mindless "savages", "gooks" … and the like. Subhumans are regarded as insensitive to maltreatment and capable of being influenced only by harsh methods.[48]

Dehumanization certainly played a role in helping JI terrorists engage in atrocities. Amrozi, convicted for his role in the October 12, 2002 Bali bombings, revealed his utter lack of empathy for the humanity of his victims when he shrugged off the suggestion that they had killed Australians instead of Americans by quipping: "Australians, Americans, whatever – they are all white people."[49] If it was bad enough that Amrozi could not see beyond the empty abstraction of "white people," his brother and senior JI leader Mukhlas himself declared that all Westerners were "dirty animals and insects that need to be wiped out."[50] Extremely noteworthy in this respect is Woodward's observation that during the Jakarta riots Chinese were denounced by the mobs as "pigs, lice, and dogs." Woodward correctly points out that for "Muslims, dogs, like swine, are defiled creatures." The clear implication here is that, as Bandura suggests, the Chinese were seen as "subhuman objects," bereft of "feelings, hopes and concerns," "insensitive to maltreatment and capable of being influenced only by harsh methods." Woodward's harrowing descriptions of the horrific rapes of Chinese women bear testimony to the insidious power of dehumanization.

It is also clear, moreover, that *ideological entrepreneurs* are needed to engage in the incendiary propaganda that desensitizes ordinary people to the ingrained self-sanctions against killing other human beings. Donald Horowitz explains that the function of ideological entrepreneurs is to seek opportunities to provide "a hostile interpretation of events."[51] Ideological entrepreneurs do so by acting as "radical unifiers" in an ontological sense. That is, they display "a tendency to interpret a precipitating incident" with reference to "instances of the targets' prior conduct." This is important, as the "cognitive propensity to act on the basis of chains of events" helps facilitate "justification of the resulting violence."[52] Woodward, in his analysis of the events leading up to the 1984 Tanjung Priok riots, points the finger at preachers in local mosques who "delivered vitriolic sermons" attacking not only the New Order regime for imposing the controversial *asas tunggal* policy but also denounced "Christians, and the Chinese and Muslims" who associated with these putative outgroups. The Maluku conflict of 1999–2000 in particular provided much raw material for the ideological entrepreneurs of JI, who made VCDs (video compact discs) and distributed them across Southeast Asia, from Indonesia to the southern Philippines. These were shown during informal teaching sessions by JI clerics, and the "eager young men in attendance, duly incensed by what they had witnessed, were then briefed on how they could join the jihad."[53]

Singapore JI leaders routinely employed fiery speeches to elicit an emotional response from members before requiring them to fill out surveys indicating what kinds of terrorist activities they wished to be involved in. "Having signed their names on the survey, members were not able to alter their decisions later on."[54] Woodward observes that Laskar Jihad leaders similarly acted as ideological entrepreneurs during recruitment rallies, showing "photographs of burned out mosques and Muslims killed by Ambonese Christians." Ideological entrepreneurs were also present on the Christian side of the Maluku conflict, particularly amongst the ranks of missionaries. Both JI and Laskar Jihad ideological entrepreneurs in sum took pains to show how the Maluku conflict fitted into the wider cosmic war between the global Islamic community and the Jewish–Crusader axis. In Juergensmeyer's terms, they helped "sacralize" the Maluku fighting.[55]

## Globalization, fundamentalism, and preventing the sacralization of conflict

In summary, the foregoing analysis suggests that religious violence is less about religion per se than about the underlying social psychological and in particular mimetic, dynamics driving it. As noted, the religious cause merely provides the *legitimation* for the violence the warring parties *already* feel compelled to commit. Religion, or more precisely the ideological frameworks derived from particularistic readings of religion, further provide overarching narratives that purport to situate local conflicts in South and Southeast Asia within wider transnational cosmic war scenarios. Regardless of the territorial, political, socio-economic – ultimately, mimetic – configurations of a conflict, when the warring parties in a conflict zone begin to view one another in *absolutized, sacralized, and transnationalized cosmic war terms*, negotiated solutions become very difficult to achieve.[56] This is why ideological frameworks derived from absolutist, rigid religious visions – that is, religious fundamentalism – are a major "sacralizer" and thus legitimator of inter-group violence.

Certainly, the chapters by Ganguly and Ayres suggest that in South Asia, religious fundamentalism is on the rise. Indian secularism has been severely battered by the Hindu Right with predictably dire implications for the rights of minority communities such as the Muslims. In Pakistan and Bangladesh, Muslim majority regimes have done little to ensure the protection of non-Muslim community rights while the growth of radical Islamic forms of fundamentalism continues unabated. Religious fundamentalism is not going to go away anytime soon. In a sense, it is the flip side of globalization. Globalization has been usefully characterized as "worldwide integration through an ongoing, dynamic process that involves the interplay of free enterprise, democratic principles and human rights, the high-tech exchange of information, and movement of large numbers of people."[57] While it is true that "the juggernaut of free enterprise, democracy, and technology offers the best chance of wealth creation," the key to "improving the human condition," globalization has been traumatic for many Third World societies.[58] By privileging "individualistic, impersonal, competitive, privatistic, and mobile" values and attitudes, globalization processes have inadvertently undermined traditional social units such as the family, clan, and voluntary association.[59] More precisely, globalization, which is to many non-Western societies synonymous with Westernization, is destabilizing because it promotes the desacralization of society; encourages religious and moral relativism; places the onus on the individual to determine his "values, career, life style and moral system"; and most disconcertingly, undermines traditional ideas about sexuality and the status of women.[60] Michael Stevens argues in this regard that for "communitarian societies, keyed to historical continuity, group coherence and security, personal rootedness, and the affirmation of moral righteousness, empowering the individual is equated with rending society asunder."[61]

This is precisely why back-to-basics movements have sprung up in many Third World states in order to counter the perceived ideologically and spiritually debilitating effects of globalization. The essential problem is that thus far these religious fundamentalist movements have not been particularly successful in accommodating the cognitive underpinnings of modernity. While for instance, many religious fundamentalists have embraced the scientific and technological training of the West, they have not quite, as Malise Ruthven suggests, undergone the necessary concomitant "epistemological revolution, the institutionalization of doubt – that made modernity possible."[62] Within the mind of the technically trained, Western-educated, and outwardly sophisticated Islamic fundamentalist, for instance, the "dual identity of village Muslim and applied scientist are imperfectly integrated."[63] This has produced a fundamentalist mindset that psychologists like J. Harold Ellens consider a form of "psychopathology":

> An essential component of this psychology is a rigid structuralist approach that has an obsessive-compulsive flavor to it. It is the mark of those who have a very limited ability to live with the ambiguity inherent to healthy human life ... Fundamentalism is a psychopathology that drives its proponents to the construction of orthodoxies ...[64]

Finally, Stuart Sim, while similarly decrying the "fundamentalist mentality," adds that not only do fundamentalists seek the "desire for certainty," they also seek "the power to enforce that certainty over others."[65] This is what makes the religious fundamentalist a problem: he is not naturally inclined to live and let live in matters of faith. Sim contends that "religious fundamentalism seems to be more to do with power than spiritual matters," and "power is a political rather than a spiritual issue."[66] Political scientist R. Hrair Dekmejian in this respect captures aspects of Sim's argument in his description of the "*mutaasib*, or Muslim fundamentalist fanatic," for example, as characterized by "rigid beliefs, intolerance toward unbelievers, preoccupation with power," and a "vision of an evil world."[67] This observation may shed some light on the motivations of violent radical religious fundamentalist movements in South and Southeast Asia as described in the chapters by Ganguly, Ayres, and Woodward.

The clear implication is that over and above strengthening democratic governance and raising living standards in the short to medium term, better quality education must be the key. Education – *both* secular and religious – with a view to encouraging critical thinking amongst current and future generations and broadening the intellectual, spiritual, and civilizational horizons of entire communities, may perhaps have the most profound effect in weeding out the psychic roots of ethno-religious violence. More precisely, broader-based secular and religious education is more likely to provide the intellectual bulwark against absolutist religious and ideological visions. Downstream, this may well keep inter-group violence *below* the sacralization threshold, thereby improving the chances for a negotiated solution. In this respect for instance, plans reportedly under consideration in Washington to provide $250 million for the modernization of Indonesia's 178,000 state schools and 10,000 "West-tolerant" Muslim-run schools, if effectively and sensitively managed, would represent an important and proactive step likely to have salutary longer-term consequences for the amelioration of religious conflict.[68]

# Notes

1 Acting Head, Centre of Excellence for National Security and Associate Professor, Institute of Defence and Strategic Studies, Nanyang Technological University, Singapore. Email: iskumar@ntu.edu.sg

2 Some elements of the argument developed in this essay draw on the author's chapter entitled "The Making of the Jemaah Islamiyah Terrorist," in *Teaching Terror: Strategic and Tactical Learning in the Terrorist World*, ed. J. Forest (Boulder, CO: Rowman & Littlefield, 2006).

3 Allport cited in J. Harold Ellens, "The Dynamics of Prejudice," in *The Destructive Power of Religion: Violence in Judaism, Christianity and Islam, Vol. 2: Religion, Psychology and Violence*, ed. J. Harold Ellens (Westport, CT: Praeger, 2004), 88.

4 Neil J. Kressel, *Mass Hate: The Global Rise of Genocide and Terror*, rev. (New York: Westview, 2002), 211.

5 Ibid.

6 Ellens, "Dynamics of Prejudice," 96.

7 Willard Gaylin, *Hatred: The Psychological Descent into Violence* (New York: PublicAffairs, 2003), 24.

8 Ibid., 26.

9 Ibid.

10 Ibid., 28.

11 Ibid.

12 Cited in Clark McCauley, "Psychological Issues in Understanding Terrorism and the Response to Terrorism," in *Psychology of Terrorism, Vol. 3: Theoretical Understandings and Perspectives*, ed. Chris E. Stout (Westport, CT: Praeger, 2002), 7.

13 Gaylin, *Hatred*, 26–7.

14 Ibid., 27.

15 Ibid., 244.

16 Paul N. Anderson, "Religion and Violence: From Pawn to Scapegoat," in *The Destructive Power of Religion: Violence in Judaism, Christianity and Islam, Vol. 2: Religion, Psychology and Violence*, ed. J. Harold Ellens (Westport, CT: Praeger, 2004), 267.

17 Ibid., 276.

18 For a discussion in this regard of the distinction between apolitical "neo-fundamentalist" Muslims and politically driven "Islamists," see Barbara D. Metcalf, "Traditionalist Islamic Activism: Deoband, Tablighis, and Talibs" (essay based on Institute for the Study of Islam in the Modern World Annual Lecture, Leiden University, Leiden, November 23, 2001).

19 Jerrold M. Post, "Terrorist Psycho-Logic: Terrorist Behavior as a Product of Psychological Forces," in *Origins of Terrorism: Psychologies, Ideologies, Theologies, States of Mind*, ed. Walter Reich (Washington DC: Woodrow Wilson Center Press, 1998), 35.

20 R.S. Ezekiel, *The Racist Mind: Portraits of American Neo-Nazis and Klansmen* (New York: Viking Penguin, 1995), xxxi, cited in Timothy Gallimore, "Unresolved Trauma: Fuel for the Cycle of Violence and Terrorism," in *Psychology of Terrorism, Vol. 2: Clinical Aspects and Reponses*, ed. Chris E. Stout (Westport, CT: Praeger, 2002), 153.

21 Gaylin, *Hatred*, 46.

22 Ibid., 48.

23 Kressel, *Mass Hate*, 209.

24 Ibid.

25 Mack C. Stirling, "Violent Religion: Rene Girard's Theory of Culture," in *The Destructive Power of Religion: Violence in Judaism, Christianity and Islam, Vol.*

2: *Religion, Psychology and Violence*, ed. J. Harold Ellens (Westport, CT: Praeger, 2004), 12.
26  Ibid., 15.
27  Ibid., 17–18.
28  Benjamin Beit-Hallahmi and Michael Argyle, *The Psychology of Religious Behavior, Belief and Experience* (New York: Routledge, 1997), 243.
29  Anderson, "Religion and Violence," 270–1.
30  Ibid., 271.
31  Michael J. Stevens, "The Unanticipated Consequences of Globalization: Contextualizing Terrorism," in *Psychology of Terrorism, Vol. 3: Theoretical Understandings and Perspectives*, ed. Chris E. Stout (Westport, CT: Praeger, 2002), 44.
32  Stephen D. Fabick, "Us & Them: Reducing the Risk of Terrorism," in *Psychology of Terrorism, Vol. 2: Clinical Aspects and Reponses*, ed. Chris E. Stout (Westport, CT: Praeger, 2002), 231.
33  Stevens, "Unanticipated Consequences," 45.
34  Jonathan T. Drummond, "From the Northwest Imperative to Global Jihad: Social Psychological Aspects of the Construction of the Enemy, Political Violence and Terror," in *Psychology of Terrorism, Vol. 1: A Public Understanding*, ed. Chris E. Stout (Westport, CT: Praeger, 2002), 60, 75.
35  Cited in Kressel, *Mass Hate*, 28; emphasis added.
36  Diane Perlman, "Intersubjective Dimensions of Terrorism and its Transcendence," in *Psychology of Terrorism, Vol. 1: A Public Understanding*, ed. Chris E. Stout (Westport, CT: Praeger, 2002), 28.
37  Ibid.
38  Mark Juergensmeyer, *Terror in the Mind of God: The Global Rise of Religious Violence*, 3rd edn (Berkeley, CA: University of California Press, 2000), 195.
39  Perlman, "Intersubjective Dimensions," 30.
40  Ibid., 32.
41  Juergensmeyer, *Terror in the Mind of God*, 211, 214.
42  Perlman, "Intersubjective Dimensions," 32.
43  Albert Bandura, "Mechanisms of Moral Disengagement," in *Origins of Terrorism: Psychologies, Ideologies, Theologies, States of Mind*, ed. Walter Reich (Washington DC: Woodrow Wilson Center Press, 1998), 163.
44  Ibid., 164.
45  Donald L. Horowitz, *The Deadly Ethnic Riot* (Berkeley, CA: University of California Press, 2001), 541.
46  Bandura, "Mechanisms," 169–70.
47  Ibid., 173.
48  Ibid., 180–1.
49  Andrew Bolt, "Why Peace is not Negotiable", *The Sunday Mail*, October 9, 2005.
50  Angel Rabasa, "Radical Islamist Ideologies in Southeast Asia," in *Current Trends in Islamist Ideology*, Vol. 1, ed. Hillel Fradkin, Husain Haqani and Eric Brown (Washington, DC: Hudson Institute, 2005), 32.
51  Horowitz, *Deadly Ethnic Riot*, 93.
52  Ibid., 531.
53  Dan Murphy, "How Al Qaeda Lit the Bali Fuse: Part 2," *Christian Science Monitor*, June 18, 2003.
54  Singaporean Ministry of Home Affairs, *White Paper: the Jemaah Islamiyah Arrests and the Threat of Terrorism* (Singapore, January 7, 2003), 16.
55  Juergensmeyer, *Terror in the Mind of God*, 163.
56  Charles Selengut, *Sacred Fury: Understanding Religious Violence* (Walnut Creek, CA: AltaMira Press, 2003), 228. See also Juergensmeyer, *Terror in the Mind of God*, 162–3.

57  Stevens, "Unanticipated Consequences," 37–8.
58  Ibid., 38.
59  Ibid., 39.
60  Selengut, *Sacred Fury*, 157–8.
61  Stevens, "Unanticipated Consequences," 40.
62  Malise Ruthven, *A Fury for God: The Islamist Attack on America* (London: Granta, 2002), 147.
63  Ibid., 124.
64  J. Harold Ellens, "Fundamentalism, Orthodoxy and Violence," in *Destructive Power of Religion, Vol. 4: Contemporary Views on Spirituality and Violence*, ed. J. Harold Ellens (Westport, CT: Praeger, 2004), 120.
65  Stuart Sim, *Fundamentalist World: The New Dark Age of Dogma* (Cambridge: Icon Books, 2004), 29.
66  Ibid., 100.
67  Cited in Kressel, *Mass Hate*, 199.
68  John Kerin, "US Aims at Terror Schools," *Weekend Australian*, October 4, 2003. Since going to press, the United States has pledged US$157 million to assist Indonesia's educational programmes and a further US$8.5 million to develop an Indonesian version of Sesame Street. See "Education Brought to the Kids by the Letters U, S and A," *The Straits Times*, March 16, 2006.

# 9

# DEBATING STRATEGIES FOR DISRUPTING VIOLENCE

## Lessons from South Asia

*Maya Chadda*

The Sabarmati Express from Ayodhya carrying 1,700 Kar Sevaks (volunteer cadres of the Vishva Hindu Parishad (VHP), a Hindu nationalist organization) was due at 2:55 am on the morning of February 27, 2002 at Godhra station in Gujarat. This small town in Uttar Pradesh had been the center of fierce controversy over the previous decade about a mosque constructed in the sixteenth century, allegedly over a destroyed Ram temple. The journey of the Sabarmati Express from Ahmedabad to Ayodhya and back to Ahmedabad had been marked by incidents between Hindus and Muslims traveling on the train and on platforms where the train had stopped en route. On the morning of February 27, an altercation took place between a Muslim tea vendor and the Kar Sevaks over the price of tea and harassment of two young Muslim women, the details of which have remained obscured by conflicting reports.[1] The quarrel led to someone pulling the emergency chain just as the train left the station. Both sides of the train tracks near the Godhra station are populated by the Muslim Ghanchi community which has a history of participation in previous Hindu–Muslim riots. While tensions escalated, a Muslim mob of 2,000 quickly gathered with homemade weapons – pickaxes, kerosene-soaked rags – to confront the Kar Sevaks. The mobs attacked the train and set fire to two compartments in which 59 Kar Sevaks including women and children perished.[2] The events that followed have been a subject of extensive reporting but briefly, the carnage at Godhra led to the most widespread retaliation and brutal killings of hundreds of innocent Muslims all over Gujarat, and particularly in the city of Ahmedabad.[3] When the violence ended, the official figures of the dead in Gujarat exceeded 1,000, nearly all Muslims, and estimates of the number of Muslims displaced from their homes and forced into relief camps went up from 50,000 to 100,000 within a few weeks.[4] The Gujarat riots were the worst incidence of communal violence since the partition of India in 1947.

This was, of course, not the first time such violence had occurred in Gujarat, or for that matter, in India. Godhra is a small town with a long and bloody history of violence between its Muslims and Hindus and the state of Gujarat, particularly the cities of Ahmedabad and Vadodara, both along the route of the Sabarmati Express, have been the scenes of many riots going as far back as 1961. But Gujarat is hardly the only state prone to Hindu–Muslim violence.[5] Other cities in the states of Maharashtra, Uttar Pradesh, and Andhra, have also faced repeated episodes of Hindu–Muslim violence. While such violence remained at a low level throughout the 1950s and early 1960s, it escalated steadily in the 1970s, reaching a peak in the early 1990s.

This history of religiously-based violence raises two broad questions: What accounts for the persistent increase in the intensity and frequency of such violence? And what strategies are available to prevent its occurrence? In this chapter, I will concentrate on the latter, namely, the question of strategies to prevent religious violence. Some discussion of the causes is however unavoidable, especially those that are implicit in the proposed preventive strategies. Religiously-based violence has haunted India since long before independence in 1947. Its stubborn persistence has naturally led to many inquiries and appointments of commissions to investigate into the causes and make recommendations to prevent it. Scholars have been equally preoccupied by this problem. There is now a large body of literature examining religious violence in India.[6]

This article will analyze the Indian experience in the context of available explanations and recommendation about how religiously-based violence can be prevented. I have divided the discussion into three parts. The first part provides the context – historical and theoretical – to clarify the nature of religiously-based violence in India. The second part deconstructs the key strategies that have been advanced to disrupt violence. The third part outlines my own reflections on what might work better to prevent conflicts and addresses what we still do not fully understand about violence in countries such as India. I argue that no single cause or single agency strategy can prevent or defuse religious violence and that available discussion of preventive strategies has only addressed either the very long-term or the immediate and short-term causes of conflict. What is needed is an interim strategy that combines several agencies and actors in a "coalition of the willing" to establish permanent road blocs in violence-prone towns and cities. This is not meant to be a comprehensive account of violence or its long history in India. The focus is on analyzing the effectiveness of preventive strategies. Although there are many religious communities in India and therefore many points of tensions emanating from conflicts over identities – Hindu, Sikh, Christian, Buddhist, and animist – I focus largely on the Hindu–Muslim divide.

Muslims constitute close to 12 percent of the Indian population and therefore a sizable minority within India. The "Muslim question," as the issues relating to this minority are referred to in India, is a test not only of India's secular democracy but also of its federal governance. The Muslim question is not however confined to domestic matters alone. It extends beyond the border to developments in Pakistan, Afghanistan, and Bangladesh, the three Muslim countries near India. The long-standing dispute over the Muslim majority region of Kashmir, now divided into India and Pakistan occupied parts, makes India's Hindu–Muslim conflict an extension of her regional security. Since the late 1980s and particularly the 1990s, *jihadi* elements in Pakistan, aided and abetted by Pakistan's intelligence agencies have linked the struggles in Kashmir to the struggles for control of Afghanistan.[7] The rise of Islamic fundamentalism in Bangladesh during the last decade and a half has made the Hindu minority in that country a target of frequent attacks, allegedly in retaliation for attacks on Muslims by Hindus within India.[8] The Indian Muslims have however been careful to separate their demands from the claims of the separatists in Kashmir. This disconnect between domestic and foreign policy on Kashmir, has spawned separate approaches to each of these problems. India perceives the struggle over Kashmir as a geopolitical conflict with Pakistan. On the other hand, the Hindu–Muslim clashes in the rest of India are believed to flow from socio-economic inequities disguised as religious ideology. This chapter concentrates on the domestic dimensions of the Hindu–Muslim conflict and the preventive strategies produced by its repeated occurrence.

## The historical and theoretical context

Any understanding of violence prevention, presumes we know the nature of what it is that we seek to prevent. In this section, I make six observations that provide a historical and theoretical context for an analysis of preventive strategies.

First, post-Mughal history, particularly the British colonial period, has played an important role in shaping Hindu–Muslim relations in India. Several leading Indian historians blame the British colonial authorities for sowing the seeds of distrust and animosity between the two communities which they argue is the main reason why India was partitioned amidst horrendous Hindu–Muslim violence.[9] When the British left in 1947, the subcontinent plunged into large-scale religious violence that took over a million lives and displaced close to 12 million people who trekked to their respective religious homes and safety across the newly created international borders – Hindus to India and Muslims to Pakistan.[10] The division of British India into two separate nation-states did not however create homogenous religious homelands. A large number of Muslims continued to reside within India, scattered across many regions and provinces of the country. Nor did the partition settle the dispute over international boundaries and territories. Pakistan continued to lay claims to majority Muslim provinces of India, particularly the territories of the former kingdom of Kashmir. Thus India's external security concerns became inextricably tied to the project of building a coherent and unified nation-state in which maintaining Hindu–Muslim amity became a key concern.

The events of 1947 left deep scars and long memories on both sides of the India and Pakistan border. The partition had led to war, with the first war in 1947 followed by three more armed conflicts, including the 1999 clash over Kashmir's Kargil sector. Pakistan's leadership had argued that there were two distinct but equal nations in the subcontinent: Pakistan, a home to the Muslims, and India, which was predominantly Hindu. Indian leaders had, however, rejected the "two-nation theory" as vehemently as it was advanced by Pakistan.[11] Indian leaders declared that the only line dividing Indian people from others was the one defined by territorial nationalism and that India was not a nation of Hindus but all who lived within its borders, Hindus, Muslims, Sikhs, and Christians alike. These rival national ideologies, intensified by the violence of the partition and the wars over Kashmir, have had an enduring impact on Hindu–Muslim relations within India as well as India's relations with Pakistan and Bangladesh.

Against this background, and given the current conditions of social, cultural, and economic discrimination, it would not have been unusual had the Indian Muslims retained some affinity to Pakistan, made common cause with the Kashmiri struggle, and extended support to the international movement of fundamentalist Islam that has swept the Islamic world in the 1990s. After all, the Indian Muslims had legitimate grievances about their minority status in India and in riot after riot, the Muslims had borne the main brunt of police firing and mob actions. The Indian Muslim community has, however, no connections with Osama bin Laden and Al Qaeda, or any connection with Pakistan and its clandestine operations in Kashmir or India. As a large minority, their principle objective is to retain a degree of cultural control over their social and personal life. Successive Indian governments have acknowledged their minority status and provided for separate Muslim personal law and economic measures to improve their social conditions but these efforts have been inadequate at best.[12]

Over the last two decades, the "Muslim question" has assumed dangerous new proportions largely because of the rise of militant Hindu nationalism and natural consolidation of votes in response to India's competitive electoral democracy.[13] Although unrelated, the revival of Hindu nationalism since the 1980s and its representative party the BJP has coincided with the outbreak of insurgency in Kashmir (1989) and increasing involvement of the *jihadi* elements from across the border from Pakistan into Kashmir. For a large number of Indians, particularly those sympathetic to the agenda of the BJP and its family of organizations (known as the Sangh Parivar), these developments were not accidental. The Muslim militancy in Kashmir was in their view the work of the Muslim "fifth column" represented by the 140 million Indian Muslims.

It is then not surprising that Gordhan Zapadia, the Gujarat Minister of State for Home Affairs said in an interview with the *Indian Express*, that: "In Godhra an outside agency like the ISI was involved and it was a pure terrorist act."[14] The Home Minister in the central cabinet, L.K. Advani, repeated these charges. The *Independent Fact Finding Mission* constituted by several leading human rights activists and secular leaders reported that these accusations "branded local Ghanchi Muslims as Pakistani agents, in other words, as agents of a long standing enemy power, thereby conforming to the traditional demonization of Indian Muslims as sympathizers and cohorts of Pakistan."[15] Beyond the issues of discrimination and lack of opportunities, the "Muslim question" has also revolved around Article 370 of the Indian constitution, which grants the state of Jammu and Kashmir (the Indian-held part of Kashmir) a special status within the Indian Union. The Hindu nationalists demand that Article 370 be abolished. Controversy also surrounds the issue of the Muslim Personal Law meant to protect Islamic identity and institutional autonomy within the frame of the Indian constitution.[16] The Hindu nationalists demand replacement of separate personal law with uniform civil code and an end to all special preference given to Muslims in government jobs and education institutions. Except in Kashmir, the bulk of the Hindu–Muslim clashes in India are local events, more a result of rivalry caused by electoral demography, poor distribution of economic resources, and self-elected ghettoization of the Indian Muslims.

Second, it is important to separate religious violence from other types of violence. Scholars disagree whether religious violence is properly a part of – or apart from – ethnic violence. For Ashutosh Varshney and Donald Horowitz, all conflicts based on ascriptive categories – caste, religion, language, and religion are essentially "ethnic" in nature.[17] There is considerable merit to this argument. For instance, in the cases of the Sikh religious community, Nagas (largely Christians), and Kashmiris (mainly Muslim), religious identity is inextricably tied to economic and political grievances. The Sikh demands have never been purely about claiming co-equal status as a religious community. Nor has it always been separatist. It is evident from the history of this conflict that long periods of peaceful coexistence within India were followed by periods of protests, marches, and violence. The most vicious and violent cycle of Sikh protest came to an end in 1992, when Punjab, that had been a scene of large-scale violence in the previous decade, was reintegrated within the Indian political system via elections. Similarly, the Nagas in the northeast, who are predominantly Christians and animists, have demanded a separate state, largely on the argument that they are a distinct ethnic nation, apart and separate from traditions common to the plains of India. Kashmiri nationalism has not revolved around Islam but has been a product of Kashmir's history and geography. At the same time, Kashmiri separatists are largely Muslims and Nagas are mainly Christians. Is the violence in Punjab, Nagaland, and Kashmir a product of economic and political grievances or is it an outcome of religious differences? It is difficult to separate the different sources of violence. In this chapter, however, I draw a distinction between nationalities (commonly referred to as ethnic conflicts) with and without geographically compact homelands. Both demand autonomy but the latter are unable to demand separation and therefore do not pose a danger to India's territorial integrity. As minorities (some may prefer to call them nationalities), they call for a different order of preventive strategy. Kashmiris are, then, a nationality; Muslims in Mumbai are part of the larger minority population of Indian Muslims. Eruption of violence calls for use of the coercive arm of the state, namely, first police and then the army in each instance, but the political context and hence the preventive measures used in Kashmir will be different from those needed to defuse riots in Mumbai.

Third, we need to consider the geography of religious violence. Religious conflicts need not be territorial in nature. One might argue that Islamic *jihadis* in Pakistan want to not only wrest the Muslim majority province of Kashmir from India but also to erase the boundaries of Pakistan. They seek to establish an Islamic republic that would include all the contiguous Muslim concentration areas in the region. In contrast, not all Sikh nationalists wanted a separate state of Khalistan. Most Punjabi Sikhs aspired to equal status, larger economic investment, and greater cultural and political autonomy from the Indian state.[18] Territoriality is not, then, implicit in religiously-based conflict. By the same token, there is the notion of sacred space that cuts across boundaries of the currently constituted territorial state. Many Sikh holy shrines are in present Pakistan; Muslim Kashmiris live on both sides of the disputed border and a large number of Pakistani citizens have families and friends cross the border in India. The extremists among the Hindu nationalists also talk about erasing the present Indo-Pakistan border and recreating the undivided India in their quest for the Hindu Rashtra (the Hindu state). History, religion, ethnicity, and ideologies thus link Pakistan and Bangladesh to India. There is, nevertheless, a tension between this sacred geography and sovereign territoriality.

Fourth, it is important to map the frequency and patterns of violence before designing a preventive strategy. While popular perception and press suggest that religiously-based violence is widespread and endemic, scholars stress that not to be the case. Most India scholars agree that such violence is largely confined to several riot-prone cities and small towns and that rural India is largely free from Hindu–Muslim violence. From his study of Hindu–Muslim riots from 1947 to 1995, Varshney concludes that riots do not occur all over India. He identifies four of India's 28 states, and primarily eight cities aas riot prone.[19]

Fifth, it is equally important to desegregate violence on the basis of organization and scope. The Hindu–Muslim conflict in India is more in the nature of a riot than an insurgency or war. Riots occur but they do not lead to wars with foreign powers. Insurgencies are in the nature of civil wars. They require a durable organization, access to weapons and planning on the part of the insurgents, and frequently support from an ethnic kin state.[20] The Kashmir insurgency could not be sustained without support from the Pakistani government at some level. While insurgencies are against a state and usually about territorial control or denying the same to the state, riots are an entirely different category of violence. They are almost always localized and move along a different ladder of escalation compared to insurgencies and wars. Riots are far from controlled events in that even those who initially trigger riots may lose control over the chain of violent retaliations. At the same time, riots are not as spontaneous as reported in the press. There is always some element of organization even if it is a jerry-rigged alliance of riot specialists and musclemen. "Rioters display a mixture of lucid calculation and irrational passion in their behavior, carefully targeting their victims but finding emotional release in their killing."[21] "Sparks that lead to the outbreak of violence can come from events at the national, state, or local level, and can range from rumors of the killing of a sacred cow to destruction of a holy place broadcast to millions by radio or TV. Responses to those sparks may be as mild as increased ethnic tension or as virulent as deadly ethnic riots."[22] On the other hand, religious wars are the kind that took place in Afghanistan during the 1990s and Sudan in recent years. Such conflicts are usually about territory, power and office.[23]

Sixth and last, that conflict cannot be avoided in an openly competitive society but frequent violence is an indication of failure to resolve conflicts through elections. Similarly, religiosity does not automatically lead to conflict and violence. And those who wage wars based on religion are not necessarily a pious lot. The destruction of the sixteenth-century mosque in Ayodhya, Uttar Pradesh in 1992, did not increase adherence to religion among Hindus. Dilip Awasthi and Uday Mahurkar describe in details how the 60,000 Kar Sevaks had been trained by retired Indian military officers prior to the December 6, 1992 onslaught on the Babri Mosque in Ayodhya.[24] Such militarist actions have no legitimacy in Hindu religious faith. The elements that are essential to the formation of identity differ from those that precipitate violence.

## Anatomy of religious violence in Asia: strategies for prevention

There are two broad strategies for preventing communal violence. In one, policy proposals revolve around what one might do before, during, and after the riots to prevent reoccurrence. The second is less event-oriented. It focuses on long-term solutions and details what is needed to establish communal harmony. The first set of proposals, largely the outcome of numerous commissions of inquiries and reports, focus on administrative, law enforcement, and policy measures that state, local, and central governments, courts and police can undertake to prevent violence. The Sri Krishna Commission report following the 1992–93 riots in Mumbai (henceforth the SKC) and Citizen's *Independent Fact Finding Mission* following the 2002 Gujarat riots (the *Mission* henceforth) are among the most comprehensive recommendations of this genre and in the following they are presented as representative of scores of similar inquiries. The second set of strategies focus on social conditions and political and economic causes of violence. Ashutosh Varshney, Steven Wilkinson, Atul Kohli, Donald Horowitz, and Paul Brass in their writings have recommended long-term reforms to prevent religious violence. Their recommendations call for a deepening of substantive democracy, creation of vibrant inter-religious civic associations or greater plurality of political parties and creation of institutions – such as a consociational political system for power sharing and local self-government. The coalition strategy I have proposed combines elements of both law enforcement and civil society organization.

### *The law enforcement perspective and the Sri Krishna Commission*

According to most public reports, the 1992 Mumbai riots were triggered by spontaneous protests by Mumbai Muslims in response to the destruction of the Babri Mosque in Ayodhya.[25] The visual pictures of Kar Sevaks destroying the mosque with pick-axes proved inflammatory and led to sporadic violence – stabbings and burning of property – all over India, but especially in Mumbai. According to *India Today*, the destruction of the Babri Mosque led to riot deaths everywhere. Within three weeks following the attack on the mosque, the death toll from police firing and Hindu–Muslim clashes was: 246 dead in Gujarat, 120 in Madhya Pradesh, 259 in Maharashtra, 100 in Assam, 32 in West Bengal, 201 in Uttar Pradesh, 48 in Rajasthan, 24 in Bihar, 12 in Kerala, 12 in Andhra Pradesh,

60 in Karnataka, and 2 in Tamil Nadu.[26] In the wake of the nation-wide campaign to mobilize Kar Sevaks, the Hindus in Mumbai, particularly in strongholds of the extreme Hindu nationalist Shiv Sena (Army of Shiva) political party, had already begun celebration rallies, shouting of anti-Muslim slogans, and aggressive displays of religious rituals in mixed neighborhoods. The SKC writes, "after a brief lull of December 1992" violence was precipitated by the Hindus who "brought to fever pitch ... propaganda unleashed by Hindu communal organizations and writings in newspapers like 'Saamna' and 'Navakal.'"[27] The Shiv Sena and its leaders continued to whip up communal frenzy by their statements and acts and writings while the Shiv Sena Pramukh (leader) Bal Thackeray continued to issue directive to his cadres. According to the SKC report:

> The attitude of Shiv Sena as reflected in the Time interview given by Bal Thackeray and its doctrine of "retaliation" ... together with the thinking of Shiv Sainiks that Shiv Sena's terror was the true guarantee of the safety of citizens, were responsible for the vigilantism of Shiv Sainiks. Because some criminal Muslims killed innocent Hindus in one corner of the city, the Shiv Sainiks "retaliated" against several innocent Muslims in other corners of the city.[28]

These riots could have been prevented had the initial killing been exposed as an act by criminals and firm action taken to prevent second-stage retaliation.

The Commission blamed the entire machinery of the state from the local police stations to the police commissioners and top officials of law enforcement, the top leadership in the Maharashtra government who delayed, prevaricated, or plainly encouraged the Shiv Sena cadres and the criminal elements employed by them to "teach Muslims a lesson" in humility. It recommended extensive reforms for the police and judicial bodies and punishment and expulsion of any government employee, police, or administrator complicit in riots or negligent in preventing violence. The report stressed the need to make law enforcement agencies free from political interference and underscored the danger in making the local police a tool of the ruling party and government in power. The commission also noted the role of media and press in spreading rumors and inciting mobs into a frenzy.

The *Mission* report of Gujarat riots in 2002 goes beyond the recommendations made by the SKC. The *Mission* recommended imposition of the president's rule in Gujarat and dismissal of the Narendra Modi's state government. It urged that the role of sections of the media, particularly the Gujarati language press, should be investigated by the Press Council, and disciplinary action be taken. The Human Rights Commission report on Gujarat 2002 urged the international donors to make all aid conditional upon implementation of many of the above recommendations.[29]

The SKC recommendations as well as other reports of previous inquiries remain confined to legal/administrative measures and depend on the state and its agencies for disrupting violence. The SKC is occupied with what can be done when violence breaks out, it does not deal with the historical, socio-economic, and deeply political dimensions of communal violence. As the section on the historical and theoretical context argues, these dimensions are critical to strategies that can prevent Hindu–Muslim violence. Not bound by constraints that limit the SKC, several social scientists have put forward alternative sets of conflict theories and preventive strategies.

### Democracy, civic associations, and party competition

In the second genre of preventive strategies, civic organizations and political institutions play a key role. Ashutosh Varshney, for instance, argues that on its own and free from popular pressure, the state is unlikely to act with speed and dispatch or remain above partisan politics.[30] Based on opposite pairs of violence-prone and violence-free cities with a comparable social milieu, Varshney concludes that "pre-existing local networks of civic engagement between the Hindu–Muslim communities are the single most important predictor of whether a community will respond violently to ethnic provocations."[31] Varshney's argument presumes a certain relationship between the structure of civic life and the presence or absence of religious violence. He found that communities that are most peaceful had local associations that made their members aware of the dangers of ethnic violence and worked to suppress the violent and criminal elements interested in exploiting ethnic antipathies. Local civic associations – including trade unions, professional organizations, and political parties – whose members cut across ethnic lines were effective in killing rumors, improving communication, and exerting pressure on violent elements at the local level.

Strategies that focus on issues of equal status and representation for the minority are a variant on the "deepening democracy" theme. Khushwant Singh has argued for a greater percentage of Muslim recruitment in police and law enforcement.[32] A slightly different emphasis emerges in Atul Kohli's reasons why violence and conflict occurs. He traces these to decay of political institutions, endemic corruption, and political interference leading to the decline in state capacities. Kohli therefore recommends strengthening governance mechanisms and introducing measures to make institutions free of partisan interference.[33] Donald Horowitz, a leading scholar of ethnic conflict, places his faith in "multi-polar fluidity," that is, the existence of a variety of cleavages which cancel out and prevent rival religious communities from violent clashes. For example he observes that in the two cities of Lucknow and Calicut where serious Hindu–Muslim cleavages did not exist, because cleavages of a different kind took precedence.[34] Civic association alone did not hold peace and was not the explanation for why these cities were more peaceful. Obviously, Horowitz thinks Varshney's faith in civil society organization as the single most important preventive strategy is misplaced. In Lucknow, the Sunni–Shia divide blunted the edge of the Hindu–Muslim divide, while in Calicut, a town in Kerala, the presence of a large Christian community prevented polarization strictly along Hindu–Muslim lines.

Steven Wilkinson's study of riot-torn cities in India leads to parallel propositions about relations between multiple political cleavages and communal peace. He

143

focuses on the implications of party competition for minority interests.[35] In Wilkinson's view, the greater the number of effective parties competing for power in a state, the more valuable minority voters become. This has long been true in Southern India. For example, Kerala and Tamil Nadu have the lowest levels of Hindu–Muslim violence, largely because of cross-cutting cleavages created by emergence of middle and lower caste-based parties, strong party competition, and frequent changes of the ruling party. A minority was better protected when it constituted a swing vote in highly contested competitive elections.

### Why the above strategies might not work

Although the above proposals provide valuable insights into the causes of religiously-based violence and ways to defuse and prevent it, their single cause and single agency focus is misleading. Let us take a closer look at why proposals based on civic organization alone or the state alone or restoration of equity and representation alone, will not work and why we need an interim strategy that combines short-term law and order proposals with measures to strengthen civil society interventions. An analysis of the above strategies also shows the importance of building a violence-control system that extends vertically through state and national government as well as horizontally into civil society and party organizations.

Reliance on the state alone is hazardous as the first genre of strategies – the SKC and other inquiries – show. The SKC is flawed in placing the state at the center of responsibility since it is also to blame for negligence and complicity. This flaw however points to the need to further disaggregate government capacity to prevent violence at different levels. If the local constabulary is implicated or incapable of performing its duty free of bias and if the local politicians are a party to violence, the Central Reserve Police Force (CRPF) and/or constabulary from other states should be deployed. The Central Reserve Police has a reputation for relatively effective and non-partisan enforcement of law and order.[36] While in the short run these can restore order, longer-term measures require reforming the police and steps to establish accountability.

Civil society dependent proposals are equally problematic. The first question raised by Varshney's proposal is: Why do pre-existing communal ties weaken, and if weakened, how can such ties be rebuilt in the middle of a riot? Second, how do we predict who will prevail in the tug of war between civic associations and ambitious politicians, particularly when the latter seek to mobilize support with appeals to religious sentiment? Following Varshney's arguments we are compelled to conclude that if peace held, civic associations are strong, if it failed, they are weak. That does not take us very far in predicting where and when riots might occur or how to rebuild civic associations once riots have broken out. It is possible to argue that peace might hold even if civic associations are weak, if the local political entrepreneurs have weak motives to incite the masses or if the "triggering event" is not emotionally potent to get the public riled up about alleged actions of a rival community or there are cross-cutting cleavages as Horowitz suggests in his analysis of violence-free Lucknow and Calicut.

We need to consider two additional questions as we look at the role of civic associations: What kind of civic associations can a deeply prejudiced and divided civil society produce? And, can common economic interests in maintaining peace and preventing destruction of property (keeping shops and businesses open) be strong enough to forestall an emotional storm created by a triggering incident? There is good reason to believe that in India's segregated society, communities will not be free from prejudices. Although local dynamics are paramount, community perceptions might become linked to national ideologies. The resulting violence then becomes symbolic of a community's identity and its vengeance.[37] The *Mission* report on the "Gujarat Carnage 2002" details the plight of Justice Kadri, a high court judge in Ahmedabad, who had to hide and run with his family after being warned by the police that many among their ranks could not be trusted, nor could he rely on his Hindu neighbors to protect him.[38] This is because there could be a vein of resentment and prejudice running deep under the surface of routine social interaction. How effective can Varshney's civic associations be under these circumstances?

Can the common economic interests of Hindus and Muslims in preserving peace triumph over the votaries of violence? While common interests will put a brake on violence and destruction of property, the connection between economic interests and peace has been tentative at best. If the proximate ethnic communities are economic competitors, rivalry might in fact widen the rift. In 1969, the Hindu criminal elements in Ahmedabad incited a riot to replace the Muslim hold over smuggling and illegal trade in liquor. "Cleansing" of neighborhoods might be incited by a cabal of interests representing real estate builders and their criminal cohorts in towns and cities of India. The suggestion that peace will hold if there are civic associations – and will not if there are none – can be turned on its head to argue that ethnic peace is conducive to formation of such association. Repeated experience of riots will, however, make it extremely difficult to forge common ties.[39] This is not to suggest that inter-communal civic associations are unimportant or not desirable. Indeed, they can play an important role in putting the brakes on the progress of a would-be riot. But they cannot alone and without the support from state authorities, stop religiously-based violence.

The third preventive measure advocated by Khushwant Singh and others, namely, greater minority representation in state-level ministries and cabinets, is desirable but not likely to be effective in itself. Andhra Pradesh and Madhya Pradesh have a far higher percentage of Muslims in the government and ministries but have far higher levels of violence than in Kerala and Bengal where the comparative percentages of Muslim ministers are much lower. Wilkinson shows that the two states with reputations for extremely weak state administration – Uttar Pradesh and Bihar – were highly successful in preventing violence when clear orders were issued by political leaders to act forcefully. Wilkinson comments that in 1995, "most strikingly the coalition BJP–BSP government successfully prevented a repeat of the Ayodhya violence by restricting VHP plans to mobilize around another disputed religious site at Mathura."[40] When the state acts it is able to prevent violence from spreading.

Although Wilkinson's highly illuminating study of religiously-based violence in India adds much to our knowledge about party competition and minority vote, we cannot always easily obtain the kind of political demography and party politics he requires for the cross-cutting cleavages to work. His argument that political leaders will hesitate to trigger or encourage riots if minority voters occupy significant position in electoral calculations, presumes the presence of a minority community in significant numbers in a state to be able to make a difference in elections. In addition, this minority must be united and well organized in a solid bloc to become a swing vote. This combination of factors is present only in some parts of India. In other places, we have to fall back on state protection, unbiased policing, political parties and leaders committed to minority rights, and policies that work to ensure a sense of safety and well-being for the vulnerable population. In other words, we must rely on a coalition of anti-riot interests activated well before sporadic violence becomes a full-scale riot.

## A coalition strategy: an alternative preventive measure

The strategies of Wilkinson, Varshney, Kohli, and Horowitz envisage a deepening of democracy, greater accountability, a balanced party competition, and a vigilant and unbiased public. Undoubtedly, more democracy is in itself highly desirable but the procedures of democracy have an ambiguous relationship with violence, at least in South Asia. Frequently, democracy has meant more competition for office, power, and control over resources of the state. Democracy then tends to be contentious and in a segmented society such as India can lead to conflict and violence. While this is true, it is also true that violence has a pattern, an identifiable political geography. It does not occur everywhere, all over India or occur all the time. This underscores the need to disaggregate the geography of violence in order to build preventive procedures for riot-prone areas.

Desegregation of the geography of violence points to windows of opportunity to build an interim process, a mechanism that can begin to mobilize state agencies in the affected areas at the first hint of communal tensions. Since riots escalate when they become linked to a wider circle of actors and demography, preventive strategies should establish coalitions of multiple actors, positioned at different levels of society ranging from the federal-national agencies to local state-level agencies. These actors must have real constituencies in political parties and civic groups that are opposed to religious polarization of society.

The answer to religious violence is in building in advance and activating when required vertical and horizontal coalitions of anti-riot interests and support groups in bureaucracy, citizenry, business association, and law enforcement agencies. These coalitions are vertical in that they include both the central state and local bodies; they are horizontal in that they include civic associations, community organizations, cultural clubs, citizen's committees, and business and student associations. It is imperative that such coalitions focus on preventing the second-stage retaliation. To counteract complicit or partisan behavior, the state and civic agencies should evolve a mechanism for reciprocal monitoring. Such coalitions are not unknown in India but unfortunately they have emerged on an ad hoc basis and been activated only after the frenzy of killings and destruction of property has occurred. For coalitions to be effective, they have to be in place and activated as soon as a situation displays potential for violent escalation.

Brass's seminal work on Hindu–Muslim violence underscores the importance of anti-riot coalitions in which the state forges a partnership with the civic associations and anti-violence constituencies. Brass's fieldwork and interviews in two instances of riots in the city of Kanpur is highly instructive. He found that riots are produced by precipitating events that generate a chain which "if not contained immediately will lead to a major conflagration."[41] He found that the absence of second-stage reaction prevented further violence. When the respondents were asked why they refrained from second-stage retaliation, the answer invariably was that they felt a sense of trust in the state government and in the local authorities that the situation would be brought under control. A combination of threats "both from another group and from the state and the authorities is required or is at least contributory to the movement of a riot into the dynamics of a chain reaction."[42] It then follows that if the police act with speed and dispatch – banning processions, preventing emotionally charged public rituals, and quickly arresting "troublemakers" (who are the riot specialists to use Brass's term) – the chain can be broken. In other words, the police, the parties, and the state at both local and national level must be involved in stopping the violence. If the local authorities fail, the federal authorities must rapidly step in to fill the power vacuum and watch over the actions of local authorities. Who will make them do this? This is where the horizontal coalition of anti-violence interests and constituencies become critical. They will make the political parties, state authorities, and even federal government pay the price for neglect.

It is important that the federal authorities do not draw hasty or inappropriate conclusions from local violence. Home Minister Advani should have refrained from linking the events in Godhra with Pakistan and its intelligence agencies the day after the burning of the rail compartments occurred. No investigation had been launched, and no evidence was available to support such a charge. If the public believes that they are participating in a larger historical movement, they are more likely to succumb to the exhortations by communal organizations encouraging them to "right the wrong." This is why, according to Brass, the public response to Ayodhya and the VHP attempt to mobilize the masses was so successful in 1992, while the attempt to mobilize around the killing of Kala Baccha in Kanpur two years later failed. The killing of Kala Baccha was not connected to any large historical memories or events. Kala Baccha was a criminal boss turned politician. The public simply saw through BJP attempts to whip up popular sentiment and did not respond to it.[43]

Is the Indian state capable of building such coalitions and undertaking the necessary reform of police and other state agencies? And if it needs to be forced into enacting reforms, can the Indian democracy generate sufficient popular pressure to push for them? Answers to these questions will depend on how one characterizes the Indian political system, its central state, the center-state relations, and competitive party democracy. Although there is no consensus among students of India about the nature of the Indian state or its democracy, it is important to remember that the Indian state is not a homogenous monolith, but a conglomeration of many conflicting factions and interests. It is necessary therefore to guard against a simplistic connection between state weakness and communal violence. According to Wilkinson, "independent investigations into the very worst cases of violence have all identified the state government's lack of purpose and clear orders, rather than any lack of state strength, as the key factor prolonging the violence."[44] He quotes the Reddy Commission appointed after the September 1969 Ahmedabad riots and notes that "the Inspector General of Police before advising the commissioner was not prepared to act on his own and was trying to seek the prior approval of the government."[45] Evidently a similar pattern of confusion and negligence explains the delays in deploying force when riots occurred in Ranchi (1967), Bhagalpur (1989), and Mumbai (1992–93).

If there is an established anti-riot mechanism that can be activated at the first hint of tensions, violence can be avoided or minimized. Some elements of the state and its agencies may be biased but others that are capable of imposing law and order may be confused rather than complicit. It is possible therefore to build a coalition of interested segments that would support reform and checkmate local riot systems by joining other segments within the state that are opposed to the weakening of political institutions. Such a coalition of interests could be reinforced by generating a degree of discrete support from those in civic society most hurt by violence.

One might argue that the number of individuals benefiting from the corrupt local nexus of politicians, police, and criminal elements that constitute a riot-ready system is still a minority. And the central government and its policing and administrative arms may have little to gain from local riots. Both these agencies can act in tandem as an arm of the anti-riot system. Can the coalition of anti-riot forces – official and civic – become stronger than those benefiting from riots and currently in power in many cities and towns of India? The answer depends on the system of incentives and rewards that the anti-riot network is able to provide. The purpose of state and party patronage needs to be reoriented, rewarding those who stand up in a sustained manner for peace as opposed to those who perpetrate violence in pursuit of immediate interests. What the coalition strategy offers is not a riot-proof system. It will not work when the local and central state belongs to the same political party with an anti-Muslim agenda. This was evident in Gujarat in 2002. Riots may not then be prevented in every instance but they can be localized and isolated and prevented from spreading in many more instances than is the case at present.

## Summation and conclusions

The above analysis of prevention shows that religious conflicts have a subtext: economic inequalities, social discrimination, and victimization. Once violence breaks out, as it did in Godhra and then the rest of Gujarat in 2002 and earlier in

148

Mumbai, the whole community belonging to a particular religion becomes a target of violence. Such violence is derived from cultural exclusiveness, arguments about living space and first claims to citizenship, desire to "right the historic wrong" or simply from desire to seek revenge for previous acts of violence. These conflicts come to be seen as "religious" conflicts irrespective of their origin and cause. They come to be so defined because of the historical context within which they occur and the ways in which they are represented in the popular discourse, media and press.

It is noteworthy that the violence in Kashmir, although waged largely by a Muslim majority in that province, is not characterized as a religious conflict. The Indian strategies to prevent violence in Kashmir range from militarization of the dispute with Pakistan to offer of greater autonomy, restoration of the special status to the state of Jammu and Kashmir, economic assistance, and fencing of the border with Pakistan. None of these strategies are applicable in the case of Hindu–Muslim violence. Although transnational connections to Hindu–Muslim violence have existed since independence, these have compelled the Indian Muslims to in fact renounce ties with Pakistan or Kashmir. On the other hand, the Hindu nationalists have found justifications in making Muslims the targets of violence by branding them as the "fifth column" for Pakistan. The rise of Hindu nationalism has no doubt made the Hindu–Muslim violence more difficult to check but it is not beyond the scope of reasonable negotiations or democratic politics. The Muslim organizations in India do not see their conditions as a "clash of values" or cultures, nor do they identify with the international agenda of Al Qaeda. The Indian Muslim demands are negotiable.

Questions still remain as to why preventive strategies have failed in the past and why even the coalition strategy proposed here offers at best, an imperfect solution to violence. The answer lies in the contradictory forces of history, modernization, and globalization. In fact, we have only a partial and largely inadequate understanding of how these forces breed violence.

If European history is an example, India's progress towards modernization and globalization should have erased or marginalized "ancient hatred" and replaced it with a new secular and humanitarian ethic. The process of modernization implies triumph of rationality over narrow claims of parochial and primordial identities. The study of social violence in India and elsewhere, however, shows that modernization has brought more, not less violence in its wake; the march to individual freedom has been a mixed blessing and at times a serious disadvantage.

Mark Juergensmeyer, Ashis Nandy, and Partha Chatterjee point out that the Indian state and its politics is artificial, predatory, and operates in a spiritual vacuum.[46] The state's modernist secular declaration prevents it from drawing on the embedded traditions of tolerance and coexistence rooted in the subcontinent's life and society. Alienated from everything that provided a sense of self-worth and community, a modern urban, middle class Indian is ready fodder to the communal nationalism, whether Hindu or Islamic. For this set of scholars, Gandhian politics which combined rational thought with traditional values of cooperation not competition, tolerance not conversion, sacrifice not aggression, represents the real and authentic, homegrown solution to the endemic violence. The question still arises as to how to select traditions that sustain the humanist ethic and abandon those that reinforce prejudice. Certain traditions sustain the said ethics of harmony and peace; other popular traditions do the opposite. Traditions do not live in a vacuum; they require an integrated set of social institutions to sustain them. These institutions can be extremely unequal and hierarchical (such as caste) as they are in India. So what do we do? Do we sacrifice social justice to secure communal harmony? It is not clear whether religious and ethnic violence in India is a product of modernization, competition and social alienation, or a result of perverted modernization. There is no going back however. Modernization is here to stay even if it only liberates individuals to participate in violence free from traditional and customary restraints.

If we don't understand the relationship between modernization and violence, we also don't fully understand the connection between violence and the point of origin. Most studies of riots indicate that it is best to keep violence confined to the locale where it breaks out. Can we prevent violence by doing just the opposite, namely integrating India into the global markets and its concomitant ideologies of universal human rights and global commons? One might argue that the Indian state could be made to pay a price for failing to arrest Hindu–Muslim violence: loss of incomes, drying up of global investments, restrictions on travel, and economic uncertainties and denial of access to loans and aid from donor agencies. The concern over international image, which is important for a steady flow of global capital, might compel cities and towns to close down riot systems and compete with each other to earn a reputation for probity, prosperity, stability, and efficiency. Unfortunately, there are other global connections that do the opposite. The Gujarat riots of 2002 show that the links can be pernicious. For the past decade and a half, expatriate Gujaratis and diasporic Indians, have been investing in real estate and other businesses in Gujarat. A large number among them however support the BJP and its family of Hindu militant organizations. The international links in fact intensified the tensions and added an edge to the violence in Gujarat. Globalization is hardly an unmixed blessing when we consider its ambiguous impact on inter-community relations.

Third, we only partially understand the links between state capacity and patterns of violence. Does a weak state produce violence? Does a strong state help prevent it or will the use of coercion in fact aggravate the inter-community tensions? It is important to define what we mean by state capacity. Equating it with coercive strength alone is patently wrong. State capacity ought to be measured in how efficiently a state is able to resolve conflicts before they go beyond electoral politics. Institutional capacity to solve tensions at the point where they originate will prevent escalation. State capacity, alone, however, is no guarantee of inter-community peace.

To sum up, there is no single strategy to prevent Hindu–Muslim violence in India. Even the coalition strategy proposed here cannot guarantee peace. It is limited by the alignment of political and ideological forces at a given time. It can however prove to be an important learning process even when it fails – an opportunity for mutual recognition among civic associations and state authorities that they have a common interest in preventing religious violence. The coalition strategy will provide the framework within which such a learning process can take place. In building coalitions, agencies and actors learn a great deal about each other, styles of leadership and strengths and weaknesses, the operational dynamics of what needs to be done, and who needs to be contacted specifically to prevent violence. These coalitions need nurturing and constant repair to make the pieces fit and work well. This is not an easy task by any measure but it is an important one if India is to build a strong and secular and liberal democracy.

# Notes

1 "Crime Against Humanity," People's Union for Civil Liberties Bulletin, January 2003, http://www.pucl. org/topics/religion-communalism/2003/gujarat-tribunal-report.htm. Also see Murad Banaji, "Recent Communal Violence in Guarat, India," August 2002, http://www.kioni.u-net.com/stopwarfiles/gujarat.html.

2 The report by the Commission of Inquiry into the Gujarat 2002 riots concluded that the fire had been accidental and not a deliberate act to murder Hindus. "Report on India Train Fire," Reuters, January 18, 2005.

3 Ibid.

4 Banaji, "Recent Communal Violence."

5 Ashutosh Varshney, *Ethnic Conflict and Civic Life: Hindus and Muslims in India* (New Haven, CT: Yale University Press, 2002), 95–106.

6 Peter Gottschalk and Wendy Doniger, *Beyond Hindu and Muslim, Multiple Identity in Narrative from Rural India* (New York: Oxford University Press, 2001); Paul R. Brass, *The Production of Hindu–Muslim Violence in Contemporary India* (Seattle: University of Washington Press, 2003); N.S. Saksena, *Communal Riots in India* (Noida: Trishul, 1990); Paul R. Brass, *Riots and Pogroms* (New York: New York University Press, 1996); Thomas B. Hansen, *The Saffron Wave, Democracy and Hindu Nationalism in Modern India* (Princeton, NJ: Princeton University Press, 1999); Ram Puniyani, *Communal Politics: Facts Versus Myths* (New Delhi: Sage Publications, 2003).

7 Ahmed Rashid, *Taliban, Militant Islam, Oil and Fundamentalism in Central Asia* (New Haven, CT: Yale University Press, 2000), 183–96.

8 T.R. Gurr, "Assessment for Hindus in Bangladesh," Minorities at Risk Project, University of Maryland, Center for International Development and Conflict Management, College Park, MD, 2000, http://www. cidcm.umd.edu/inscr/mar/ assessment.asp?groupId=77102.

9 Mushirul Hasan, *Legacy of a Divided Nation: India's Muslims Since Independence* (Mumbai: Oxford University Press, 1997), 25–57; Tai Y. Tan and Gyanesh Kudaisya, *The Aftermath of Partition in South Asia* (London: Routledge, 2000), 14.

10 Hasan, *Divided Nation*, 168–77.

11 Kuldip Nayar, "The Two-Nation Theory," *Countercurrents.org*, August 10, 2003, http://www. countercurrents.org/ipk-nayar100803.htm.

12 Hasan, *Divided Nation*, 281–7.

13 Ibid., 260–9.

14 Kamal M. Chenoy et al., *Gujarat Carnage 2002: A Report to the Nation by an Independent Fact Finding Mission* (New Delhi: Jawaharlal Nehru University, 2002), 14.

15 Ibid., 13.

16 Hasan, *Divided Nation*, 264.

17  Varshney, *Ethnic Conflict*, 4.
18  Maya Chadda, *Ethnicity, Security and Separatism in India* (New York: Columbia University Press, 1997), 126.
19  Varshney, *Ethnic Conflict*, 119–71.
20  Rajat Ganguly, *Kin State Intervention in Ethnic Conflicts* (New Delhi: Sage Publications, 1998), 9–38.
21  Judy Barsalou, "Lethal Ethnic Riots: Lessons From India and Beyond," Special Report 101, United States Institute for Peace, Washington DC, February 2003, 1.
22  Ibid.
23  Larry Goodson, *Afghanistan's Endless War: State Failure, Regional Politics and the Rise of the Taliban* (Seattle: University of Washington Press, 2001), 54–91.
24  Dilip Awasthi and Uday Muhurkar, "Orchestrated Onslaught," *India Today*, December 31, 1992, 54.
25  Sri Krishna Commission, Government of India, *Preventive Measures and Riot Control Measures Taken by Police*, Chapter 4, http://www.dalitstan.org/mughalstan/qat/frishna.
26  "Bloody Aftermath," *India Today*, December 31, 1992, 58–61.
27  SKC, *Preventive Measures*.
28  Ibid.
29  Smita Narula, "'We Have No Orders to Save You' State Participation and Complicity in Communal Violence in Gujarat," HRW Report 14, no. 3, Human Rights Watch, April 2002, 11, http://www.hrw.org/ reports/2002/india/Gujarat.pdf.
30  Ashutosh Varshney, "Making the State Behave Well," *Indian Express*, April 23, 2002.
31  Barsalou, "Lethal Ethnic Riots," 8.
32  Khushwant Singh, *Hindustan Times*, October 15, 1969, cited in Omar Khalidi, *Indian Muslims since Independence* (New Delhi: Vikas, 1995), 37.
33  Atul Kohli, "Roots of Sectarian Conflict" (lecture for Asian Social Issues Program, New York, March 7, 2002), http://www.asiasource.org/asip/kohli.cfm; Atul Kohli, *Democracy and Discontent: India's Growing Crisis of Governability* (Cambridge: Cambridge University Press, 1990), 217.
34  Barsalou, "Lethal Ethnic Riots," 9.
35  Steven Wilkinson, "Putting Gujarat in Perspective," *Economic and Political Weekly* 37, no. 17 (2002): 1579–83, http://www.epw.org.in/showArticles.php?root=2002&leaf=04&filename=4387&filetype= html.
36  National Commission for Minorities, *Second Annual Report (FY 1994–1995)*, Government of India (New Delhi, 1997), 111–12. The Rapid Action Force, specifically raised to deal with the problem of communal riots, had only slightly higher Muslim representation than the CRPF, at 6.9 percent.
37  Internal migration had led to violence between Biharis and Assamese when the Ranvir Sena in Bihar and the United Liberation Front of Assam clashed in incidents of retaliatory violence. See Paolienlal Haokip, "Bihar–Assam Violence," IPCS Issue Brief, Institute of Peace and Conflict Studies, New Delhi, December, 2003.
38  Chenoy et al., *Gujarat Carnage 2002*, 16.
39  Rajesh Joshi, "Test Flights of the Hindutva Dream, For the Sangh, Gujarat is Ideal for its Saffron Experiment," *Outlook*, 1999, http://www.geocities.com/indianfascism/fascism/role_govtpolice.htm.
40  Wilkinson, "Gujarat in Perspective."
41  Paul R. Brass, *Theft of an Idol, Text and Context in the Representation of Collective Violence* (Princeton, NJ: Princeton University Press, 1997), 257.
42  Ibid.
43  Ibid., 258.
44  Wilkinson, "Gujarat in Perspective," 1579–83.
45  Ibid.

46 Mark Juergensmeyer, *The New Cold War? Religious Nationalism Confronts the Secular State* (Berkeley, CA: University of California Press, 1993); Ashis Nandy, "The Politics of Secularism and Recovery of Religious Tolerance," in *Mirrors of Violence: Communities, Riots, and Survivors in South Asia*, ed. Veena Das (New York: Oxford University Press, 1990), 69–93; Partha Chatterjee, "Secularism and Toleration," *Economic and Political Weekly* 29, (1994): 1768–77, reprinted in Partha Chatterjee, *A Possible World: Essays in Political Criticism* (Delhi: Oxford University Press, 1997).

# 10

# VIOLENCE AND THE LONG ROAD TO RECONCILIATION IN SOUTHERN THAILAND[1]

*Joseph Chinyong Liow*

... the fact remains that religious violence is not, ultimately, about economics, political power, or even territory. It is about conflicting sacred visions, prophetic pronouncements, and eschatological expectations. ... The goal of the violence is religious and spiritual and the rewards are based upon divine promise and eternal life – Charles Selengut, Sacred Fury.

... they were bloody crazy, which means they must be high on drugs. I have never seen normal people who are as courageous and crazy – General Chaisit Shinawatra on the 32 militants killed in Krisek Mosque on April 28, 2004.

You must kill all of them, those outside the religion around you, so they will know you, who have faith, are strong as well – Excerpt from Chapter 7, Berjihad di Patani.

These lunatics do it every day ... They are insane and I am insane enough not to be scared of them. The attacks were carried out indiscriminately by mad people and radical Islamic terrorists – Prime Minister Thaksin Shinawatra on the bomb blast in Narathiwat on August 26, 2004, a day before he made a visit to the province.

Against the backdrop of a century-long ethno-nationalist conflict between the Thai state and its restive Malay-Muslim provinces in the south, January 2004 witnessed for the first time the targeting of religious targets when three monks were murdered by men apparently clad in Islamic dress. Later on April 28, 2004, Thai security forces decimated a 400-year-old mosque in the process of quelling an outbreak of violence that proved to be the boldest attack by militants in recent history. Copies of a manuscript, written in Jawi, titled *Berjihad di Patani* (The Conduct of Holy War in Pattani) were found on the bodies of seven of the militants killed in the violence. Following this incident, bomb blasts rocked three Buddhist temples in the Muslim-dominated Narathiwat province in May, and Muslim religious teachers continue to "mysteriously disappear" as security forces indiscriminately raid Islamic schools throughout the south.

This train of violence has fundamentally ruptured the texture of socio-political life in southern Thailand, which consists of the Malay-Muslim dominated provinces of Narathiwat, Pattani, Yala, Songkhla, and Satun, and polarized society by creating a climate of mutual distrust and suspicion between Muslim and Buddhist communities.[2] This chapter examines the seemingly endless stream of violence and bloodshed in southern Thailand. It begins with an attempt to capture, conceptualize, and articulate the nature of the latest manifestations of southern Thai violence. Following this, it reflects on the short and long run strategies of disrupting and delegitimizing violence by way of a discussion of the problems and prospects associated with present policies of the Thaksin administration. This reflection is all the more imperative, insofar as the fight against religious violence and terrorism is about winning hearts and minds. The chapter essentially makes two arguments: 1) against a historical backdrop of ethno-nationalist resistance, the nature of violence in Thailand's predominantly Malay-Muslim southern provinces has taken on a more religious flavour, and insofar as the broader political and security situation is concerned this "Islamization" process will intensify more as a result of the Thaksin administration's own policies than the exertions of militants attempting to mobilize the Islamic idiom for their own causes, and 2) while not necessarily absolutized, the increasingly religious character of violence and the government's commitment to existing strategies, premised on a national security culture that perceives pluralism as a threat and questionable surveillance policies and tactics including the application of force and intimidation, both pose substantial hurdles to prospects for reconciliation and the delegitimization of violence in the south.

## Prevailing perspectives on southern Thai militancy

There has been a tendency among certain security experts to approach the topic of long-standing tensions between Muslim communities and secular states with the ongoing international war on terror as a point of entry. The problem with such an approach is self-evident when one considers how such works have privileged simplistic assumptions of Muslim resistance as expressions of a broader international *jihadi* struggle being conducted by well-connected Islamic terrorists, rather than complex and localized Muslim contestations against prevailing power configurations. Southeast Asia has not been spared such simplifications, and this is clearly evident in the phraseology of terrorism studies in the region today, where assumptions that it is a "crucible of terror" and "hotbed" of international terrorist activity comprising states that are "countries of convenience"; "hotbeds" are etymologically founded on rudimentary observations of Islam's greater visibility in everyday life and mainstream politics.[3] This tendency also underscores how, for example, many security experts tend to explain away Muslim resistance as a function of the negative influence of "fundamentalist" Wahhabi and Salafi theological strains with little attempt to consider how these abstract philosophies and ideologies relate specifically to Muslim concerns against the sociological, historical, and political backdrop of Southeast Asia, which may or may not invest them with meaning for everyday Muslims. This consideration is particularly trenchant in the case of the Malay-Muslim community in Thailand, where its long-standing resistance has never been driven by abstract or ideological rejection of modernity or "the West," but rather in opposition to Bangkok's attempts at assimilation. As to the question of international terrorist links, no experts or security and intelligence agencies (including the Thais themselves) have been able to demonstrate conclusively the existence of such links despite extravagant claims.[4] While there is no doubt that broad ideological links with Muslim struggles elsewhere in the world exist, insofar as the conduct of violence in southern Thailand is concerned there are primarily three characteristics to it that suggests it remains primarily an internal phenomenon. First, suicide bombing, which has been the key tactic of Al Qaeda and Jemaah Islamiyah strategies of asymmetrical warfare, has not surfaced in southern Thailand. Second, violence has primarily been targeted at symbols of the Thai state – police and military personnel, state officials, teachers, and Buddhist monks – and not the Western targets associated with many acts of international terrorism today. Finally, the arsenal of southern rebels consists predominantly of firebombs, machetes, and pistols. The elaborate use of explosive devices, used to devastating political effect by the Al Qaeda globally and Jemaah Islamiyah in Indonesia, has yet to characterize the conduct of violence in the south.

Discussions on the "Islamic" character of southern Thai violence also need to be reconciled with some empirical and historical facts. First, while some 80 percent of the estimated four million Muslims in Thailand reside in the five southern provinces known for historically harboring separatist tendencies, one should not forget that another 20 percent or so are scattered elsewhere in the country and play no part in the struggle in the south. Second, in the Malay world (of which southern Thailand is a part), Islam has traditionally found greatest political resonance as a component of Malay ethnicity. While Thailand enjoyed a rich tradition of Muslim reformist intellectual scholarship, leadership of Malay-Muslim resistance has in most cases, at least traditionally, not arisen from this pool, but from Malay nobles and aristocrats displaced by annexation.[5] To that effect, it is worth stressing that the struggle of the Malay-Muslims of southern Thailand has long been premised primarily on the notion that the community possessed an ethno-cultural identity distinct from the dominant Thai nation. In other words, it has been the ethno-religious nexus that has traditionally motivated the political struggle.[6]

## Roots of violence, pre-2004

In order to understand the roots of southern Thai resistance, one must invariably come to terms with Thai history and nationalism. Here concerns for territorial integrity in the face of predatory colonialism, historical antagonisms, and in the

156

case of southern Thailand, territorial expansion, informed the acute sense of vulnerability among Siamese monarchs and set the parameters for ethnic relations within Siam's territorial boundaries.[7] In fact, it was in response to these threats that leaders of Siam constructed a "Thai" national identity in order to foster a sense of nationalism. This was pursued through policies of assimilation aimed at diluting the cultural identity of minority groups, since "ethnicity was seen as a potential threat to national sovereignty."[8] It was this outlook that set the stage for the Malay-Muslim community's resistance to the assimilation strategies of the Thai state.

Traditionally, a distinct Malay-Muslim identity in southern Thailand was predicated on the historical legacy of the kingdom of Patani and the cultural congruence it enjoyed with the Malays of the peninsula, and in particular those in the Northern Malay state of Kelantan.[9] Consequently, the cumulative effect of Bangkok's attempts to assimilate the southern Malay-Muslim provinces after their annexation in 1902 was the creation of a wider and stronger Malay-Muslim consciousness, which has expressed itself in resistance since 1903, ranging from political protests and demonstrations to violence and claims of independence.[10]

What is of interest is the role of Islam in this historical resistance. Several points stand out. While the general consensus has been that the 1979 Afghan conflict and Iranian Revolution inaugurated Muslim radicalism in a grand fashion, one notes, curiously enough, that violence in southern Thailand peaked before, not after, 1979.[11] And while Islam was being mobilized throughout the Muslim world to undermine existing domestic secular political structures, throughout the 1980s, under the governments of Prem Tinsulanond and Chatchai Choonvahan the Thai state made great strides in reconciling with the Muslim population in the south and marginalizing separatist forces through a range of socio-economic and cultural policies. Moreover, it was also noticeable that the key separatist parties in the 1980s, namely the Patani United Liberation Organization (PULO) and Barisan Revolusi Nasional (BRN), were largely secular in ideology even if their members were Muslim, and not averse to collaboration with the Malaysian and Thai communist parties. Finally, the democratization of Thai politics since the 1980s afforded a voice for the Malay-Muslim community in government. The Democrat Party and New Aspiration Party in particular have reinforced their presence in the south by incorporating a number of Muslim politicians into their ranks.[12] In fact, it has been suggested that the formation of the Bersatu (United) coalition of separatist organizations in 1989 was itself demonstrative of the government's successful marginalization of these groups.[13] While mutual suspicions might have lingered, through these initiatives the government managed to roll back the expansion of separatist ideology that characterized the climate of the 1970s and prompted the surrender of hundreds of separatists by the mid-1990s.

While the preceding discussion is not to suggest that Islam and the politicization of Muslim consciousness after 1979 was of little consequence, it does offer several insights. First, it is erroneous to read into the history of resistance an overpowering religious motivation. Rather, in the narrative of violence and separatism in Thailand the relevance of Islam lay in its traditional role as a marker of Malay ethnicity and its appeal, through that channel, as a means to articulate and express discontent and disenfranchisement felt towards the central government. Second, Islam is not a monolithic phenomenon, but rather needs to be situated in a temporal mode that is linked to a particular context. This is clearly evident in how the traditional separatist struggle employed Islam primarily "in defence of the Malay nation," and only after that for "the true religion of God."[14] For many Muslims in southern Thailand, this is the "Islam" that has justified their struggle; and it has little direct relation to abstract, "authentic" Wahhabism or teachings of radicals such as Sayyid Qutb or Maulana Maududi, whose names many "terrorism experts" cite liberally.

## Krisek and the "Islamization" of resistance

While religion per se has not played a crucial role in the history of separatism in southern Thailand, recent developments suggest that shifts are occurring within the ethno-religious nexus. The violence that took place on April 28, 2004, when more than a hundred youths conducted eleven coordinated pre-dawn attacks on a series of police posts and security installations in Yala, Songkhla, and Pattani, resulting in 108 militants and 5 police and military officials being killed and 17 arrests, and in particular the raid on Krisek Mosque in Pattani, is most alarming. Inasmuch as the general Malay-Muslim population no longer support militant resistance to the state, the Krisek massacre threatens to "Islamize" the conflict in southern Thailand and radicalize Muslim sentiments. Given the monumental impact of Krisek, the event is worth recounting here.

According to eyewitness accounts, a number of Muslim youths had streamed into Krisek Mosque on the evening of April 27 at around 8 pm, whereupon they conducted prayers and read the Quran throughout the night. At 4 am the following morning, they issued a call to jihad through the audio system of the mosque (which was used for the *azaan* or call to prayer) and invited others to join them. A short while later this group set out with machetes and attacked police posts and government installations in surrounding villages. Similar attacks took place in other provinces at around the same time. Despite having ample time and opportunities to disperse into the surrounding villages and forests, the militants in Pattani chose to return to Krisek, knowing full well that they would easily be surrounded. In point of fact, many of the militants were already prepared to be *shahid*, martyrs for Islam, and in the tradition of Muslim martyrdom had instructed family members not to wash their bodies after death, for the blood of the *shahid* is pure in the eyes of Allah.[15] By 6 am, Thai security forces had massed outside the mosque. At noon orders were given by Panlop Pinmanee, Deputy Director of Internal Security Operations, to seize the mosque. Heavy weaponry such as rocket launchers and M-16 assault rifles were employed against the militants after the failure of a tear-gas attack, resulting in the massacre of all 32 individuals.

During a senate inquiry into the attacks, Kraisak Choonhavan, Chairman of the Senate Foreign Affairs Committee, revealed that some of the militants were found with bullets through the head; further evidence surfaced that ropes had been used to bind their wrists.[16] This indicated that contrary to statements made by security officers, several militants had in fact surrendered and were summarily executed. Post-mortems on the bodies also uncovered traces of the hallucinogen Aprazolam in their blood. A similar hallucinogen was previously found in the blood of Al-Maunah militants who had engaged the Malaysian police authorities in a shoot-out several years earlier after an arms heist in the state of Perak.[17] This evidence drew attention to the prospects that a new group might have surfaced in southern Thailand.[18]

The Krisek massacre, however, was symbolic far beyond the massive violation of human rights and abuse of power that took place, for it marked the first acts of martyrdom in the long history of southern resistance. Moreover, the choice of Krisek itself carried great political significance. In Malay-Muslim folklore, the Krisek Mosque is a 400-year-old symbol of Muslim identity. Legend tells of a Chinese lady of noble birth, Lim Ko Niew, who came to southern Thailand 400 years ago in search of her brother. Upon hearing that he had converted to Islam and refused to return to China, she laid a curse on the mosque that was then being constructed at the site of Krisek before committing suicide. The fact that the mosque remains standing today is seen, by Muslims in the region in the context of this folklore, as emblematic of Islam's resilience in the face of trial and adversary.[19] Further, the date of April 28 was equally striking for the fact that several previous incidences of rebellion against the Thai state have taken place in the south on or around that date.[20] Both these facts point to a calculated attack, meticulously orchestrated and executed in order to maximize the symbolism and arouse Malay-Muslim fervour, where "a martyr's death also is not a cause for mourning but for respect and celebration. Political and religious revisions of history, and interpretations of present situations based on such revisions, exacerbate the conflict with fanatic intensity."[21]

With the events of April 28, 2004 resistance in southern Thailand has assumed a religiosity that threatens to alter the nature and character of what was primarily an ethno-nationalist struggle; and with the increasing religious character of violence in the south, illustrated most profoundly by the bloodstained floors and Qurans in Krisek Mosque, resistance may well be increasingly predicated on religious symbols and meanings which will continue to feed resentment as Islam takes on greater potency as an organizing principle to comprehend, rally, articulate, and express resistance against the central state.[22] In some respects this has already happened, with the desecration of the Lim Ko Niew shrine, ironically located right next to Krisek Mosque in Pattani, on June 1, in what was obviously a retaliatory attack.

## Prospects for reconciliation

As violence in southern Thailand escalates, so does pressures for the Thaksin government to resolve the problem. Prospects for reconciliation will hinge on the Thai government's ability to generate a coherent plan that encompasses strategies to disrupt the operations of militants and contain the violence in the short term, and delegitimize their causes in the longer run. In order to deal with the former, the Thaksin administration needs to prioritize matters of governance and focus on the implementation of social and economic policies at the grassroots level and, to the extent that surveillance and intelligence-gathering are required, facilitate monitoring of suspected militants within the community without alienating the majority of the population. In the longer run however, the objective of the delegitimization of violence will be best served with a strategy aimed at transforming the *weltanshauung* of both the Thai national security elite as well as the Malay-Muslim community in a manner that facilitates the integration of southern Thailand into the larger nationalist project without dilution of Malay-Muslim socio-cultural identity. At the heart of this objective would be the return of political, cultural, and ideational space for the Malay-Muslim community that was in the process of being carved out by previous administrations but subsequently confiscated by force by the Thaksin government. Rather than focusing on specific policy initiatives or proposals, this section proposes to reflect on the key themes that should frame the Thai government's attempt to de-escalate, and eventually delegitimize and eliminate, violence.

## *Governance*

Given that militancy in southern Thailand is often a potent concoction of religion and specific local and temporal configurations of power, and that it is not merely religious ideas themselves, but the "local, institutional, spatial and historical contexts of religious expression and interaction, conflict and reconciliation" that frames state–society interaction on this account, the issue of administration and governance is paramount.[23] Here, the Thaksin administration has been found wanting over the past two years.

Analysts trace the genesis of the current phase of violence to Thaksin's dismantling of the Southern Border Provinces Administrative Committee (SBPAC) and its intelligence arm, the Civil-Military Unit 43, in March–April 2002 and the replacement of this system with a Southern Border Provinces Coordination Centre (SBPCC) in the following July. Unlike the previous institutions, however, the SBPCC is essentially manned by police and reports to a CEO-style governor, signalling a centralization of power in the hands of a Bangkok appointee.[24] In many ways, this change speaks directly to two problems hampering operational governance in the south – police misadministration and corruption, and the accentuation of turf battles.

At the heart of police administration has been the ruthless and uncompromising application of force in dealing with suspected "militants."[25] Mistreatment during interrogation, abduction of suspects, and extra-judicial killings epitomize the current security policy in the south and have done little more than foster a climate of fear.[26] Even the policy of amnesty, so successful in enticing communists to surrender and recently extended to the separatists, is in danger of failing given the prevailing perception among the Muslim population that Thai security forces have executed some among those who have accepted amnesty.[27] This abuse of power is aggravated by rampant corruption within the southern administrative establishment. It is common knowledge, for example, that incompetent police personnel are often "banished" to the south from Bangkok and proceed to create their own fiefdoms.[28] Such a state of affairs has sowed much ill-feeling within the region for police administration, and the Thaksin administration's continued reliance on the policy of Martial Law that privileges the use of force and intimidation by the police will not only hamper the implementation of other policies in the south, but also influence the manner in which these policies are perceived and accepted by the Malay-Muslim population.

Turf battles have also proven a further obstacle to the government's ability to address the problems of the south. This was expressed most profoundly in the tension between the military and police over jurisdiction, where the matter of the dismantling of the SBPAC, which was essentially run by the military, and its replacement by police administration was very intensely and publicly debated by both security agencies. Public differences in opinion over the sources of violence between the Prime Minister (who blames drug gangs and bandits), the National Security Council (NSC) (corrupt officials), the military (local separatists and bad intelligence), the police (disgruntled military elements), and the interior ministry (Muslim extremists) were a further manifestation of turf battles, as was the matter of negotiation with Wan Kadir Che Man, leader of the Bersatu umbrella separatist organization, which witnessed officials repeatedly contradicting each other over Bangkok's negotiation policy. At one level, these differences certainly highlight the complex nature of the security situation in the south, in particular the range of actors' intent on capitalizing on the confusion. Yet it also draws attention to the severe lack of co-ordination between agencies and officials who horde information accrued in the course of their respective investigations in order to undermine the efforts of their competitors.[29]

Another facet to the problem of governance is the question of access to the state and power structure, which often determines the content and context of relations between central governments and marginalized minorities. The previously discussed problem with Muslim representation in Bangkok has been accentuated in the south by the current administration's reluctance to include Muslim voices in discussions on the problems.[30] It is this lack of established and institutionalized outlets of expression that makes violence an appealing avenue of "symbolic empowerment."[31]

Strategies for surmounting the problem of bureaucratic impediments, inter-agency rivalries, and turf battles need to be found. These efforts should focus on the centralization of information gathering and dissemination under an NSC empowered to enhance the scope and depth of dialogue with the Muslim community so as to permit balanced assessments of intelligence reports and information. Furthermore, while existing cooperation with and participation of Bangkok-based Muslim politicians must continue, the NSC will need to make greater efforts to engage religious leaders from the south and concentrate its outreach on Islamic schools and mosques.[32] The reintroduction of a centralized administrative body in the mould of the SBPAC to work closely with the NSC would open further avenues for authorities to listen and investigate complaints from southern Muslims concerning corrupt or inept Thai officials, and then transfer them out of the provinces should the accusations prove true.[33] The current strategy of focusing on surveillance will also need to be tweaked in a manner that focuses on enhancing "human factor" intelligence instead of relying on hardware, as is the case at present. Rather than extensive investment in "state-of-the-art" surveillance equipment, the Thai government would do well to recruit and/or train a much larger pool of civilian officials (as opposed to uniformed security officers) with some degree of competence in Malay and Jawi, if not Arabic, who will be able to integrate themselves into the community and relate to Malay-Muslim culture.

## *Economics and Development*

The southern provinces have always been among the poorest in Thailand. Globalization has forced the pace of industrialization and development in the country to the extent that the south has become increasingly left behind owing to its traditional lifestyle and rural economy. Pressures of development have led to mass rural migration, the break-up of the traditional family and community structure, and a widening income gap between the Malay-Muslims and other Thai communities. This state of affairs has accentuated the sense of marginalization, which in turn provides a ready pool of support for radical movements and ideologies.[34] It is because of this that the economic and developmental imperative has featured prominently in the Thai government's policies towards the south. Yet the manner in which the Thaksin administration has conceptualized and implemented such policies has in fact had the opposite effect of aggravating tension.

Since 2001, the Thaksin administration has apparently injected 28 billion baht into the region for infrastructure and development projects. Much of this money has however been siphoned off through corruption; the rest of the money has gone into economic and developmental policies that in truth do little more than amplify the Bangkok government's lack of sensitivity to Malay-Muslim culture. For instance, state-led economic projects have privileged the tourism industry rather than agriculture and fishing, the traditional cornerstones of the southern Thai economy.[35] Moreover, the lack of competence in the Thai language, particularly among the older generation, has further hampered the trickle-down effect of government economic policies. The creation of a Village Fund, a generous loan programme purportedly introduced to assist Malay-Muslim entrepreneurship, was rejected because interest was charged in violation of Islamic law.[36] Scholarship funds made available to Muslim students were discovered to have come from the Government Lottery Agency, which had legalized the underground lottery in mid-2003, sparking further resentment from the Muslim community.[37]

At another level, a central problem that urgently needs redress is the fact that the tradition-bound Malay-Muslim communities of the south do not possess the education required to appreciate the modernity and development that the Thai government purports to bring to them. Given this consideration, rapid industrialization of the south, Thaksin's chosen economic policy route, has seen job opportunities fall to more qualified personnel from outside of the region as opposed to members of the local community. This will almost certainly alienate the southern population even further.

Be that as it may, the Thai government should also be cautioned against over-emphasizing the "poor" and "poverty-stricken" economic conditions in the south. While there is little doubt that southern Thailand can benefit from further development, the sentiments of the Malay-Muslim community are that economic development should be given significantly less priority than cultural and religious autonomy insofar as government policy directions are concerned.[38]

### Discourse, dialogue, and dissonance

Area studies experts argue (at least prior to April 28, 2004) that as a consequence of two decades of concerted attempts at reconciliation, separatism and Muslim ideologies of militancy now lack currency among southern Thai Muslims who have come to consider themselves Thai by nationality, and Muslim by religion. That said, the Thai state's continued threat perception towards plurality, has led it to view Malay-Muslim ethnic consciousness as a concern. The Thaksin administration's shortcomings in terms of operational policies in the south dealing with the Muslim population have set the reconciliation process back substantially and rejuvenated the fading dissonance between the Muslim community and the central Bangkok authorities.

Over the past two years the contest over the symbols and meaning of religion, in this case Islam, in political discourse and representation in southern Thailand has evolved in a manner that has shrunk the available space in the socio-political sphere, previously built up through the process of democratization and non-governmental organization (NGO) activism, for a "Thai Islam" that is clearly distinguishable from, and more conciliatory than, the ethno-nationalist Islam of separatism and the extremist brand of Islam epitomized by the Tariqah movement and propagated in certain religious schools. As violence escalates, so too does the urgency of regaining lost socio-political space for Muslims who remain opposed to extremism, but are increasingly finding themselves presented with a *fait accompli*.

In more recent times, two particular attempts at expanding this practical and discursive space for Islam in Thailand stand out, not only for the enlightened nature of their proposals, but also for the fact that they were discarded by the Thaksin administration. The National Security Policy for the Southern Border Provinces (1999–2003) was an initiative of the NSC during the Chuan Leekpai administration that had as its basis the celebration of cultural plurality and participation of the southern population in economic development and the political process. Underlying this initiative was the recognition that separatism was only appealing because of the denial of rights and respect to the southern provinces. The most striking feature of this policy was the fact that it was arrived at in consultation with local leaders from the south.[39] Similarly, in April 2004, Deputy Prime Minister Chaturon Chaisaeng presented a "Peace Plan" in the form of a seven-point proposal to draw down the violence that had re-ignited. These included the gradual lifting of Martial Law, support for the *pondok* education system, maintenance of the dual-nationality system, and the provision of amnesty to militants.[40] The National Security Policy was eventually allowed to lapse by the Thaksin administration without any effort being made to review its achievements or discuss renewal. It was also Prime Minister Thaksin who, despite expressing initial support, eventually scuttled the Chaturon Peace Plan before it even surfaced in Cabinet for official deliberation. Clearly then, the current administration has not displayed the necessary political will and commitment to support initiatives (which ironically have been prompted by these very same people) to find durable solutions to the fundamental causes of problems in the south. In place of carefully crafted inclusivist policies aimed at recognizing and reconciling with the Malay-Muslim provinces, the Thaksin administration has chosen tactics such as bribery (free haj trips and money are offered to Muslim informants who are prepared to turn over "suspected separatists" from their own villages) and "Nationalism Boot Camp" courses which operate as little more than interrogation and indoctrination centres.[41]

To be sure, there are also considerable structural challenges to issues of consultation, dialogue, and expansion of political space for a "Thai Islam" under current circumstances that need to be acknowledged and addressed. The first of these problems lies in what Surin Pitsuwan describes as "the belief on the part of government officials that national security demands the full integration of its population. It tolerates no diversity among the people within the state."[42] If this mindset prevails, it is easy to see how ethno-cultural plurality remains antithetic to the strategic culture and worldview of the state. Its leaders will remain resistant to permitting the necessary space for Muslim identity. Second, while there is a need for a community of committed Muslim leaders to interface with the state, it is increasingly difficult to see such a community surfacing against the current backdrop of tension and suspicion. "Moderate" Muslims in Bangkok find themselves in a difficult position: neither trusted by the government, nor accepted in the south. Third, Bangkok-based politicians are acutely aware that in any case it is not likely to be in their political interests to speak out, which partly explains their relative silence in the wake of the recent outbreak of violence. Finally, in the current milieu defined by US power and Washington's binary "for us or against us" policy ultimatum to the world, it is difficult for Muslim leaders from countries aligned with the United States to speak out in opposition to "extremist Islam" precisely because of the danger that doing so can be read as collaboration in Washington's war on Islam.

### Identity reconstruction

As suggested above, delegitimization of violence hinges on the expansion of discursive and, equally importantly, practical space for Muslims to talk, teach, and live an Islam that is congruent with principles of peaceful co-existence and harmony. This is important as it undercuts the claims to legitimacy and authenticity on the part of extremist renditions of Muslim ideology. Islamic education is highly instrumental in facilitating this process.[43]

Islamic education has long been a potentially explosive issue in the politics of southern Thailand. In 1922, Tengku Abdul Kadir Qamaruddin launched one of the largest campaigns against Bangkok in Thai history in reaction to legislation that required all Malay-Muslim children to attend government schools and learn Siamese. Later attempts at assimilation under Phibun Songgkram in the 1930s and Sarit Thanarat in the 1960s also sparked considerable outrage from the community and set the stage for several decades of separatist resistance.[44]

The centrality of the *pondok*, the Islamic religious school in the Malay world, to the lives and identity of Malay-Muslims in southern Thailand stems from its role as a rite of passage for Malay youths into adulthood, as well as a place of reflection and contemplation for older members of the community.[45] In the context of everyday Muslim life, the religious teachers in the *pondok*, known as Tok Guru, play a major role as spiritual guides; but they also command great political influence. As Surin Pitsuwan presciently described, "one of (their) duties is necessarily the sporadic outbursts of political opposition to the central government in their quest for a higher degree of self-rule."[46]

The biggest challenge for the Thai government to this day remains the regulation of the curriculum of the *pondok* education system in a manner that would not be viewed as threatening to Malay-Muslim identity. While policies have been formulated to this end, their effectiveness has been unconvincing. For instance, recent parliamentary laws have legislated government support for *pondok* schools.[47] In practice however, this has not been the case as much of the funding has disappeared through corruption.[48] Since April 28, 2004 the Thai government has attempted to register the approximately 500 *pondok* schools in the southern provinces by promising funding for those that comply.[49] Responses to this policy have however been markedly muted, and Muslim community leaders and village headmen express concern that participation in the registration exercise would invariably open their schools to greater government intervention and even raids by security forces.

Much of the difficulty surrounding the government's policy on *pondok* education stems from the suspicion that Islamic schools, particularly those that remain unregistered, breed militancy and separatism.[50] Thai security forces believe that since 28 April, 2004 masterminds behind violence in the south are using *pondok* schools to recruit a new wave of militants to replenish their ranks. Because of this, the security apparatus has subjected *pondok* schools to Martial Law regulations, random checks, and the arrest of Tok Guru suspected of preaching violence.[51] Two developments are of particular concern to the Thai government. First, they believe that some of these *pondok* schools are part of the small but troublesome Tariqah (the Path) movement, a Sufi mystical movement that has traditionally been involved with separatism in Thailand, and that promotes the use of hallucinogens and holy water and oils in their meditation in the belief that these elements have the power to ward off bullets.[52] Second, government sources are also concerned about *pondok* schools that receive funding and scholarships from Middle Eastern charities, which are suspected to be cogs in the financial network of international terrorism.

While the government's concern for the curriculum of *pondok* schools is well-taken, regulation remains a decidedly difficult task. Given that "the methodology of *Pondok* education in Southern Thailand was and is ... similar to the widely recognized system of the intellectual learning process among the institutions in medieval Islam," a primary objective must be to modernize general Islamic education in a manner that fosters not only knowledge of religion, but also practical skills that will empower and equip graduates from the Muslim education system for mainstream life.[53] Discussions on the possible creation of a Pondok Institute Association initiated by the Central Islamic Committee of Thailand and currently under way are welcomed and should be supported at the highest levels by the central government so as to encourage self-reflection on the part of the community and hopefully facilitate the modernization of the curriculum and infrastructure of religious schools. Even then, any policy will have to first be predicated on the government's ability to locate these schools amidst a system that is highly arbitrary. *Pondok* schools are often established by Muslim scholars who return from the haj and time in Middle Eastern institutions. A *pondok* can be established in a *kampung* (village) and have as little as three students on its roster. Furthermore, any move to register and regulate *pondok* schools, if not done adroitly and with caution, will only drive these schools underground, and further beyond the reach of the state's regulatory mechanisms.

At another level, the government should also consider the matter of increasing tertiary Islamic education opportunities in the south that espouse a foundation in advanced religious education with secular subjects. Moreover, the existence of an Islamic university would provide a means of further education for Muslims and limit outflow to Middle Eastern and South Asian tertiary Islamic institutions.

In the main, government policies, however they are implemented, should be seen as encouraging Islamic education, not curtailing it as has been the case with previous such attempts. As Surin Pitsuwan articulated, "it must be realized that in these *Pondoks* lie not the extremist separatists but a future leadership that offers hope for the region."[54] In other words, the government's perspective of and discourse on *pondok* education needs to change drastically. Previously, when Muslim Islamic education has been denied by state policies, Muslims have responded either by departing to Muslim centers of learning for further Islamic education, or by taking *pondok* schools underground.[55] Both scenarios are undesirable on the part of the government.[56]

On the other hand, even if a certain measure of monitoring is required, attempts at doing so thus far have been marked by an excessive use of force. *Pondok* schools are subject to surprise searches by soldiers (as opposed to civilian bureaucrats or state representatives) wielding guns and manhandling Tok Guru. Mosques are regularly monitored as well, but not so much for their teaching (there is a severe shortfall of state officials who are sufficiently competent in Jawi to make any sense of what is taught in mosques) as for the presence of weapons and explosives. Even more disturbing is the fact that soldiers regularly conduct these searches with dogs, and have been known to enter the sanctuary with their shoes on and rifles in hand. Such methods of "monitoring" need desperately to be changed, because they are offensive to Muslims.

## *Influence of international events*

There should be little doubt that the conflict in southern Thailand is framed by the ongoing "global" war on terrorism, whose parameters are both being defined by the policy elite in Washington and embraced by their counterparts in Bangkok. Since the invasion of Afghanistan, the policy of the Bush administration has generated tension between secular states (and some Muslim states as well, it should be added) aligned with the US and Muslim communities, and in a few cases this tension has found violent expression. Of immediate concern is Bangkok's alignment with the US (Bangkok expelled three Iraqi diplomats in March 2003 in a move that sparked widespread protest in the south, dispatched 420 troops to Iraq in September, and was consequently allocated "major non-NATO ally" status by Washington in October) on its own security predicament. Southern Muslims interviewed by the author, for instance, responded to questions of why the April 28 violence was perpetrated by suggesting that anger and frustration with US foreign policy towards the Muslim world, and Bangkok's support of this policy, was a key motivator.[57] The Malay-Muslim community continues to boycott US products. The Islamic committees of all five southernmost provinces recently passed resolutions calling for the government to explain their staunch support of the US, while 50,000 Muslims took part in a protest against the US immediately after the outbreak of the Afghan campaign.[58] In this respect, talk of American involvement in southern Thailand is fundamentally misplaced, and will only aggravate tension given that under current circumstances the Thaksin administration's support of American policy is tantamount to presenting Thailand's Muslim population with a *fait accompli*.[59] Rather, Bangkok's immediate interest in stemming violence in the south would be better served with lower profile support and judiciously-crafted policies with respect to cooperation with the US on the war on terrorism.[60] This should include less focus on military operations, and more on the humanitarian aspects of nation-building in Iraq and Afghanistan.

Another external dimension to the southern Thai problem is the so-called Malaysia connection, and violence has on several occasions posed considerable challenges to Thailand–Malaysia relations. The Thai government harbours suspicions of Malaysian sympathy for their co-religionists and ethnic kin and continues to pressure Kuala Lumpur to play an active role in assisting Bangkok to track down militants and separatists who use dual-citizenship and the porous borders between the southern provinces and northern Malaysia to seek sanctuary in the latter. For their part, the Malaysian government holds grave reservations towards Bangkok's handling of southern Thai sentiments and in closed-door meetings has diplomatically suggested that their Thai counterparts tone down the use of force.[61] Of interest is the outcome of recent meetings between the top leadership of the two states, in particular the decision to recruit Malaysian religious leaders to "advise" their counterparts in southern Thailand and "instruct" Thai *pondok* school pupils. This policy is problematic at several levels. First, as with many other Thaksin administration initiatives, it was undertaken without consultation with locals in the south. Second, given the highly politicized nature of the religious school system in Malaysia itself, in particular the fact that Islamic schools are one of the grounds where the UMNO–PAS Islamization race is played out, such a move threatens to import Malaysian Muslim politics into southern Thailand. Finally, given the proud Muslim intellectual history of Patani which in the past has seen Muslim scholars from the peninsula come to southern Thailand for further instruction, Muslims in south Thailand give little credence to Bangkok's suggestion that Malaysian religious teachers have anything to impart to their counterparts in the south.

## Conclusion

Any discussion on the resolution of the security problems in southern Thailand must begin with the Thai government's own recognition that acts of violence have not been the work of a few lunatics but are symptomatic of a deep malaise that has crept into southern Thailand over the past three years after a long hiatus. Moreover, it threatens to swiftly transform again into a full-blown insurgency, this time with an increasingly religious dimension. Despite the increasing religious flavor of violence evident in the targeting by both parties of religious institutions and symbols, the Thai government must realize that this state of affairs is less as a consequence of a global *jihadi* influence than of the government's own ignorance, policy miscalculations, mismanagement, and provocations.

Containing violence and fostering a mood of reconciliation in southern Thailand has proven an increasingly onerous task for the Thaksin government. In all likelihood this task will be made considerably more difficult by the tenor of current government attempts to deal with the conflict, which continue to privilege the use of force and appear to address more the symptoms than the causes. In this regard, it is a profound irony that while the Thaksin administration has made great efforts to deny the religious character of violence that has taken place in the restive south since his inauguration in 2001, it has been his government's heavy-handed policies, manifested most profoundly at Krisek, which has ensured the "Islamization" of resistance and increased its momentum.

While creating a secure environment is an important objective, securitization measures will not contain, let alone solve, the problem. History has shown time and again that the delegitimization, or even disruption, of violence in southern Thailand cannot be premised on the extension of state strength to the south, and that policies of this nature more often than not heighten rather than reduce tension. In order to disrupt the violence, the primary emphasis of the Thaksin government should be to discredit and delegitimize the cause of separatism and Islamic militancy in southern Thailand through a political process that sends a message to the Muslims in the south that they will be accorded cultural, economic, social, and political space in a manner that celebrates pluralism as an expression of, as opposed to a threat to, Thai national identity. Policies aimed at empowering the Muslim community and preserving their culture and identity will ensure that support for anti-establishment movements are reduced. That said, it is clear that many of the potentialities explored in this chapter entail a fundamental shift in the style and objective of governance of the Thaksin administration; and it has yet to demonstrate any inclination in this direction. The fact that the Thai state continues to privilege the use of force as a primary policy instrument in the south is illustrated by persistence of Martial Law in the deep south (Yala, Pattani, and Narathiwat), and the recent re-appointment of hawkish former Defense Minister and current Deputy Prime Minister Thamarak Isarangura and former Fourth Army chief Panlop Pinmanee, both of whom were responsible for the April 28 massacre at Krisek Mosque and transferred after the incident to positions in the southern administration.[62]

The paradox will prove a challenging one for the Thai government. While the problem of southern Thailand is a complicated one with deep historical roots, and any attempts to resolve it demand sensitivity and caution, given the recent turn of events it has also become increasingly urgent that solutions be found to address the religiously-inspired violence. While it remains doubtful that external players have entrenched themselves in the south, there is a real and grave danger that unless successful policies are implemented, and implemented fast, foreign militants may capitalize on resentment and internationalize Thailand's internal conflict. Once that happens, an already convoluted security situation will deteriorate further, given the Thaksin administration's open flirtation with a US government whose foreign policies are read in the villages of southern Thailand as nothing short of a war against Islam.

# Notes

1  I would like to thank Saroja Dorairajoo, Chaiwat Satha-Anand, Panitan Wattanayagorn, Surat Horachaikul, Kavi Chongkittavorn, and Ahmad Somboon Bualuang for sharing their vast knowledge and insight in the form of comments on the main arguments of this chapter.

2  To illustrate this mood, a Thai-Buddhist state official I met in Narathiwat informed me that he now carries a gun everywhere he goes for his own safety, and that the Thai-Buddhist community in the south now feel like an oppressed minority. On the other hand, a Muslim community leader informed me that only a day before our meeting, August 13, and in the coffee shop outside the very hotel where I was staying (CS Pattani), two Muslim men dressed in Jubah were arbitrarily accosted by Thai police and taken into custody. They were returned about an hour later, visibly shaken.

3  A case in point is Zachary Abuza, Militant Islam in Southeast Asia: Crucible of Terror (Boulder, CO: Lynne Rienner Publishers, 2003), 1-31. Abuza's arguments are premised on sweeping, controversial, troubling, and ultimately unjustifiable claims. For instance, he suggests in one broad brushstroke (13), without documentation, references, or qualification, that "The madrasas and pesantren ... in Southeast Asia ... have advocated a stricter, more intolerant brand of Islam and condemn the secular nation-state. They are the core of a growing and powerful radical Islamic movement and have established networks within the region and with the Middle East." There is now a critical mass of students studying in Islamic universities (including Al Azhar) and madrasas, which Abuza argues (12) "teach rigid Wahhabi interpretation of Islam and has produced the most radical firebrands in the Muslim world ... who are reinforced in their conviction that Malaysia, Indonesia, and Mindanao must become Islamic states." He also argues, again without documentary support, on (14–15) that the presence of Hadramauts in Southeast Asia has been a key source of violence and

radicalism. This claim was made notwithstanding the fact that Hadramaut Muslims constituted only a fraction of alleged JI members taken into custody throughout the region.

4 See Frank Bures, "Muslim Unrest Flares in Thailand," *Christian Science Monitor*, January 7, 2004; Joseph C. Liow, "Thailand: Are Al-Qaeda and Jemaah Islamiyah in Southern Thailand?" Asian Analysis, ASEAN Focus Group and the Australian National University, Sydney, September 2004.

5 Key leaders of the Malay-Muslim resistance, for instance, include Tengku Mahmud Mahyiddeen, Tengku Abdul Jalal, Tunku Abdul Yala Nasae, and Tunku Bilor Kortor Nilor, all of whom were related to Malay royalty from the peninsula.

6 See R.J. May, "The Religious Factor in Three Minority Movements," *Contemporary Southeast Asia* 13, no. 4 (1992): 403–4.

7 Thongchai Winichakul, *Siam Mapped: A History of the Geo-Body of a Nation* (Chiangmai: Silkworm Books, 1994).

8 Saroja Dorairajoo, "Violence in the South of Thailand," *Inter-Asia Cultural Studies* 5, December 2004.

9 Clive J. Christie, *A Modern History of Southeast Asia: Decolonisation, Nationalism and Separatism* (London: I.B. Tauris Publishers, 1996), 174; See also Connor Bailey and John Miksic, "The Country of Patani in the Period of Re-awakening: A Chapter from Ibrahim Syukri's Sejarah Kerajaan Melayu Patani," in *The Muslims in Thailand, Vol. II: Politics of the Malay-Speaking South*, ed. Andrew Forbes (Bihar: Centre for Southeast Asian Studies, 1989).

10 Surat Horachaikul, "The Far South of Thailand in the Era of the American Empire, 9/11 Version, and Thaksin's 'cash and gung-ho' Premiership," *Asian Review* 16, (2003): 137–9.

1 1 For example, it was in late 1975 that 70,000 Malay-Muslims protested in Narathiwat against the alleged murder of five Malay villagers by Thai marines. This was the largest example of mass resistance from the Malay-Muslims in Thai history. Another landmark incident was the bombing of the Don Muang International Airport in June 1977.

12 Malay-Muslims have since taken on key government positions that have included Speaker of the House as well as the ministerial posts in the Ministry of the Interior and Foreign Affairs, and Deputy Prime Minister.

13 See "Primer: Muslim Separatism in Southern Thailand," GlobalSecurity.org, July 22, 2002, http:// www.globalsecurity.org/military/library/report/2002/Muslim_ Separatists_%20Primer_Jul02.doc.

14 These phrases were found in the document *Berjihad di Patani* allegedly found on the bodies of militants who conducted the April 28, 2004 attacks in Pattani and Narathiwat. Chaiwat Satha-Anand had seen the document, and had informed the author during an interview, Bangkok, August 17, 2004.

15 I was informed that many of these youths had left these instructions in the form of notes to their family members before they departed for the mosque the night before. Author's interview with Ahmad Somboon Bualuang, Pattani, August 15, 2004. This was confirmed by Chaiwat Satha-anand in Bangkok, August 17, 2004. I was also informed that in Narathiwat province there are tombstones with the word *shahid* written on them, and where the bodies were buried after April 28, 2004.

16 "Inquiry into the Pattani's Krue Se Mosque Killings A Cover Commission of Thailand," ACHR Review, Asian Centre for Human Rights, New Delhi, May 5, 2004, http://www.achrweb.org/Review/2004/19-04.htm.

17 The Al-Maunah militants had believed that by drinking this hallucinogen, their bodies would be impervious to bullets. Similar drugs were believed to have been used by the Afghan *mujahidin* fighters during the campaign against the Soviet Union.

18 Thai media reported a group by the name of Talekat Hikmahtullah Abadan (Direction from God Towards Invincibility), but I have not been able to confirm the existence of

such a group. See "Imam Admits Contact with Separatists," *The Nation*, September 1, 2004.

19 This point was stressed during an interview conducted with Saroja Dorairajoo, an anthropologist who has worked in southern Thailand for the past six years, on August 6, 2004.

20 For example, on April 28, 1948 Malay peasants clashed with police forces of the Phibun Songgkram government in Kampung Dusun Nyor in Rang-ae district of Narathiwat, which allegedly resulted in 400 Malay-Muslim and 30 police deaths. On April 29, 1980 a noodle shop in Pattani was bombed, resulting in 14 injuries. On April 28, 2003 a guerrilla unit armed with automatic rifles raided an armoury of the Thaksin Pattana 2 outpost in Narathiwat's Sukhirin district at 2:30 am, killing four soldiers before stealing more than 30 machine guns. Half an hour later, an outpost in Tharn Toh district, Yala, was raided, with 20 more guns stolen and many soldiers wounded. I would like to acknowledge Saroja Dorairajoo for this information.

21 Rona M. Fields, Salman Elbedour, and Fadel A. Hein, "The Palestinian Suicide Bomber," in *The Psychology of Terrorism, Vol. 2: Clinical Aspects and Responses*, ed. Chris E. Stout (Westport, CT: Praeger, 2002), 208.

22 Events since April 28 give further credence to concerns that the violence in the south is fast taking on a religious flavour. In July, three Buddhist temples in the south were desecrated in attacks that quickly reminded Thailand's Buddhist majority of the demolition of the Buddhas of Bamiyan by the Taliban in February 2001. Weapons have allegedly also been found in the homes of Muslim religious teachers after surprise raids by security forces.

23 Thomas Scheffler, "Introduction" in *Religion Between Violence and Reconciliation*, ed. Thomas Scheffler (Beirut: Orient-Institut, 2002), 13–14.

24 "Thai Opposition Leader Slams Government's Scrapping of Previous Mechanisms in South," *The Nation*, July 18, 2002.

25 A classic case of this is how southern police have conducted searches in mosques with guns, dogs, and without taking off their shoes. See "Primer: Muslim Separatism in Southern Thailand."

26 For instance, Muslim community leaders have informed the author that numerous religious teachers have "disappeared" since the violence of April 28 and the resultant crackdown on *pondok* schools.

27 "In the South, an Iron Fist in a Velvet Glove," *Far Eastern Economic Review*, August 12, 2004. This was highlighted to me in an interview with a Muslim community leader in an interview in Pattani, August 15, 2004. I have also been informed by an official from the Malaysian Home Ministry that the Malaysian government has decided not to extradite separatists caught on Malaysian soil because they had knowledge of such executions. Interview with Malaysian Home Ministry official, March 14, 2004. It is likely that this reluctance on Malaysia's part to assist Thailand that accounted for Thaksin's harsh criticisms and accusation that Malaysia continues to harbour separatists. See Joseph C. Liow, "The Security Situation in Southern Thailand: Towards an Understanding of Domestic and International Dimensions," *Studies in Conflict and Terrorism* 27 (2004).

28 So too do some ex-separatists, it must be added, who use their separatist "credentials" to create their own "spheres of influence."

29 Author's interview with former National Security Council member, Bangkok, August 17, 2004.

30 "PM Brushes off Muslim Leaders' Call," *The Nation*, February 10, 2004. Various sources have informed me that Thai-Buddhists constitute up to 70 percent of members on provincial councils and other local administrative bodies.

31 Mark Juergensmeyer, "Holy Orders: Religious Opposition to Modern States," *Harvard International Review* 25, no. 4 (2004): 36.

32 Needless to say, rebuilding Krisek Mosque itself should be an immediate and major project in this regard.

33 One of the notable strengths of the SBPAC was the fact that it was authorized to transfer any senior civilian government or military official out of the province within 24 hours if accusations levelled on them proved to be accurate.

34 In this respect, it is not surprising that several of the youths killed at Krisek were found with 1,000 baht bills in their pockets.

35 Joseph C. Liow, "Bangkok's Southern Discomfort: Violence and Response in Southern Thailand," IDSS Commentaries, Institute of Defence and Strategic Studies, Singapore, May 2004. For the Muslim community, the tourism industry, with its emphasis on secular enjoyment, epitomizes all that is anathema to Islam.

36 This went against the Muslim prohibition on interest.

37 Surin Pitsuwan, "Abode of Peace," *Worldview Magazine* 17, no. 2 (2004): 3.

38 This came across clearly in my interviews with Muslim community leaders from the south.

39 This differed markedly from Thailand's previous three national security documents on the south, which were essentially top-down instructions emanating from Bangkok and blamed foreign elements for aggravating the situation in the south.

40 For details, see "Southern Peace Initiative Wins Cabinet Approval," *The Nation*, May 6, 2004.

41 See "Boot-camp Course in Nationalism," *The Nation*, August 30, 2004.

42 Surin Pitsuwan, *Islam and Malay Nationalism: A Case Study of the Malay-Muslims of Southern Thailand* (Bangkok: Thai Khadi Research Institute, Thammasat University, 1985), 276.

43 See Hasan Madmarn, *The Pondok and Madrasah in Patani* (Bangi: Penerbit Universiti Kebangsaan Malaysia, 1999); Joseph C. Liow, "The *Pondok* Schools of Southern Thailand: Bastion of Islamic Education or Hotbed of Militancy?" IDSS Commentaries, Institute of Defence and Strategic Studies, Singapore, August 2004.

44 In fact, the BRN was made up of students and teachers from Islamic schools in Narathiwat that had closed in protest to moves by the Sarit government in 1960 to forcibly bring Islamic schools under the control of the Ministry of the Interior.

45 Pitsuwan, *Islam and Malay Nationalism*, 183.

46 Ibid., 179.

47 This, I was informed, is stipulated in Article 15.1.2 of the Private Education Act instituted under the Chavalit government in 1989.

48 Author's interview with Muslim community leader, Pattani, August 15, 2004.

49 I was informed by Thai military intelligence sources that of the 500 identified, only some 300 have been registered.

50 A Thai intelligence informant (military) approximates that there are 30 such *pondok* schools in the south.

51 "Teacher, Student Arrested," *Bangkok Post*, August 13, 2004.

52 Pitsuwan, *Islam and Malay Nationalism*, 251–6.

53 Madmarn, *The Pondok and Madrasah*, 66.

54 Pitsuwan, "Abode of Peace," 5.

55 Author's interview with Muslim community leader, Pattani, August 15, 2004.

56 A scholar researching the *pondok* phenomenon informed me that approximately 85 percent of Muslim students from Thailand studying abroad are being sponsored by their host institutions. Author's interview, Bangkok, August 17, 2004.

57 Various interviews conducted in Pattani, August 13–14, 2004, and in Narathiwat, August 15, 2004.

58 Horachaikul, "The Far South of Thailand," 141.

59 See, for example, J.C. Lumbaca, "Use Special Forces in Thailand's Troubled South," PacNet, no.35A, Pacific Forum CSIS, Honolulu, Hawaii, August 20, 2004.

60  Ideally, Washington could play an important role in pressuring the Thai government to scale down the use of force in the southern region. Unfortunately, it appears that the current policy of the Thai government is likely to have its supporters in the uppermost echelons of American political leadership.
61  The problems and aspects of Thailand–Malaysia cooperation on this issue have been dealt with in Liow, "Security Situation," 515–8.
62  "Thamarak Gets Deep South Job Again," *The Nation*, July 28, 2004; "Controversial Thai General Sent Back to Muslim South," Reuters, August 24, 2004. It is worth nothing that both remain recalcitrant, and insist publicly that the use of force was legitimate.

# 11

# LÉVINAS AND THE QUESTION OF CIVILIZATIONAL AMITY AFTER SEPTEMBER 11

*See Seng Tan*

As long as people keep labeling other people as terrorists, it seems like we'll always have terrorists. – The artiste (again known as) Prince[1]

The premise of this essay is that in the present age of growing religious militancy, the best prospects for amity among contending communities and ideologies – conveniently lumped together here as "civilizations"[2] – are likely to be found in *an a priori ethical responsibility toward the other*. This entails recovering an ethos of criticism that can provide a sustained critique of processes of materialization that produce settlements, particularly the notion of subjects as already given, upon which the criteria for evaluation and judgment are based. What I have in mind here is the settlement regarding subjectivity as inextricably tied to *sovereignty*, without which all notions of subjectivity (or agency) are, according to this modernist logic, deemed impossible. Despite their manifold differences, what state practitioners and religious militants share in common is an adherence to sovereign subjectivity, whether predicated upon terms that are affirmative (self or "us") or abject (other or "them"). In contrast, I argue that any serious attempt at addressing this enduring problem of subjectivity, which has long plagued security studies in general and aspects of which attend to religious militancy after September 11 in particular, would find better purchase in an understanding of subjectivity that is *decoupled* from the long-cherished supposition of sovereignty.[3] With reliance on the ideas of Emmanuel Lévinas, I propose, in place of the given sovereign subject that enjoys pride of place in established international theory and practice, *a notion of subjectivity that necessarily begins with an ethical obligation vis-à-vis the other, without which subjectivity itself would be unthinkable.*

This may seem an inapt, perhaps overly philosophical, introduction for a review of ostensibly policy-oriented studies in strategies to disrupt and delegitimize violence perpetrated on religious grounds. For many, September 11 has come to symbolize civilizational enmity writ large, underscoring, as two observers put it, "the difficulty of understanding colliding thought-worlds."[4] All too often, however, security analysts and practitioners have largely sought to circumvent that difficulty by either deferring or simply ignoring it altogether, either of which holds serious implications for strategies crafted in response to religious conflict, or, for that matter, already existing policies that may have some bearing on the conflicts themselves. But there is an even more basic concern. Quite apart from the important question of determining whether this or that strategy is more apposite for disrupting and delegitimizing religious violence, there is the question of the "ideas and communities that lie behind the acts" (as previously stated by Juergensmeyer) not just of the militants who commit atrocities, but also of the governments and societies against whom those atrocities have been directed and whose forceful reprisals – the recent wars in Afghanistan and Iraq come most readily to mind – may have left their intended targets and ancillary communities shocked but not necessarily awed.

In invoking an ethos of criticism, we call into question the modernist-rationalist logic of evaluating and judging the verity of narratives – or, for that matter, of choosing sides in clashes between and within civilizations – by a criterion *outside* the narrative, which is what sovereignty-based discourses presuppose and, importantly, utilize to elect, endorse, and where necessary, exonerate actions and reactions of violence. This refers equally to the official narratives/histories of the state as well as the violent revisionist or counter-narratives/histories of religious militant groups,[5] both of which are united in their shared belief in their own given sovereign and autonomous subjectivity and in the refusal to acknowledge the other in ways that promote civilizational amity. Heeding Spivak's caveat regarding the "irretrievably heterogeneous" quality of subaltern subjects for – or, conversely, against – whom we should not so confidently presume to speak, this essay does not pretend to know or represent in any essentialist manner the religious militant subject.[6] Rather, the focus here is on discourses and practices, secular and state-sponsored as well as religiously affiliated, which tacitly assume if not unequivocally advocate the eradication of the other on the grounds of *moral necessity*.[7] In that sense, both states and their militant adversaries are united in the goal to destroy the identity of the other – a goal rationalized on *ethico*-political grounds – without acknowledging their respective complicities in generating and prolonging civilizational enmity. According to James Young, "world views may have both generated the catastrophe and narrated it afterwards."[8] Although portrayed as an unfortunate but necessary realism, the logic shared by both sides nevertheless embodies a perilous idealism that could likely produce the very outcomes it seeks to eschew.[9]

I am not implying that the problem confronting us would be readily resolved with the decoupling of subjectivity and sovereignty. But what a Lévinasian approach allows us to recognize is the *intrinsic role of the ethical in all understanding*. As Lévinas once put it, "Ethics redefines subjectivity as this heterogeneous responsibility, in contrast to autonomous freedom."[10] His approach thereby encourages us to apply the ethos of criticism first and foremost in an exercise in *self-critique* that discourages the easy and all-too-familiar recourse to simplistic exclusivist formulas in inter-civilization relations. Assuredly, this is not an invitation to yet another round of self-flagellation – as opposed to "other-bashing" – as has been the case, say, with works by US pundits highly critical of not just post-September 11 counter-terror and Iraq policies of the Bush administration, but of America's growing unilateralism in the post-Cold War period in general. Rather, my contention is that it is likely only by way of such a social-cum-communitarian logic that civilizational amity in Asia could conceivably have a chance, if at all, of succeeding. Conversely, in obdurately transfixing ourselves to a subjectivity whose ontology is decidedly treated as given and autonomous, we fail to appreciate the extent to which our very self or identity is effectively bound up with the other, including even a violent other seeking to destroy us. As Partha Chatterjee once observed about the paradoxical reliance by sovereign identity on the other/difference without which the former is inconceivable: "For Enlightenment itself, to assert its sovereignty as the universal ideal, needs its Other; if it could ever actualize itself in the real world as the truly universal, it would in fact destroy itself."[11] Simply put, *by demolishing the subjectivity of the other we end up destroying our own.*

## Religion and violence in South and Southeast Asia

In his chapter on southern Thailand, Joseph Liow maintains that the present policies of the Thaksin administration are fundamental to an understanding of the growing Islamization and concomitant violence in Thailand's deep south. In that respect, Liow makes two interrelated arguments. First, the intensification of religious militancy and violence in Thailand's Malay-Muslim dominated provinces, in his view, can be attributed more to the Thaksin government's flawed policy toward the south "than the exertions of militants attempting to mobilize the Islamic idiom for their own causes." Second, the government's mulish commitment to existing strategies, which are informed by "a national security culture that perceives pluralism as a threat and questionable surveillance policies and tactics including the application of force and intimidation," likely poses the most significant obstacle to the delegitimizing of violence in the south. Indeed, Liow argues that long-standing resistance in the south has never been motivated by abstract or ideological rejection of modernity or the "West," but rather opposition to Bangkok's policy of assimilation. As such, Liow takes umbrage against the proclivity of many security analysts to attribute militancy and conflict to the undue "negative influence of 'fundamentalist' Wahhabi and Salafi theological strains" without considering how these ideologies and philosophies relate specifically to Thai Malay-Muslim concerns in the light of the latter's social, historical, and political backdrop. It is precisely this interaction between ideas and milieus where events come to be invested with intelligibility and meaning, thereby endorsing particular courses of action.

Liow indicts the Thaksin government for its complicity in partly triggering and exacerbating grievances in the Thai south. Such complicity constitutes a liability, he argues, which must be acknowledged and redressed if strategies to disrupt and delegitimize militant violence can hope to succeed. Debilitated by a weak state capacity and legitimacy as well as unhelpful inter-agency rivalries, Bangkok must not only centralize its intelligence and information collection apparatuses and efforts but also engage meaningfully with the Malay-Muslim community. Other recent findings lend support to this argument.[12] Bangkok's development policies need to be balanced with an appreciation for the demand in the south for cultural and religious autonomy. Thaksin's assimilation/integration imperative, Liow concludes, should be discarded and replaced with the very initiatives of the previous Chuan administration that celebrated cultural pluralism – initiatives dropped by the Thaksin administration when it assumed power – on the grounds that the appeal of separatism arises "because of the denial of rights and respect to the southern provinces." On this point Liow is certainly correct given that assimilation/integration, even in communities where it could conceivably be argued "to have worked," continues nevertheless to be highly problematic for minorities, not least those in the United States.[13]

Maya Chadda begins her chapter on India with two important distinctions. First, she notes the need to distinguish between identity and conflict since religion, by itself, does not automatically produce violence – an obvious but nevertheless noteworthy consideration – whose causes may be different than religious ones in some cases. Second, there is also the need to distinguish between the geography and sociology of ethno-religious conflicts since the latter need not be territorial in nature. Various plausible causes of civilizational enmity and violence are discussed: absence of inter-ethnic civic associations (Varshney); absence of multiparty political competition and inability of minorities to tilt the balance in electoral contests (Wilkinson and Horowitz); presence of an institutionalized riot system (Brass). Questioning the efficacy of solely emphasizing ecological approaches, Paul Brass in particular, in Chadda's view, highlights the importance of differing interpretations that could provide the requisite spark in igniting the tinder comprising a combination of economic disparity, demographic imbalance, denial of political and cultural autonomy, governance failures, and the like. Two variants of strategies aimed at preventing communal violence are discussed. The first set of strategies addresses the challenge of restoring law and order, which involves policy proposals focused on possible preventive measures before, during, and after a conflict's duration, particularly administrative, law enforcement, and policy measures that can be adopted by the federal, state, and local governments. The second set emphasizes long-term political, economic, and social solutions aimed at fostering communal harmony, like the elimination of discrimination, creating greater economic equality and opportunities, and improving the enfranchisement of minorities into the political process.

The preventive, coercive, and reconstructive strategies enumerated in both essays are comprehensive, necessary, and, importantly, fundamentally sound. However, two significant impediments likely stand in the way of their implementation: state incompetence and paucity of political will. In the case of the former, recent studies suggest that where Southeast Asia (and conceivably South Asia as well) are concerned, weak and effete institutions and intra-bureaucratic rivalries in many countries have stymied efforts against terror and insurgency.[14] In the case of the latter, deficient political will has long proved the bane of good and effective governance at the state as well as regional levels in Asia. Regarding the ASEAN region where the collective regional good is all too often trumped by the primacy of national interests, that has certainly been the case, although others elsewhere have suggested that recent region-wide developments hint at the likelihood of increased participation by civil society actors in areas long considered the exclusive preserve of governments, such as conflict management, which could conceivably lead to an improvement in mediation prospects.[15] Indeed, the two are in an important sense interrelated: states lack the requisite will for cooperation precisely because they lack the institutional capacity to make cooperative ventures work.

Furthermore, to complicate matters, the urgent need to disrupt and delegitimize violence all too often opens the door to *state-sanctioned terrorism*, namely, the sort of draconian, anti-democratic national security culture and policies with which Liow in particular is understandably concerned. As Amitav Acharya recently observed regarding Asia's counter-terror efforts:

> While it is certainly important to fight terrorism – no one complains about this – it is just as important to note the potential for abuse. First, the anti-terrorism campaign has led to renewed justification for internal-security laws feared by many ... The labeling of indigenous separatists as "terrorists" distracts attention from the root causes of such movements in neglect and poor governance ... Fighting terrorism is necessary to maintaining security. But Asia must be on guard that in doing so it doesn't add to regional instability or discord, or undermine the process of democratization.[16]

Taking the argument a few notches further, one of the Bush administration's more vociferous critics, US scholar Noam Chomsky, has this to say about his own country's war on terrorism:

> To call this a "war against terrorism" however, is simply propaganda, unless the "war" really does target terrorism. But that is plainly not contemplated, because the Western powers could never abide by their own definition of the term, as in the U.S. Code or army manuals. To do so would reveal at once that the U.S. is a terrorist state, as are its clients.[17]

Another point of interest is that despite notable differences in their respective arguments, the two essays are complementary. On his part, Liow draws attention to the interaction between ideas and environs – between text and context, as it were – where events are infused and imbued with intelligibility and meaning that legitimize specific acts of violence. In a sense, we may agree with Booth and Dunne's view that, "Terrorism is an act, not an ideology."[18] By the same token, as Liow's insight suggests, violent actions are defined as *terrorist* precisely because of the contextual conditions – political, economic, social, and/or of course ideological – that frame those actions. Again, as Juergensmeyer has intimated:

178

Whether or not one uses "terrorist" to describe violent acts depends on whether one thinks that the acts are warranted. To a large extent the use of the term depends on one's world view: if the world is perceived as peaceful, violent acts appear as terrorism. If the world is thought to be at war, violent acts may be regarded as legitimate. They may be seen as preemptive strikes, as defensive tactics in an ongoing battle, or as symbols indicating to the world that it is indeed in a state of grave and ultimate conflict.[19]

As for Chadda, she cautions against privileging an unwarranted structuralism in the over-emphasis of root causes of conflict to the exclusion of any consideration for how local agents may have interpreted and defined their conditions as justifying the resort to violence. In this respect, Chadda attempts to trace the interactions between structure and agency, as it were, to which Liow refers, by exploring at length the kinds of strategies relevant to different stages of a conflict in the South Asian context. Both studies make very clear the importance of redefining the terms of collective existence, enlarging the political and social spaces for negotiation, accommodating the specific interests of the other, and allowing for cultural and religious diversity and plurality.

Both studies place the onus of redress and restitution largely on *the state*, and ostensibly for good reason since the state remains, for all intents and purposes, the principal agency and institution that maintains (theoretically at least) a relative monopoly on power, capacity, and legitimacy. As bleak as things may appear, as weak, incapacitated, and/or lacking in political will and rectitude as states may be, we seem bound somehow to recur to the state. In an essay on human security, Barry Buzan makes the same point:

> States may not be a sufficient condition for individual security, and they may even be the main problem ... But they are almost certainly a necessary condition for individual security because without the state it is not clear what other agency is to act on behalf of individuals. Because states hold this position, they can claim their own right of survival over and above that of their individual citizens.[20]

Furthermore, it is maintained that efforts to transcend the state when deciding on new security referents find it exceedingly problematic to do so without reverting to the state: "Versions of human security that seek to reduce all security to the level of the individual," Buzan continues, "have somehow to confront the dilemma that bypassing the state takes away what seems to be the necessary agent through which individual security might be achieved."[21] We may push for greater accommodation by states of cultural and religious diversity and civil society, we may even lambaste them for failing to provide for the security of humans, including their own citizens, or worse yet, being the direct cause of at times untold human suffering. We may look towards "transnational" settings, such as the international order, an international regime or organization, or a broader international community for answers. But somehow we end up returning to the state. There is, as it were, a shared commitment and disposition vis-à-vis the state, despite all its shortcomings, as a given and unparalleled mode of collective existence. In short, we turn to the subject, which constitutes, for international theory and practice, the ultimate emblem of sovereignty.

## Modernity as paradox

A theoretical comment on constructivism in international relations study is useful at this juncture given that a fair amount of the debate on religion and violence, to my mind, seems to inadvertently mirror the embedded rationalism within constructivism. This unintentional mimicry is not particularly helpful, especially the way in which the debate is shaped by claims and counterclaims that are essentialist in orientation. In other words, they engage in various naturalizing and delimiting practices similar to the sort found in mainstream constructivism. Despite the proliferation within security studies of so-called constructivist insights, which claim to have succeeded in marrying structural and rationalist approaches with sociological perspectives, security thinking and practice in the main has for the most part subscribed, if only tacitly, to an individualism that divests constructivism of the social logic it ostensibly espouses and centering the methodology within the economic logic of rationalism.[22] The propensity to conflate sovereignty and subjectivity renders it difficult if not impossible to inquire into how subjectivity itself is produced. This is especially true of works that share an epistemological and ontological commitment, even if only a tacit one, to rationalism and positivism. Yet this unproblematic correspondence is necessary if the myth of the subject as essentially given and sovereign, if only as an ideal rather than reality, is to be upheld. In this respect, *the norm of territorial and cultural alignment, with its nexus between sovereignty, on the one hand, and identity on the other, is thereby central to the social construction of the world as comprising sovereign presences in an anarchic space.*[23] Hence Chadda's allusion, rightly so, to the difficulty in separating religious nationalism from territory even as she wants to talk about the ostensibly transnational quality of cultural and religious identity.

It is precisely this sort of *ontopology* that has informed and continues to inform not only the thinking and doing of governments and societies seeking to protect and preserve the status quo and their "way of life," but, curiously enough, that also of Islamist militant groups seeking to destroy the former in the hope of realizing their preferred vision of collective existence, be it a theocratic state or the equally nebulous notion of some region-wide caliphate. Although states and militants differ markedly in terms of their agendas, beliefs, and values, both nevertheless share a similar "nostalgia for the politics of place," as William Connolly has called it,[24] whether defined in terms of geographically demarcated territories or imagined virtual spaces, *but a place nevertheless*. All this marks a relentless search for essence or, more properly, the desire, if not for the reality of essence then certainly its ideal. And perhaps it is within this shared ideal where we find the commonplace distinction between *modern and traditional*, which operates in quite a fair bit of analysis on religion and conflict, increasingly destabilized and unsettled. To be sure, we are left in no doubt as to who the "traditionalists" are as evinced in the following statement by US President George W. Bush, in the immediate aftermath of September 11, where in religious militants "an enemy has emerged that rejects every limit of law, morality, and religion. The terrorists have no true home in any country, or culture, or faith. They dwell in dark corners of earth"[25] – an unambiguously malignant other that leaves modern states with no recourse other than to seek its destruction.

Yet it is clear as well, in their shared sense of the fundamental significance of sovereign, autonomous, and exclusivist subjectivity/identity/presence/place, that religious militants can equally be considered *modern*. Or, at the very least, they are not anti-modern; recall Liow's point about the Malay-Muslim militants being motivated less by abstract or ideological rejection of modernity or the "West" than the Thaksin administration's imprudent policies *vis-à-vis* the south. In this respect, modernity is not quite the same thing as *secularism*, except that both secularist moderns and religious moderns, as we have already seen, are conjoined in their obdurate devotion to a given subjectivity that readily discounts all traces of the other within it and without which it cannot exist, no matter their fashionable allusions to "identity-formation" and the like. From this vantage point, subjectivity can no longer be understood as given, autonomous, and complete – the hallmarks that render it *sovereign*. Instead, it is, to borrow from Richard Ashley, "a social totality that is never really present, that always contains traces of the outside within, and that is never more than an effect of the practices by which ... dangers are inscribed."[26] If such is the other, and the other is, in the sense conveyed here, part and parcel of that which makes us, well, *us*, then prospects for civilizational amity in all probability have their origins in, among other things, just such an acknowledgment. As Kevin Robins has noted about Saddam Hussein, an observation which could easily accommodate, in varying extents, militants from Peshawar to Pattani:

> Two distinct, though interrelated, forces have shaped modern Western culture and identity. The first ... has been the centrality of reason as the constitutive principle of modernity itself ... The second ... has been the intensive and intense encounter with other cultures brought about by imperialism expansion ... Saddam is not an alien monster, a monster against modernity, but rather a monster born of modernity, a monster within modernity.[27]

It should be obvious by now that what is not being claimed here is that religious violence possesses no social agency and therefore moral culpability of its own. The point here is simply that no amount of strenuous attempts at disrupting and delegitimizing ethnic and religious conflict could bring about meaningful, sustainable communal harmony and stability – unless and until a serious effort is made by communities and cultures throughout to grapple critically with the exclusivist and ethnocentric suppositions that underpin our views about global life. In that sense, what is also interesting is *how* the so-called modern, civilized secular "West" is being urged to deal with militancy born not from without but within a modernity that is at best existential. Neil Livingstone cites a counter-terror expert on how Western governments should prosecute the war on terrorism:

> "In combat there is no such thing as a fair fight," observes one counter-terrorism specialist. Anything short of draconian methods that will give the West an edge in its struggle against terrorism, therefore, "should be encouraged." In this connection, the war against terrorism has gone high tech and, in the final analysis, it may well be that technological superiority will be the most important factor in the West's ability to withstand the terrorist challenge.[28]

It is true that the *combination of radicalism with technology* would prove combustible, as the US National Security Strategy of 2002 has warned, cannot be denied. But the recommendation of the employment of "draconian methods" by the supposedly modern West against the supposedly anti-modern militants and terrorists raises the question of who precisely is mixing radicalism and/or fanaticism with technology. Written in the context of America's Pacific War against Japan, Michael Sherry's words are an eerie description of the United States' own potent admixture of fanaticism with technology:

> The lack of a proclaimed intent to destroy, the sense of being driven by the twin demands of bureaucracy and technology, distinguished America's technological fanaticism from its enemies' ideological fanaticism. That both were fanatical was not easily recognizable at the time because the forms were so different. The enemy ... had little choice but to be profligate in the expenditure of manpower and therefore in the fervid exhortation of men to hatred and sacrifice – they were not, and knew they were not, a match in economic and technological terms for the Allies. The United States had different resources with which to be fanatical: resources allowing it to take the lives of others more than its own, ones whose accompanying rhetoric of technique disguised the will to destroy. As lavish with machines as the enemy was with men, Americans appeared to themselves to practice restraint, to be immune from the passion to destroy that characterized their enemies and from the urge to self-destruction as well.[29]

Thanks in part to the acute influence of the so-called "neoconservatives" over US defense and foreign policy, nowhere do we get a more vivid sense – so evident in the ongoing imbroglio Washington has created for itself in Iraq – of the appalling consequences that could arise and indeed have arisen from mixing technology *and* radical ideology together. Whichever brand of fanaticism, whether technological, ideological, or both, the ubiquitously religious idiom in which it is expressed is unmistakable, *particularly when it is fused with ethico-political justifications.*[30] But it is through such inquiry that we are painfully reminded that the "monsters" of and within modernity are not only Saddam Hussein, Osama bin Laden, Abu Bakar Ba'asyir, Hambali, or the latest militant/terrorist/tyrant to hog the news headlines and counter-terrorism blacklists. They can also be found treading the corridors of power in Delhi, Islamabad, Bangkok, or Singapore, not to mention Canberra or Washington. Ultimately, in refusing to recognize and acknowledge the other within us, states and militants consign themselves to an unending spiral of violence and destruction that humanity can ill afford.

## Effacing/erasing the other

So we all get used to it. I understand now that nothing but "otherness" killed Jews, and it began with naming them, by reducing them to the other. Then everything became possible.

Slavenka Drakulić [31]

A couple of illustrations of the concerns raised in the foregoing discussion are in order. In an editorial in *The Australian* dated September 3, 2004, the following opinion was tendered in the light of a recent series of terrorist attacks against Russian targets, including the Beslan school in North Ossetia where hundreds of children and adults were taken hostage, many of whom subsequently perished in the botched rescue effort by Russian security forces:

It is simplistic to assume that all these evil acts are directly connected. The bombers and hostage-takers have their own separate short-term objectives and are not all acting on the orders of Osama bin Laden. But from the Caucasus mountains, through the Middle East to Southeast Asia, the world is at war with Islamic fundamentalists, men and women who place no value on their own lives, or anybody else's. And their uncompromising commitment to absolute victory makes them enemies with no interest in any negotiated peace. This is not a war against a conventional enemy with rational goals. The objective of the al-Qa'ida movement, and its allies, is for nations to be ruled according to their fundamentalist interpretation of the Koran. Nor is it a war between Muslims and those who hold any other, or no, religious faith. Rather it is a worldwide fight between those who desire peaceful, prosperous lives and hope their children will live long and happily, and a handful of men and women who believe those who do not share their values deserve death.[32]

That I have selected a press editorial as an illustration of a secular state-sponsored perspective (or at least a version of it) should not pose a problem given the significant role played by the fourth estate in defining terrorism.[33] This lengthy statement provides a sense of how representations of the other as violent, irrational, uncompromising, and devoid of any concern for life help to foster the view that little would be achieved were attempts to be made to negotiate with terrorists. Accordingly, no negotiation could be possible for the express reason that no compatibility is thought to exist between terrorists and the residents of the "modern world." This is not to imply that there is little or no truth to those representations. The consequences of the violence unleashed by religious

183

extremists – whether in New York, Bali, or North Ossetia – were palpably real, the spilled blood and broken bodies an undeniable reality. Yet what is equally real and undeniable is that quite specific meanings as to what all that violence really represented have clearly something to do with how our narratives about those events and the subjectivities involved have been constructed and framed.[34] The editorial closed with the following thought:

> This is not an easy argument to accept for people who live in the modern world, where change is possible, and who have a right to run their own lives. But understanding that Islamic terrorists have no interest in the way we live now is the only way to make sense of their behavior. The nonsensical arguments we heard after September 11, that terror is a response to poverty or is caused by American power, are based on the false expectation that terrorists have achievable goals. This makes it essential to distinguish between the madness of the terrorists and some of the causes they claim to defend.[35]

With this finale the closure is complete, and the people of the "modern world" are left with no further recourse other than the tacit but unavoidable conclusion, based ostensibly on a logic of *moral necessity*, that the only approach to disrupting and delegitimizing religious violence is to eliminate, by force, the alleged perpetrators of that violence (in the above case, "Islamic terrorists"). But a *just* violence at that; after all, there are many who regard the war on terrorism, at least the campaign in Afghanistan if not Iraq, as, to use Booth and Dunne's words, "a just war because the threat posed by Osama bin Laden could not be resolved through dialogue given its genocidal intent against Americans and Jews, and its goal of waging unlimited civilizational war."[36] Accordingly, no quarter can or ought to be granted to those who refuse us the right of dialogue, who have no "achievable goals." Although that is, as the editorial put it, "not an easy argument to accept" for the civilized moderns to whom the terrorists are diametrically opposed, annihilation is the only fate permissible under the circumstances. The assumption inherent here is well articulated by Juergensmeyer: "The implication is that such terrorists are hell-bent to commit terrorism for whatever reason – sometimes choosing religion, sometimes another ideology, to justify their mischief. This logic concludes that terrorism exists because terrorists exist, and if we just got rid of them, the world would be a more pleasant place."[37] Furthermore, arguments that highlight either root causes or chariness and resentment at perceived excesses in US foreign policy are derided by the editorial, willy-nilly, as "nonsensical" without supporting evidence.

Not dissimilar logics underpin governmental counter-terror discourses as well, especially those of the United States. In an address before the US Congress immediately following September 11, President Bush ruminated: "Americans are asking, why do they hate us? They hate what we see right here in this chamber – a democratically elected government. Their leaders are self-appointed. They hate our freedoms – our freedom of religion, our freedom of speech, our freedom to vote and assemble and disagree with each other."[38] Here the other is inscribed as something so unmistakably different from *us* and *ours* that no room for dialogue with much less comprehension of the other is conceivable. Indeed, no room for considering whether the reason the president proffered in explaining the horrors of September 11 (such as "they hate our freedoms") could have been erroneous is conceivable, even though the *other* may have provided, at least according to one example, a not unreasonable answer.[39] Elsewhere the American president, in comparing Osama bin Laden and Al Qaeda to Hitler and the Nazis, has also stated: "Our nation faces a threat to our freedoms, and the stakes could not be higher. We are the target of enemies who boast they want to kill – kill all Americans, kill all Jews, and kill all Christians. *We've seen that type of hatred before – and the only possible response is to confront it, and to defeat it.*"[40] Note that this appeal is defined in terms of a previous danger, which makes this new threat knowable and known without any actual knowledge of the motives and causes behind it. Perhaps none is really necessary. As one analyst has noted concerning Washington's counter-terror policy at large: "They [US government officials] don't look at why people resort to terrorism. Cause? What cause?"[41]

On the other side of the "civilizational divide," at least in discursive terms, the following statement by an alleged perpetrator of the Bali bomb attacks in October 2002, Samudra, rendered under interrogation is equally telling in its representation of the other, in this case the US and its allies:

> To oppose the barbarity of the U.S. army of the Cross and its allies ... to take revenge for the pain of ... weak men, women and babies who died without sin when thousands of tons of bombs were dropped in Afghanistan in September 2001 [sic] ... during Ramadan ... To carry out a [sic] my responsibility to wage a global *jihad* against Jews and Christians throughout the world ... So that the American terrorists and their allies understand that the blood of Moslems is expensive and valuable; and cannot be – is forbidden to be – toyed with and made a target of American terrorists and their allies. So that the [American and allied] terrorists understand how painful it is to lose a [sic] mothers, husbands, children, or other family members, which is what they have so arbitrarily inflicted on Moslems throughout the world. To prove to Allah – the Almighty and most deserving of praise – that we will do whatever we can to defend weak Moslems, and to wage war against the U.S. imperialists and their allies.[42]

The language and terms of reference are somewhat different if archaic, but the logic underpinning it and the discursive effects that are produced are more or less similar to those from the earlier illustrations. As bomb attacks in Morocco, Turkey, Indonesia, and Egypt – significantly, all states with Muslim majorities – appear to indicate, traces of the other within the amorphous social totality of Islamic communities worldwide are disallowed even as militant discourse in some quarters has shifted from exonerations of Muslim deaths by the militants' hands in the past as collateral damage, to fearsome rationalizations of the same today as rightly deserved due to their collusion with the West and their ostensibly dubious

Muslim credentials: the militants' version of "either you are with us or against us," if you will. In both cases, the appeal is to moral and religious necessity – executing Allah's orders by executing the other.

To be sure, not every member of the "modern world" or every government presently engaged in the war on terrorism would necessarily agree with the conclusion that terrorists are not amenable to negotiation or even conciliation.[43] It is tempting, for instance, to view the Spanish withdrawal from Iraq following the Madrid bombings and in response to "guarantees" from the militants as a possible indication that negotiation should not be prematurely ruled out, or that terrorists, contrary to the editorial from *The Australian*, do in fact pursue "achievable goals." Indeed, that Washington and Moscow successfully brokered a 1987 landmark agreement to eliminate their respective intermediate nuclear forces, despite then US President Reagan's infamous vilification of the former Soviet Union as the "evil empire," implies that rhetorical absolutism does not automatically preclude negotiation. But whether a comparable readiness to relax absolutist claims and practices exists today among opposing sides of civilizational enmity is debatable.[44] For the most part, contemporary arguments that reject all possibility of dialogue and negotiation tend to be ignorant of anthropological, sociological, as well as theological debates about the politicized nature of religion and ethnicity. Such arguments are therefore unaware of how they are implicated in their essentializing and primordializing of the peoples and groups they claim to merely represent. Despite the alleged conformity to facts on the ground, what these arguments demonstrate is a dubious dependence upon implications the speakers have drawn from their own opinions about the actuality of the situation, which are then projected back into their assertions concerning reality. Almost without exception, such claims are rendered and sanctioned, as it were, by an appeal to necessity.

Nevertheless, a crucial lesson of contemporary civilizational enmity is just how untenable such appeals are, particularly those founded upon an idealized sovereign subjectivity. In this respect, what is especially intriguing is *how we moderns, who presuppose objectivity and a scientific realism to all our claims, in fact employ, egregiously so, ethico-political reasons in justification of our evaluations and judgments in everyday life.* All too often the basis for choosing between competing visions of history, far from being the objective and scientific modes of evaluation and judgment as averred by positivist-rationalists, is *moral* or *aesthetic* in kind.[45] If so, then it is likely the case that no extra-ideological ground exists by which conflicting conceptions of global life and knowledge can be adjudicated. If so, then much of what stands for knowledge claims in international relations and security involve invocations of ethico-political considerations in the finalizing of those claims. In White's words: "since these conceptions have their origins in ethical considerations, the assumption of a given epistemological position by which to judge their cognitive adequacy would itself represent only another ethical choice."[46] As the discussion in preceding sections has shown, such ethical choices are made, again and again, by both state practitioners as well as religious militants in legitimization of their violent actions – *without, however, any concomitant sense of ethical responsibility to the other*. When planning strategies to disrupt and delegitimize violence, which themselves are reliant on specific ethical choices, these concerns must necessarily be factored in.

## Emmanuel Lévinas and prospects for civilizational amity

Enter Lévinas, whose ideas arguably provide an understanding of subjectivity and responsibility that is vital in order for a successful reconfiguration of inter-civilization relations.[47] In essence, his approach regards ethics as first philosophy, without which the entire philosophical enterprise is, in his view, doomed always to the possibility of evil precisely because it privileges presence, the self, without consideration for the other except in instrumental or utilitarian terms, broadly defined. At least four points are noteworthy.

First, perhaps the most visibly apparent overarching theme in Lévinasian thought is *responsibility*, not to the self but to and for the other. In contradistinction to the Enlightenment-inspired notion of being as autonomous, given, and therefore sovereign – a notion whose ideological preservation by various self-ordained gatekeepers, curiously enough, has not necessarily comported with the ethos of Enlightenment – Lévinas understands being as a radically interdependent condition rendered possible only by virtue of one's responsibility to the other that enables one to be "devoted to the other man before being devoted to [oneself]."[48] Lévinas regards just such a responsibility as an ontologically prior or primitive condition, one that is, in Derrida's terms, "without limits ... before memory ... [and] before the very concept of responsibility."[49] Responsibility to the other therefore comes before everything else; indeed, it is the very thing that renders *thought* possible at all.

Second, when responsibility is comprehended in just such a way, it reshapes our traditional conceptions of *subjectivity* for the reason that *the origin of the subject is now found in its very subjection to the other*. More specifically, this subjection takes place prior to any consciousness, identity, or even freedom; indeed, subjects are constructed by dint of their relationship with and to the other.[50] There is, as such, an ever-present indebtedness to the other that marks our very own identity and subjectivity.[51] As Lévinas has intimated: "The fundamental experience which objective experience itself presupposes is the experience of the Other."[52] Hence, being or subjectivity can only be properly affirmed in terms of *a right to be in relation to the other*, which raises fundamental questions for ethics.

Third, if subjectivity is only properly apprehended in terms of a right to be in relation to the other, then it is precisely this condition that serves as the only viable foundation for an effective ethics wherein subjectivity undergoes *sustained de-centering* to prevent reducing everything to itself.[53] The following comment sums up nicely the ways in which responsibility, subjectivity, and ethics relate to one another within a Lévinasian framework:

> This unique lack of choice comes about because in Lévinas's thought ethics has been transformed from something independent of subjectivity – that is,

from a set of rules and regulations adopted by pregiven, autonomous agents – to something insinuated within and integral to that subjectivity. Accordingly, ethics can be understood as something not ancillary to the existence of a subject; instead, ethics can be appreciated for its indispensability to the very being of the subject. This argument leads us to the recognition that "we" are always already ethically situated, so making judgments about conduct depends less on what sort of rules are invoked as regulations, and more on how the interdependencies of our relations with others are appreciated.[54]

To the preceding three themes central to Lévinas' thought a fourth may be added: *the failure of ethical systems, whose foundations are in the Enlightenment and its derivative, liberal humanism, in securing civilizational amity.* As Lévinas has intimated, "We must ask ourselves if liberalism is all we need to achieve an authentic dignity for the human subject. Does this subject arrive at the human condition prior to assuming responsibility for the other man in the act of election that raises him to this height?"[55] Against the potential allegation that Lévinas is "anti-human," it may be argued that the sort of "anti-humanism" in his thought is neither inhuman nor inhumane for the reason that it does not eradicate the human but "clears the place for subjectivity positing itself in abnegation, in sacrifice, in a substitution which precedes the will." As such, Lévinas advocates the denouncement of liberal humanism precisely "because it is insufficiently human" as a consequence of its inconsideration of alterity and otherness.[56]

Against this Lévinasian backdrop, the dubious nature of Washington's "regime change" policy as evidenced by the current debacle in Iraq, where "democratization" has ironically meant, in many respects, anarchy for many Iraqis, raises serious questions regarding the viability of the sort of liberal democratic experimentation the United States has in mind for the Middle East. By this I am not implying that democracy is irrelevant to the Middle East region. Thanks to Lévinas' sustained attack on liberal humanism and his reflections on the failure of Western philosophy to sufficiently insure itself against evil, we are able to discern and appreciate fundamental weaknesses in Western liberal democratic systems, the most significant of which is its neglect of the processes and practices which produce new identities, including the "Islamization" – or perhaps radicalization might prove more apropos a term – of Western and/or Westernized societies. As William Connolly has argued:

Liberalism remains a philosophy of tolerance among culturally established identities more than one of attentiveness to how these identities are established and the ways in which new possibilities of identity are propelled into being. In other words, liberalism is attentive to "difference" as already defined, heterodox identities in an existing network of social relations, but tone-deaf to "*différance*" as that which resides in an existing network of social relations, *but has not yet received stable definition within it.* As a result of this thinness in the appreciation of difference, dominant forms of liberalism remain unattuned to the crucial role new *enactments or performances* play, first in generating new claims to identity, and second in *retroactively* crystallizing violence in previous patterns of being.[57]

In other words, tolerance does not permit any inquiry into *how* difference is constituted in the first place. Nor does it permit inquiry into how the dominant identity, purportedly in question, is able somehow to preserve its dominance – precisely because tolerance also functions to keep the powerful in power. Since both Chadda and Liow place the bulk of the onus of redress and restitution on the state in advancing civilizational amity, whatever such policies governments may commit to, whether predicated upon multicultural, consociational, or other premises, must necessarily take the foregoing concerns seriously. That said, the onus here does not and cannot denote the reinstallation and re-endorsement, no matter how inadvertent and unintentional, of the state as the principal if not *only* institution involved in the reconfiguration of inter-civilization relations, which basically amounts to the sort of largely state-centric recommendations allowed, say, by Samuel Huntington in his positivist-realist-oriented analysis of civilizational enmity.[58]

Alternatively, a process truly committed to a democratic pluralistic promotion and preservation of civilizational amity would necessarily have to include, among other things, the encouragement of multiple sources of knowledge and analysis in various institutions within and without the communities in question, such that non-sovereign and non-state perspectives are accorded greater legitimacy; the gratuitous support of peace initiatives and proposals by local communities and civil society groups, including non-governmental organizations (NGOs), which all too often are overlooked by established actors in diplomacy and governance; the development of new understandings of political, economic, and cultural spaces that resist essentialist and exclusivist formulations, and so forth.

The prospects for a reconfiguration of inter-civilization relations after September 11 are likely the most robust within the context of a Lévinasian understanding of a subjectivity that is not already fixed and given, but open to – indeed, utterly dependent upon – an a priori responsibility to the other, including even violent others that seek to harm it. When subjectivity is defined in terms of an autonomous being or presence, always and already demarcated and delineated from everything else – a bounded self-contained identity that needs no other – it resembles what Hans-Georg Gadamer has called a "closed horizon":

> The closed horizon that is supposed to enclose a culture is an abstraction. The historical movement of human life consists in the fact that it is never utterly bound to any one standpoint, and hence can never have a truly closed horizon. The horizon is, rather, something into which we move and that moves with us. Horizons change for a person who is moving. Thus the horizon of the past, out of which all human life lives and which exists in the form of tradition, is always in motion.[59]

Conversely, a Lévinasian reading of horizons – of subjectivity and identity, or being and presence, that is – sees them as open, changing, and fluid. From this standpoint, the dynamic interaction between official histories or narratives, on the one hand, and counter-histories or counter-narratives on the other need not be violent.[60] Ultimately, it is unclear whether such a conjoining of social and cultural horizons would be sufficient to prompt ideologues and extremists on both sides to abandon violence. Without it, however, the outcome is undeniably and horrendously clear. The fact that Lévinas' suspicions about liberal humanism, with its presupposition of subjectivity as autonomous, given, and sovereign, as being "insufficiently human" are well founded, is borne out by our reflection on modernity and its paradoxes. How, we might ask, could liberal humanism, with its laudable goals and intentions, end up producing "monsters" of the sort elaborated above and on every conceivable side of the civilizational divide? I have suggested that a fair part of the answer possibly lies in the fundamental presupposition of sovereign subjectivity, which both states and militant groups seem to share. Lévinas supplies an infinitely more satisfying answer: The possibility of evil as a product of reason, he proposes, is a very real one for grand acts of evil are, according to his understanding, not to be found in the aberration of reasoning or an accident of ideology and religion. Rather, it can be found in "the essential possibility of *elemental Evil* into which we can be led by logic and against which Western philosophy had not sufficiently insured itself."[61] As Jean Bethke Elshtain once put it, "Virtue without limits becomes terror."[62] And so perhaps too the sort of idealistic, evangelical, and terrifying virtue promulgated and forcibly imposed by liberal humanists against which its recipients have so violently militated.

## Conclusion

In closing, it is perhaps apposite that we turn to the late Jacques Derrida, whose own writings can, in at least one sense, be understood as an advocacy, critique, and reformulation of Lévinasian themes: "Nothing seems to me less outdated than the classical emancipatory ideal. We cannot attempt to disqualify it today, whether crudely or without sophistication, at least not without treating it too lightly and forming the worst complicities."[63] If anything, this is a rather odd statement, especially coming from a thinker who, much like Lévinas, has proved such a worthy adversary of the subjectivity-as-sovereignty claim that has long served as a hallmark of modernity. In that sense, not unlike Derrida's surprising gesture to emancipation, the suggestions for celebrating difference and pluralism discussed in these concluding remarks do not differ markedly from the many admirable recommendations raised in the two essays that were reviewed here. Nevertheless, the Lévinasian approach invoked here compels us to walk a road less traveled precisely because it invites, indeed it necessitates, an attitude of humility that is alien to many states, societies, and particular faith communities, which, in their alienation from one another, have largely resorted to forms of mediation that are reliant on metaphysical conceits and cultural-cum-ideological hubris. Ultimately, any hope of civilizational amity after September 11 can rest on no other foundation other than *the ethical acknowledgment of the other as intrinsic to any appreciation of the self.*

# Notes

1  Quoted in *The Straits Times*, October 7, 2004, L16.

2  See, for example, Mark Juergensmeyer, *Terror in the Mind of God: The Global Rise of Religious Violence*, 3rd edn (Berkeley, CA: University of California Press, 2003), 12–13.

3  Richard K. Ashley and R.B.J. Walker, "Reading Dissidence/Writing the Discipline: Crisis and the Question of Sovereignty in International Studies," *International Studies Quarterly* 34, no. 3 (September 1990): 367–416; Jenny Edkins, Nalini Persram, and Veronica Pin-Fat, eds, *Sovereignty and Subjectivity* (Boulder, CO: Lynne Rienner, 1999).

4  Ken Booth and Tim Dunne, "Worlds in Collision," in *Worlds in Collision: Terror and the Future of Global Order*, ed. Ken Booth and Tim Dunne (New York: Palgrave Macmillan, 2002), 1.

5  Edward W. Said, *Culture and Imperialism* (New York: Alfred A. Knopf, 1993), 324.

6  Gayatri C. Spivak, "Can the Subaltern Speak?" in *The Post-Colonial Studies Reader*, ed. Bill Ashcroft, Gareth Griffiths, and Helen Tiffin (New York: Routledge, 1995), 26.

7  Let me be clear, however, that I neither privilege linguistic or ideational determinism, on the one hand, nor local agency on the other, in making this claim.

8  James E. Young, *Writing and Rewriting the Holocaust: Narrative and the Consequences of Interpretation* (Bloomington, IN: Indiana University Press, 1988), 4–5.

9  David Campbell, *National Deconstruction: Violence, Identity, and Justice in Bosnia* (Minneapolis, MN: University of Minnesota Press, 1999), 116.

10  Emmanuel Lévinas and Richard Kearney, "Dialogue with Emmanuel Lévinas," in *Face to Face with Lévinas*, ed. Richard A. Cohen (Albany, NY: State University of New York Press, 1986), 27.

11  Partha Chatterjee, *Nationalist Thought and the Colonial World: A Derivative Discourse* (London: Zed, 1986).

12  See Seng Tan and Kumar Ramakrishna, "Interstate and Intrastate Dynamics in Southeast Asia's War on Terror," *SAIS Review of International Affairs* 24, no. 1 (2004): 91–105.

13  As Nirmala Puru Shotam has noted of Chinese-Indonesians who emphasize their identity as Indonesians, they "can never be the authority on Indonesian-ness and hence claim to speak as an authority, insofar as indigeny and other essentialist forms are given precedence." Quoted in C.J.W.-L. Wee, "Introduction: Local Cultures, Economic Development, and Southeast Asia," in *Local Cultures and the "New Asia": The State, Culture, and Capitalism in Southeast Asia*, ed. C.J.W.-L. Wee (Singapore: Institute of Southeast Asian Studies, 2002), 15.

14  For example, see various essays in "Fighting Terrorism on the Southeast Asian Front," Asia Program Special Report, no. 112, Woodrow Wilson International Center for Scholars, Washington DC, June 2003. Also see Kumar Ramakrishna and See S. Tan, eds, *After Bali: The Threat of Terrorism in Southeast Asia* (Singapore: Institute of Defence and Strategic Studies, 2003). In Southeast Asia, Singapore and Malaysia are likely the two exceptions to the norm where state efficacy is concerned.

15  See Seng Tan, "NGOs in Conflict Management in Southeast Asia," *International Peacekeeping* 12, no. 1 (2005): 1–18.

16  Amitav Acharya, "Fight Terrorism – But Carefully," *Far Eastern Economic Review*, September 9, 2004, 26.

17  Noam Chomsky, *9–11* (New York: Seven Stories Press, 2001), 16.

18  Booth and Dunne, "Worlds in Collision," 8.

19  Juergensmeyer, *Terror in the Mind of God*, 9.

20  Barry Buzan, "Human Security in International Perspective" (paper prepared for the ISIS Malaysia 14th Asia-Pacific Roundtable on Confidence Building and Conflict Reduction, Kuala Lumpur, June 3–7, 2000), 1, 8.

21  Buzan, "Human Security," 8.

22  For a useful debate on the merits and problems of constructivism, refer to: "Forum on 'Social Theory of International Politics'," *Review of International Studies* 26, (2000): 151–63; and Ronen Palan, "A World of Their Making: An Evaluation of the Constructivist Critique in International Relations," *Review of International Studies* 26, (2000): 575–98.

23  A similar point is made in Campbell, *National Deconstruction*, 165.

24  William E. Connolly, "Democracy and Territoriality," *Millennium: Journal of International Studies* 17, (1991): 463–84.

25  President Bush's remarks at the Department of Defense Service of Remembrance, October 11, 2001. For a full account see http://www.whitehouse.gov/news/releases/2001/10/print/20011011-1.html.

26  Richard K. Ashley, "Living on Border Lines: Man, Poststructuralism, and War," in *International/Intertextual Relations: Postmodern Readings of World Politics*, ed. James D. Derian and Michael J. Shapiro (New York: Lexington, 1989), 304.

27  Kevin Robins, "The Mirror of Unreason," *Marxism Today*, March 1991, 42.

28  Neil C. Livingstone, *The Cult of Counterterrorism* (Lexington, MA: Lexington Books, 1990), 129–40.

29  Michael Sherry, *The Rise of American Air Power: The Creation of Armageddon* (New Haven, CT: Yale University Press, 1987), 253–4.

30  And, we might add, essentialist and exclusivist as well. As Correa has put it, "by sacred one does not mean only the religious, but the primordial as well." C. Correa, "The Public, the Private, and the Sacred," *Daedalus* 118, no. 4 (1989): 93–114.

31  A Croatian writer, quoted in Campbell, *National Deconstruction*, 11.

32  Editorial, "No Hope of Negotiating with Terrorists," *The Australian*, September 3, 2004, http:// www.theaustralian.news.com.au/common/story_page/0,5744,10652292% 255E7583,00.html.

33  As Juergensmeyer has written, "Hence the public response to the violence – the trembling that terrorism effects – is part of the meaning of the term. It is appropriate, then, that the definition of a terrorist act is provided by us, the witnesses – or more often our public agents, the news media – who affix the label on acts of violence and destruction that makes them terrorism. These are public acts of destruction, committed without a clear military objective, that arouse a widespread sense of fear." *Terror in the Mind of God*, 5. If anything, media discourse can be considered as "semi-official narratives that authorize and provoke certain sequences of cause and effect, while at the same time preventing counter-narratives from emerging." See Said, *Culture and Imperialism*, 324. See also Edward W. Said, *Covering Islam: How the Media and the Experts Determine How We See the Rest of the World*, rev. (New York: Vintage, 1997).

34  See Seng Tan, "Enemy of Their Making? US Security Discourse on the September 11 Terror Problematique," in *After Bali: The Threat of Terrorism in Southeast Asia*, ed. Kumar Ramakrishna and See S. Tan (Singapore: Institute of Defence and Strategic Studies, 2003), 261–80.

35  Editorial, "No Hope."

36  Booth and Dunne, "Worlds in Collision," 12.

37  Juergensmeyer, *Terror in the Mind of God*, 7–8.

38  President Bush's speech before a Joint Session of Congress, September 20, 2001. For a full account see http://www.whitehouse.gov/news/releases/2001/09/print/20010920-8.html.

39  "We are not against America or Americans," Mohammad Sohail Shaheen, the second-highest ranking diplomat who represented the Taliban government in Pakistan, reportedly said. "We are against the arrogance of intimidation ... I like America. I like Americans. I just don't like American foreign policy." Asra Q. Nomani, "At Home with the Taliban," *Salon.com*, October 10, 2001.

40 President Bush's address to the nation at the World Congress Center, November 8, 2001, emphasis added. For a full account see http://www.whitehouse.gov/news/releases/2001/11/print/20011108-13.html.

41 Eqbal Ahmad, *Terrorism: Theirs and Ours* (New York: Seven Stories Press, 2001), 14–15.

42 Quoted in Ramakrishna and Tan, "Southeast Asia a 'Terrorist Haven'?" 26–7.

43 A. Khaminwa *et al.*, "Commentary: Negotiating with Terrorists and Non-State Actors: The Journey to World Peace," *Cardozo Journal of Conflict Resolution* 4, no. 2 (2003).

44 Dan Balz, "Reagan, Bush Contrasts are as Telling as Parallels," *The Washington Post*, June 11, 2004.

45 Hayden White, *Metahistory: The Historical Imagination in Nineteenth-Century Europe* (Baltimore, MD: Johns Hopkins University Press, 1973), 432–3.

46 White, *Metahistory*, 26.

47 My following discussion on Lévinas is indebted to David Campbell's reflections in National Deconstruction, 165–91.

48 Emmanuel Lévinas, "Ethics as First Philosophy," in *The Lévinas Reader*, ed. Sean Hand (Oxford: Blackwell, 1989), 83–4.

49 Jacques Derrida, "Forces of Law: The Mystical Foundations of Authority," in *Deconstruction and the Possibility of Justice*, ed. Drucilla Cornell, Michel Rosenfeld, and David G. Carlson (New York: Routledge, 1992), 19.

50 See Ernesto Laclau and Chantal Mouffe, *Hegemony and Socialist Strategy: Towards a Radical Democratic Politics* (London: Verso, 1985), 108.

51 Lévinas, "Ethics as First Philosophy," 82.

52 Emmanuel Lévinas, "Signature," in D*ifficult Freedom: Essays on Judaism* (Baltimore, MD: Johns Hopkins University Press, 1990), 293.

53 Lévinas and Kearney, "Dialogue with Emmanuel Lévinas," 27.

54 Campbell, *National Deconstruction*, 176.

55 Emmanuel Lévinas, "Reflections on the Philosophy of Hitlerism," *Critical Inquiry* 17, (1990): 63.

56 Emmanuel Lévinas, *Otherwise Than Being or Beyond Essence* (The Hague: Martinus Nijhoff Publishers, 1981), 127.

57 William E. Connolly, *Political Theory and Modernity* (Ithaca, NY: Cornell University Press, 1993), 178.

58 Samuel P. Huntington, *The Clash of Civilizations and the Remaking of World Order* (New York: Simon and Schuster, 1996).

59 Hans-Georg Gadamer, *Truth and Method*, ed. and trans. Garrett Barden and John Cumming (New York: Seabury Press, 1975), 271.

60 As Osman Bakar has alluded: "A Muslim does not go against the teachings of his or her religion if he makes the claim that Confucius was a prophet of Islam ... The Chinese, being an ancient race and civilization, surely must have received at least one message from Heaven. Confucius deserves to be considered a candidate for the recipient of that message. If he were indeed a prophet, then his prophetic function would be that of a Law-bringer, that is, one who brings the Shari'ah to the Chinese people. The *Analects* is, in fact, basically a source of moral and ethical teachings for the organization of society, which is what the Shari'ah is all about." Osman Bakar, "Confucian Analects in the Light of Islam," *Pemikir* 1, (1995), 98–9.

61 Lévinas, "Philosophy of Hitlerism," 63.

62 Jean Bethke Elshtain, *Democracy on Trial* (New York: Basic Books, 1995), 123.

63 Derrida, "Forces of Law," 28.

# INDEX

Abouhalima, Mahmud 23–4, 26–7
Abu Bakar complex 46
Abu Sayyaf 10, 11, 18, 43
Acharya, Amitav 178
Afghanistan 41–2, 45, 96, 112–13, 137,
  184
Ahmadis (Ahmadiyya sect) 77–8, 111
alienation 5, 64, 150, 190
*aliran* 39–40
All Burma Young Monks' Union
  (ABYMU) 59, 66–7n20, 68n32
Al Qaeda 10, 17, 24, 28–9, 33, 42
Ambon 12, 95, 96, 97, 98
Anderson, Paul N. 126
Arya Samaj 72
Ashley, Richard 181
Azam, Maulana Tariq 113

Ba'asyir, Abu Bakar 46–7, 182
Bali bombings 33, 42, 47, 185
Bandura, Albert 127, 128, 129
Bangkok: assimilation attempts 15,
  19, 156, 157, 165, 176–7; Thaksin
  administration 159–64, 167–9
Bangladesh 6, 79–81, 114–16, 117–18
Barisan Nasional party 5, 157
Bengal 80
Beslan school, North Ossetia 183
Bhindranwale, Sant Jarnail Singh 22, 25,
  28
bin Laden, Osama 19n4, 25–6, 28–9, 115,
  128, 182, 184
Bombay bombings 6; *see also* Mumbai
  riots
Booth, Ken and Dunne, Tim 178, 184
Brahmo Samaj 72
Brass, Paul 64, 141, 147, 177
British colonialism *see* colonialism
Buddhism: authenticity 62–3; doctrinal
  espousal of nonviolence 52, 65n2;

*Mahamuni* Buddha image in Burma
  59, 67–8n27; political and ritual
  hegemony 52; relation of sangha and
  state in modern Theravada Buddhism
  6, 53, 54–63, 66n16, 67n23; Tibetan
  Buddhism 52–3, 65n4; veneration of
  relics 52, 57–8
Burma: 1977 anti-Muslim persecution
  58–60, 68n31; 1988 uprising 56–8,
  66–7n20; Dipeyin ambush 60–1;
  *Mahamuni* Buddha image 59, 67–8n27;
  relation of sangha and state 6, 53,
  55–61, 66n16; violence instigated
  through Buddhist symbols 6
Bush, George W. 19–20n4, 181, 184–5
Buzan, Barry 179

Cambodia 53
Chatterjee, Partha 176
China: attack on Buddhism in occupation
  of Tibet 52–3; Chinese Indonesians 87,
  92–5
Chomsky, Noam 178
Christianity: Christian Chinese
  Indonesians 87, 92–5; depicted as
  victim of global Muslim aggression
  95, 98–100; images of cosmic war 25;
  missionaries 6, 36–7; sectarian violence
  34
civic associations 143, 144–5, 146
civilizations: clash of 3, 5, 175; enmity and
  amity of 174–90
colonialism: in Burma 55, 65n9, 68n35;
  Indonesian anti-colonial war 40; in
  Malay–Indonesian archipelago 36–7;
  secular power as ethnographic concept
  of 51, 55; as a source of ethno-religious
  conflict in South Asia 70, 72–4, 137
communal religious violence: anatomies
  of religion and conflict 63–4; in Burma

194